EVANGELISM

EVANGELISM

HOW *to* SHARE THE GOSPEL FAITHFULLY

JOHN MACARTHUR

and THE PASTORS AND MISSIONARIES
OF GRACE COMMUNITY CHURCH

THOMAS NELSON
Since 1798

Published in Nashville, Tennessee, by Thomas Nelson. Thomas Nelson is a trademark of HarperCollins Christian Publishing, Inc..

Published in association with the literary agency of Wolgemuth & Associates, Inc.

Book composition by Upper Case Textual Services, Lawrence, Massachusetts.

Thomas Nelson titles may be purchased in bulk for educational, business, fund-raising, or sales promotional use. For information, please e-mail SpecialMarkets@ThomasNelson.com.

ISBN 978-0-310-13669-9 (softcover)

ISBN 978-1-401-67554-7 (eBook)

Library of Congress Cataloging-in-Publication Data
978-1-4185-4318-1

Contents

Section 4: Evangelism in the Church

Introduction
Rediscovering Biblical Evangelism

John MacArthur and Jesse Johnson

"Evangelism is one beggar telling another beggar where to get bread"

—D. T. Niles (Sri Lankan church leader and educator, 1908–70)

Virtually everyone knows the word *gospel* means "good news," and every true Christian understands that the gospel of Jesus Christ is the best news in all of time and eternity.

Of course when someone is in possession of good news, the natural inclination is to want to tell it to everyone. When the news is especially good, our impulse might be to proclaim it from the rooftops. If we think carefully about the gospel message—pondering its meaning, its implications, its simplicity, its freeness, and the eternal blessedness of those who receive it—the urge to tell it to others should be overpowering.

That is precisely why new Christians are often the most passionate evangelists. Without any training or encouragement whatsoever, they can be amazingly effective in bringing others to Christ. They are not obsessed with technique or stymied by fear of rejection. The sheer, grand glory of the gospel fills their hearts and their vision, and they want to talk to everyone about it.

Unfortunately, that passion can—and often does—diminish over time. The young believer soon discovers that not everyone thinks the gospel is such good news. Some respond to it the way they would respond to the stench of death (2 Cor. 2:16). Multitudes despise the message or become offended by it, because it punctures human pride. Many simply love their sin so much they do not want to hear a message of redemption that calls them to repent. Repeated encounters with vehement gospel-rejecters can dampen the enthusiasm of even the most gifted evangelist.

On top of that, the cares of this world and the distractions of daily life vie for our time and attention. Eventually, as the disciple becomes more and more familiar with the gospel, that profound initial sense of wonder and amazement fades somewhat. The gospel is still good news, of course, but we begin to think of it as old news, and that sense of urgency is lost.

It is therefore necessary to remind ourselves constantly how utterly vital the task of evangelism is, and how desperately in need of the gospel this fallen world is. Evangelism is not merely one incidental activity in the life of the church; it is the most urgent duty we as Christians have been given to do. Virtually every other spiritual exercise we do together as members of Christ's body we will still be able to do in heaven—praising God, enjoying fellowship with one another, savoring the richness of God's Word, and celebrating the truth together. But now is the only time we have for proclaiming the gospel to the lost and winning people to Christ. We seriously need to be redeeming the time (Eph. 5:16).

A Christian does not need to be individually called or specially gifted to be a herald of the good news; we are commanded to be witnesses of Christ, commissioned to train others to be disciples. This is an individual obligation, not merely the collective responsibility of the church. No duty is more significant, and none bears more eternally rewarding fruit.

Furthermore, the fields are white for harvest (John 4:35). The current generation is as ripe for the gospel message as any other generation in history. No matter what aspect of contemporary culture you examine, what you will discover are crying spiritual needs—and people whose souls are parched and famished for truth. The answer to such a spiritual famine in our land is not the artificial arousal of religious sentiment, not more political activism, not a better public relations campaign, and certainly not for Christians to adapt their message to the prevailing secular worldview.

The central thesis of this book is that the true answer is the unadulterated gospel itself—proclaimed clearly, powerfully, without any gimmick, in all its powerful simplicity. The gospel is the instrument of God's power for the salvation of sinners (Rom. 1:16). The key to biblical evangelism is not strategy or technique. It is not primarily about style, methodology, or programs and pragmatics. The first and preeminent concern in all our evangelistic efforts must be the gospel.

The apostle Paul emphatically repudiated cleverness, gimmicks, eloquence, philosophical sophistication, and psychological manipulation as tools of gospel ministry: "When I came to you [I] did not come with excellence of speech or of wisdom declaring to you the testimony of God. For I determined not to know anything among you except Jesus Christ and Him crucified" (1 Cor. 2:1–2).

What is particularly interesting about Paul's single-minded resolve to preach the undiluted gospel is his immediate admission that he struggled with the same feelings of apprehension and intimidation all of us experience when we contemplate our duty to proclaim it. As he reflected on his early ministry in Corinth, here is how he characterized it: "I was with you in weakness, in fear, and in much trembling" (1 Cor. 2:3).

And yet, not because of any technique or innate personal proficiency of Paul's, his ministry to them was a powerful "demonstration of the Spirit and of power" (1 Cor. 2:4). He simply unleashed the gospel in Corinth, and souls were saved. They were only a handful at first, and they came amid fierce opposition (Acts 18:1–8). But from those small beginnings, a church was founded and the gospel spread still further.

That is what we mean by "biblical evangelism." Its success is not measured by immediate numeric results. It does not have to be retooled or completely redesigned if at first glance it does not seem to be working. It stays focused on the cross and the message of redemption, undiluted by pragmatic or worldly interests. It is never obsessed with questions like how people might react, what we can do to make our message sound more appealing, or how we might frame the gospel differently so as to minimize the offense of the cross. It is concerned instead with truth, clarity, biblical accuracy, and (above all) Christ. Its message is about Him and what He has done to redeem sinners; it is not about the hurting person's felt needs, or what he or she must do to merit God's blessing.

Keeping those things straight is the key to biblical evangelism. Throughout this book we will be reminded of those principles repeatedly, from several biblical perspectives. In part 1, we will deal with the theology of evangelism, beginning with Christ's teaching on the topic from Mark 4. One thing you will see clearly as we examine the theological presuppositions and biblical foundations of evangelism is the folly of trying to win the world to Christ with worldly methods. In part 2 we will look at evangelism from a pastoral perspective, and in part 3 we will deal with issues related to personal, one-on-one evangelism. Part 4 draws all the threads together with a careful look at how an evangelistic ministry fits into and shapes the life and activities of the local church.

We think you will be blessed and edified as you study the principles set forth in this book. Our prayer is that what you gain will not be merely theoretical knowledge, but that you will come away with a passion for evangelism befitting the urgency and the sheer exhilaration of the joyful good news Christ has entrusted with us.

Section 1

The Theology of Evangelism

1

Theology of Sleep: Evangelism According to Jesus

John MacArthur

The Scripture's longest and most detailed instructions concerning evangelism are found in Mark 4. This series of parables is our Lord's Magna Carta on evangelism, and the foundation of His teaching is the parable of the soils. The point of this illustration runs contrary to much of today's evangelistic thinking as it demonstrates that neither the style of the evangelist nor his adaptation of the message ultimately has an impact on the results of his efforts. Jesus' understanding of evangelism is a resounding rebuke to those who suppose that a pastor's dress, style, or music helps him reach a particular culture or crowd, or that diluting the gospel to make it more acceptable produces true conversions. The reality is that God's power comes through the message, not the messenger.

The disciples were confused. They had left their homes, lands, extended families, and friends (Mark 10:28). They turned their backs on their former lives to follow Jesus, whom they believed to be the long-awaited Messiah, and they expected to see other Israelites make similar sacrifices and believe in Jesus as well. Rather than national conversion, the disciples found much animosity.

Jewish leaders hated Jesus and His teachings, while many of the masses were only interested in signs and wonders. Few were repenting, and doubt was beginning to grip the Twelve.

The problem was not Jesus' ability to attract an audience. As He traveled around Galilee teaching, the crowds were huge, often numbering in the tens of thousands. The disciples were often pressed tightly together. Occasionally Jesus would have to get into a boat and push offshore into the lake to teach, merely to escape the crushing weight of the desperate miracle seekers.

But as fascinating and impressive as the scene was, it was not producing true believers. People were not genuinely repenting and embracing Jesus as Savior. Even the disciples' own expectations were not being realized. The prophecies of Isaiah 9 and 45 spoke of a day when the Messiah's kingdom would be global and without end. By the time the events of Mark 4 occurred, the Lord's ministry had been public for two years, and the notion that Jesus was establishing that kind of kingdom seemed far from reality. Consequently, few people were sincerely following Him. The Old Testament described the Messiah as bringing to Israel both national salvation and international supremacy. Thus the massive crowds were only interested in miracles, healings, and food—not salvation from sin.

So it was not surprising for the disciples to have questions. If Jesus was truly the Messiah, why were many of His followers so obviously superficial? How could the long-awaited Messiah come to Israel, only to be rejected by the nation's religious leaders? And why did He not exact power and authority to establish the promised kingdom with the fulfillment of all that was pledged in the Abrahamic, Davidic, and New covenants?

The issue was this: Jesus was preaching a hard message that required radical sacrifice from His followers. On the one hand, following Christ was very appealing. It offered freedom from the labyrinth of oppressive man-made regulations imposed by the Pharisees (Matt. 11:29–30; cf. 17:25–27). On the other hand, following Christ was daunting, because it required finding the narrow gate, denying oneself, and obeying Him even to the point of death (Matt. 7:13–14; Mark 8:34). To follow Jesus required recognizing that He was divine, and that apart from Him there is no salvation and no other means to reconciliation with God (John 14:6). It also meant completely abandoning Judaism that focused on religious practice instead of a penitent heart turned to God.

Many Jews expected the Messiah to liberate them from Roman occupation, but Jesus refused to do so. Instead, He preached a message of repentance, submission, sacrifice, radical devotion, and exclusivity. The crowds were drawn to Him because of the miracles He performed and the power He possessed; the disciples, however, recognized that His approach, as powerful and truthful as it was, was not turning the curious into converts. When the disciples asked, "Lord, are there just a few who are being saved?" it was an honest question born from the reality of what they experienced (Luke 13:23 NASB). One can even imagine the disciples entertaining the idea that perhaps Jesus' message should be altered, even if just slightly, to manipulate the people's response.

THE MESSENGER IS NOT THE MEANS

In many ways, current evangelicalism is similarly confused. I have often noted that the dominant myth in evangelicalism is that the success of Christianity depends on how popular it is.[1] The perceived mandate is that, if the gospel is to remain relevant, Christianity must somehow adapt and appeal to the latest cultural trends.

That kind of thinking used to be limited to the seeker-sensitive crowd, but it has recently made the leap into more Reformed circles. There are entire movements that would agree to the truths of predestination, election, and total depravity, but then also, inexplicably, demand that pastors act more like rock stars than humble shepherds. Influenced by the emotional rhetoric of bad theology, people tolerate the idea that the cultural shrewdness of a pastor determines how successful his message is and how influential his church will be. Current church growth methodology claims that if an evangelist wants to "reach the culture" (whatever that means), he must emulate the culture in some way. But such an approach runs contrary to the biblical paradigm. The power of the Spirit in the gospel is not found in the messenger, but in the message. Thus, the motivation behind the seeker-driven mind-set might be noble, but it is seriously misguided.

Any effort to manipulate the outcome of evangelism by changing the message or stylizing the messenger is a mistake. The idea that more people will repent if only the preacher were cooler or funnier invariably causes the church to suffer through a ridiculous parade of entrepreneurial types who act as though their personal charm can draw people to Christ.

This error leads to the harmful notion that a pastor's conduct and speech should be determined by the culture in which he ministers. If he is trying to reach an "unchurched" culture, some would argue, he should speak and act like the unchurched, even when their behavior is unholy. There are many problems with that kind of logic, but foremost is the false assumption that a pastor can manufacture true conversions by looking or acting a certain way. The bottom line is that only God is in control of whether or not sinners are saved as a result of any preaching.

In reality, the hard truths of the gospel are not conducive to gaining popularity and influence within secular society. Sadly, however, many preachers crave cultural acceptance so much they are actually willing to alter God's message of salvation and His standard of holiness in order to achieve it. The result, of course, is another gospel that is not the gospel at all.

Such compromises do nothing to increase the church's witness within the culture. In fact, they have the opposite effect. By creating a synthetic gospel, they facilitate filling churches with people who have not repented of their sins. Instead of making the world like the church, such efforts succeed only in making the church more like the world. This is precisely what Jesus' teaching in Mark 4 was designed to avoid.

THE PARABLE OF THE SOILS

The disciples, having a genuine burden that others would believe, were astounded that the masses were not repenting. There must have been times when they questioned the indicting, hard, demanding message Jesus preached.

The Lord responded to this rising tide of doubt by telling the disciples a series of parables and proverbs about evangelism. A year before He would give the Great Commission, He used this series of parables as His basis for instruction concerning evangelism (Mark 4:1–34). Mark devotes more space to it than to any other teaching in his Gospel and the focal point is the initial parable, a story about a farmer sowing seed:

Listen! Behold, a sower went out to sow. And it happened, as he sowed, that some seed fell by the wayside; and the birds of the air came and devoured it. Some fell on stony ground, where it did not have much earth; and immediately it sprang up because it had no depth of earth. But when the sun was up it was scorched, and because it had no root it withered away. And some seed fell among thorns; and the thorns grew up and choked it, and it yielded no crop. But other seed fell on good ground and yielded a crop that sprang up, increased and produced: some thirtyfold, some sixty, and some a hundred. (Mark 4:3–8)

This illustration is a paradigmatic explanation of what evangelism should look like. It is designed to answer a basic question that all evangelists eventually ask: why do some people respond to the gospel while others do not? The answer to this question clarifies the essence of evangelism.

The Missing Sower

The parable of the soils begins with a farmer. What is surprising about him is how little control he actually has in the growing of the crops. There are no adjectives used to describe his style or skill, and in a subsequent parable our Lord depicts a sower as one who plants, returns home, and goes to sleep:

And He was saying, "The kingdom of God is like a man who casts seed upon the soil; and he goes to bed at night and gets up by day, and the seed sprouts and grows—how, he himself does not know.

"The soil produces crops by itself; first the blade, then the head, then the mature grain in the head. But when the crop permits, he immediately puts in the sickle, because the harvest has come." (Mark 4:26–29 NASB)

Jesus states that the farmer is ignorant of how the seed transforms itself into a mature plant. After sowing the seed, the farmer "goes to bed at night and gets up by day, and the seed sprouts up and grows—how, he himself does not know."

This ignorance is not unique to this particular farmer, but rather is true of everyone who sows. The growth of the seed is a mystery that even the most advanced farmer cannot explain. And this reality is the key to the entire parable. Jesus explains that the seed represents the gospel, and the farmer represents the evangelist (v. 26). The evangelist scatters the seed—that is, explains the gospel to people—and some of those people believe and receive life. How this happens is a divine mystery to the evangelist. One thing is clear, however: though he is the human means, it does not ultimately depend on him. The power of the gospel is in the working of the Spirit, not in the style of the sower (Rom. 1:16; 1 Thess. 1:5; 1 Peter 1:23). It is the Spirit of God who raises souls from death to life, not the methods or techniques of the messenger.

The apostle Paul understood this principle. When he brought the gospel to Corinth, he planted the church and left it in the care of Apollos. Later he described the experience this way: "I planted, Apollos watered, but God gave the increase" (1 Cor. 3:6). God was the one who actually drew sinners to Himself, changed their hearts, and caused them to be sanctified. Paul and Apollos were both faithful, but they most certainly were not the explanation for the supernatural life and growth. This truth caused Paul to say, "So then neither he who plants is anything, nor he who waters, but God who gives the increase" (1 Cor. 3:7).

Jesus intentionally highlights the farmer's lack of influence over the growth of the seed. In fact, Jesus stresses that the farmer, after planting, simply went home and fell asleep. This is directly analogous to evangelism. For a person to be saved, the Spirit of God has to draw him, and regenerate his soul (John 6:44; Titus 3:5). This runs counter to the notion that the results of evangelism can be influenced by the wardrobe of the pastor or the kind of music that is played before the message. A farmer could have a burlap or a cashmere seed bag, and neither would have any effect whatsoever on the growth of the seed. The pastor who thinks designer jeans will make his message more palatable is akin to a farmer investing in a designer seed bag so that the soil will be more receptive to his seeds.

Do not mistake this as an apologetic for wearing blue suits. The point Jesus makes is not that the evangelist should wear a tie and sing hymns. The entire parable is making the statement that as far as evangelism goes, it simply does not matter what the evangelist wears, or how he does his hair. Such externals are not what makes the seed grow. When people argue that a pastor who behaves like a particular segment of a culture is better able to reach that culture, they fail to understand Jesus' point.

All the farmer can do is sow, and all the evangelist can do is proclaim. As a preacher, if I thought someone's salvation was contingent upon my adherence to some subtle aspect of the culture, I could never sleep. But instead I know that "the Lord knows those who are His" (2 Tim. 2:19). It is not coincidental that the New Testament never calls evangelists to bear the responsibility for another person's salvation. Rather, having proclaimed the message faithfully, we are called to rest in the sovereignty of God.

Of course, the fact that the farmer went to sleep is not an excuse for laziness. It is wrong to think that the style of the evangelist determines who and how many will be saved. But there is the equally serious error of using God's sovereignty as an excuse not to evangelize. Often called hyper-Calvinism, this view incorrectly assumes that since evangelists are not capable of regenerating someone, then evangelism itself is not necessary.[2]

But that perspective likewise misses the point of Jesus' teaching. The farmer did sleep, but only after he diligently sowed his seed. A farmer who thinks, "I can't cause the seed to grow, so why bother even planting?" will not be a farmer for long.

The truth is, Jesus' description of the farmer provides the model for evangelism. The evangelist must plant the gospel seed, without which no one can be saved (Rom. 10:14–17). Then he must trust God with the results, since only the Spirit can give life (John 3:5–8).

WASTED SEED

Not only is the farmer's style irrelevant to the success of his crops but Jesus also does not suggest that the sower should alter his seed to facilitate growth. The parable of the soils portrays six results from the sowing process, but at no point do those results depend on the skill of the sower.

The absence of discussion about the seed likewise corresponds to evangelism. Jesus assumes that Christians will evangelize, using the true seed—the gospel. Altering the message is not an option. Believers are warned against tampering with the message at all (Gal. 1:6–9; 2 John 9–11). The only variable in this parable is the soil. If a frustrated evangelist looks at how difficult his task is, or how closed his culture seems to be to the gospel, the problem is not with the faithful messenger or the true gospel. Rather, it lies in the nature of the soil into which the true seed falls.

Jesus describes different kinds of soil where seeds are sown—some do not produce salvation's fruit, but others do. All four of these soils paint a picture of inevitable responses to evangelism, as the soils represent various conditions of the human heart.

Sowing on the road

The first kind of soil is not receptive at all. Matthew 13:4 describes some of the seed as falling "by the wayside." Fields in Israel were not fenced or walled in. Instead of fences, there were paths that crisscrossed the fields, making borders. These paths were purposely uncultivated. Since the climate in Israel is arid and hot, the paths were roads, beaten as hard as pavement by the feet of those who traversed them. If seed fell on these paths, birds following the sower would swoop down and snatch it.

Jesus relates this seed snatching to the activity of Satan. The compacted soil of the road represented the hard heart that the gospel seed does not penetrate, setting instead on the surface like food for the birds. It is a picture of those who, being held in bondage to Satan, have no interest in the truth. Having rejected the gospel, their hard hearts only grow more and more calloused. The more the farmer treads the path, though he frequently sows seed, the harder the ground becomes.

You might think that this soil describes the hearts of the worst, most outrageous, and irreligious sinners imaginable. But in reality, Jesus is referring to the religious leaders of Israel who were intensely and devotedly committed to external morality, religious ceremony, and traditional forms of worship. But, having rejected the Messiah, they were also utterly lost. They were proof that being "religious" is no indication of a soft heart. Rather, the deeper one's heart is entrenched in man-made religion, the more impenetrable it becomes. The only hope in such cases is to forcefully break up of the hard soil—like the smashing of stone fortresses referred to by Paul in 2 Corinthians 10:3–5 (NASB):

> For though we walk in the flesh, we do not war according to the
> flesh, for the weapons of our warfare are not of the flesh, but divinely

powerful for the destruction of fortresses. We are destroying specula-
tions and every lofty thing raised up against the knowledge of God,
and we are taking every thought captive to the obedience of Christ.

Sowing on the rocky ground

The second type of soil is compared to "stony ground, where it did not have
much earth" (Mark 4:5; see also 4:16). Before farmers sowed their fields, they
would remove all of the discoverable rocks, which was no small effort. In fact,
some rabbis used to say that when God placed rocks on the earth, He dumped
most of them in Israel. But below the reach of the plow there was often lime-
stone bedrock.[3] This is what Jesus was referring to here.

When seed fell onto this kind of ground, it would settle in the rich, soft
soil tilled by the plow. As it found water, the seed would develop and burrow,
beginning to spread roots and grow upward. But the young roots would not be
able to anchor the plant because they would soon hit that bedrock. Whatever
nutrients were in the soil, the plant would process immediately, and shoot up.
As it sprouted up into the sunlight, it would require more moisture. But because the roots could not penetrate the bedrock to get its nutrients, the fragile
plant would dry up in the sun.

Jesus compared this soil to a person who hears the gospel and immediately
responds with joy (Matt. 13:20). His quick response might fool the evangelist
into thinking that the conversion was genuine. Initially, this "convert" shows
dramatic change, as he or she absorbs and applies all the truth around him or
her. But like the seed that is quickly scorched, the apparent life is superficial
and temporary. Because there is no depth to the sinner's emotionally driven or
self-centered response, no fruit can come from it.

The true nature of this false conversion is soon revealed in the heat of suffering, self-sacrifice, and persecution. Such hardships are too much for the
shallow heart to endure.

Sowing among the thorns

The third kind of soil is filled with thorns (Mark 4:7, 18). This soil is de-
ceptive. It has been plowed and appears fertile, but below the surface lurks a
network of wild roots ready to produce an infestation of weeds. When good
seed is forced to compete for life against these dormant thorns and thistles, the

farmer's crops will be choked out. Eventually, the weeds steal the seed's moisture and veil its sunlight. As a result, the good seed dies.

The word Jesus uses for *thorns* is from the Greek word ἄκανθα (akantha), which is a particular kind of thorny weed common in the Middle East and frequently found in cultivated soil. In fact, it is the same word used in Matthew 27:29 to refer to the crown of thorns placed on our Lord's head. These unwanted plants were common and dangerous to crops.

Jesus compares this weedy soil to people who hear the gospel, but "the cares of this world, the deceitfulness of riches, and the desires for other things entering in choke the word, and it becomes unfruitful" (Mark 4:19). If the rocky soil stood for shallow emotion, and if the wayside represented religious deception driven by self-love and self-interest, then the thorny soil describes a double-minded person. When someone's heart is captive to the things of the world, his contrition over sin is not genuine. His heart is divided between earthly, temporal pleasures and heavenly, eternal realities. But those things are mutually exclusive.

The thorns correlate to the "cares of this world," and this phrase could even be better rendered "the distractions of the age" (Mark 4:19). The heart with thorns is occupied by whatever worldly things preoccupy the culture. This is the heart that loves the world and all the things that are in the world, and therefore the love of God is not in it (see 1 John 2:15; James 4:4).

Those who try to evangelize by accommodating the culture cannot avoid cultivating this kind of soil. The seed may land well enough, but as it grows, the love of the world will expose the token profession of faith for what it really is: another temporary, superficial action from a heart that is still held captive to the world.

The seeds of the gospel fall on the roadside hearers, rocky-soil hearers, and thorny-ground hearers. But in each case, it is rejected. In giving this powerful and clear analogy, the Lord never suggests that the negative response should be blamed on the farmer. The problem is not an evangelist who was not clever or popular enough. Rather, the problem is in the soil. Sinners reject the gospel because they hate the truth and love their sin. That's why the gospel, faithfully proclaimed, can be snatched by Satan, killed by self-love, or smothered by the world.

Sowing on good soil

There may be hearts that reject salvation, but Jesus also describes hearts that receive the gospel. Encouragement comes when Jesus says, "But other seed fell on good ground and yielded a crop that sprang up, increased and produced: some thirtyfold, some sixty, and some a hundred" (Mark 4:8). Good soil is deep, soft, rich, and clean. Neither Satan, the flesh, nor the world can overpower the gospel when it is planted in this kind of heart.

Nearly all of Jesus' parables contain a shocking and unexpected element in them, and the parable of the soils is no exception. So far, this agricultural analogy would have been familiar to the disciples, or for that matter, to any Israelite. They subsisted off of their farming, and their land was checkered with grain fields. They understood the danger of birds, rocks, and thorns. All of that was very common. But Jesus abandons the familiar by then describing a result no one would have ever expected—a crop of thirty-, sixty-, and even a hundredfold. An average crop could yield sixfold, and a crop that produced tenfold would be considered a once-in-a-lifetime harvest. So when Jesus said that just one of the farmer's seeds could produce as much as a hundredfold, that would have shocked the disciples.

If you are not from an agrarian society, you might miss the absurdity of Jesus describing a seed that can produce 10,000 percent. All illustrations break down at a certain point, and this is precisely the point where the farming analogy is no longer applicable to evangelism. By describing such a massive harvest, Jesus is making the point that the gospel can produce spiritual life in multiples that are impossible except by God's own power.

Heart preparation for the gospel is the work of the Holy Spirit. He alone convicts (John 16:8–15), regenerates (John 3:3–8), and justifies (Gal. 5:22–23). Heart work is God's domain:

> Then I will sprinkle clean water on you, and you will be clean; I will cleanse you from all your filthiness and from all your idols.
>
> Moreover, I will give you a new heart and put a new spirit within you; and I will remove the heart of stone from your flesh and give you a heart of flesh.

I will put My Spirit within you and cause you to walk in My statutes, and you will be careful to observe my ordinances. (Ezek. 36:25–
27; cf. Jer. 31:31–33)

As Solomon asked rhetorically, "Who can say, 'I have made my heart clean, I
am pure from my sin'?" (Prov. 20:9). The answer, of course, is no one.

While there are explanations for why people reject the gospel—both satanic and human—true repentance is supernatural. Nowhere is this truth seen
more clearly than in the conversion of the thief on the cross (Luke 23:39–43; cf.
Matt 27:38–44). His conversion could not have been more unlikely, as it occurred at a time when Jesus appeared to be a colossal failure. The Lord seemed
weak, defeated, victimized, and without power to save Himself, much less anyone else. Jesus was disgraced, His enemies triumphant, and His followers absent. The tide of public opinion was against Him, and sarcasm—provided by
the first thief—was the fitting and understandable response.

God worked His supernatural saving ability on the second thief and, contrary to natural reason, he repented and believed. Why did this dying rebel
embrace as Lord a bleeding and crucified man? The only answer is that it was a
miracle of grace and the result of divine intervention. Before the supernatural
earthquakes, darkness, and open graves, this man believed because the seed of
the gospel landed in fertile soil, prepared by the hand of God. His conversion
bears witness to the fact that it is not the style or strength of man that saves,
but the power of God.

Because God produces that heart-change, the result will be evident in every transformed life, though different in extent—and far beyond what the disciples could ever have dreamed. The gospel would soon explode in a spiritual
harvest, starting at Pentecost and continuing exponentially until the last day
of Christ's earthly kingdom. The power for this multiplication is supernatural,
but the means is the faithful witness of true believers.

The wonder of the gospel is that it is God's doing. We sow the seed by sharing the gospel, then we go to sleep, and the Spirit works through the gospel to
give life. We do not control who is saved, because the Spirit goes wherever He
wills (John 3:8). We do not even know how it happens, any more than a farmer
knows how a seed in the ground becomes food. Our job is not to impart life,

only to implant the seed. Once we have done that, we can rest in the sovereign power of God.

APPLICATION FOR EVANGELISM

The truth in this parable should have a profound effect on how we view evangelism. It should cause us to evangelize strategically, humbly, obediently, and confidently.

Strategically

Jesus teaches that certain kinds of soil allow the seed to grow with joy before it is choked out or dried up. That fact should sufficiently demonstrate the folly of making gospel appeals that aim for only the emotions. There is hardly a less-reliable guide concerning true faith than the emotions—since neither joy nor sorrow is necessarily indicative of true repentance (see 2 Cor. 7:10–11). When the evangelist primarily targets the sinner's feelings, or bases assurance of salvation on an emotional experience, he is directing the gospel at shallow hearts. Such an approach may initially appear impressive, since shallow soil looks good for a short while. But it does not result in lasting conversions.

Evangelism should also not manipulate the will by appealing to the sinner's natural desires. It is normal for sinners to wish for better things for themselves—like health, wealth, success, and personal fulfillment. But the gospel never offers what the uncommitted, impure heart already wants. Only false teachers use the pride and lusts of the flesh to coerce a positive response from people. By contrast, the true gospel offers what is incongruous to natural human desire. As Jesus told His followers:

> Do not think that I came to bring peace on earth; I did not come to bring peace but a sword.
>
> For I came to set a man against his father, and a daughter against her mother, and a daughter-in-law against her mother-in-law; and a man's enemies will be the members of his household.
>
> He who loves father or mother more than Me is not worthy of Me; and he who loves son or daughter more than Me is not worthy of Me.

And he who does not take his cross and follow after Me is not worthy of Me.

He who has found his life will lose it, and he who has lost his life for My sake will find it." (Matt. 10:34–39 NASB)

True repentance and faith in Christ denies the usual depraved longings of the human will.

Truly, truly, I say to you, unless a grain of wheat falls into the earth and dies, it remains alone; but if it dies, it bears much fruit.

He who loves his life loses it, and he who hates his life in this world will keep it to life eternal.

If anyone serves Me, he must follow Me; and where I am, there My servant will be also; if anyone serves Me, the Father will honor him. (John 12:24–26 NASB)

If neither raw emotion nor rational desire is a reliable gauge for true faith, then what is? As Jonathan Edwards rightly observed, a dependable indicator is a "humble, broken-hearted love for God."[4] He wrote:

The desires of the saints, however earnest, are humble desires; their hope is an humble hope; their joy, even when it is unspeakable and full of glory, is an humble and broken-hearted joy that leaves the Christian more poor in spirit, more like a little child, more disposed to a universal lowliness of behavior.[5]

According to Edwards, evangelism should not aim to influence emotion or manipulate the will because those things are not only easily accomplished, but are unsafe signs of conversion. Rather, "a holy life is the chief sign of grace."[6] A holy life flows from a holy heart, which produces holy affections directed at the Holy One. This is only possible when the mind of the sinner is persuaded to see his sin for what it is and the gospel as his sole solution.

Humbly

The truth is that the power of the gospel is in God's hands—not ours. Hence, we should evangelize with humility. By "humility" we do not mean uncertainty, ecumenical tolerance, or any other postmodern distortion of the term. Rather, we mean humility in the biblical sense of trembling before God and His Word (Isa. 66:2)—avoiding any prideful notion that might make us so brash as to change His message or so conceited as to take credit for His work.

The power of the gospel is in its unchanging truth, and a mutant seed will produce a mutant crop. Moreover, the evangelist should not try to make Jesus attractive to sinners. Jesus is attractive by Himself. But people are blinded to His attributes by their sin. It is not enough to encourage people to activate their selfish wills or excite their fickle emotions. Instead they must be called to mourn over their sin, to the point of genuine repentance. Thus, explaining the depth of sin and the punishment it deserves is an essential part of biblical evangelism. A sinner must hear that his sin indicts and condemns him because it offends God, and only the Spirit of God can take that truth from the sinner's ears to his heart.

It is exactly this kind of evangelism that is the first to suffer in the name of attracting more people to Jesus. In a bid to make the message more popular and the results more noticeable, evangelists too often appeal to emotions and will, rather than to the mind.

But when the real gospel is preached to the mind—a message that includes the hard calls of discipleship, the radical nature of conversion, and the glorious work of Christ—then the right seed is sown in the heart, and divinely prepared hearts will be receptive to the seed.

Obediently

When He finished explaining the parable of the soils, Jesus asked the disciples, "Is a lamp brought to be put under a basket or under a bed? Is it not to be set on a lampstand?" (Mark 4:21). He was telling His disciples that after His death and resurrection, they would have in their possession a great light. That light is the "light of the gospel of the glory of Christ, who is the image of God" (2 Cor. 4:4). It is to be preached faithfully by Christ's slaves (v. 5), but the results are as much in the sovereign power of God as the original creation was: "For God, who said, 'Light shall shine out of darkness,' is the One who has shown in our hearts to give the Light of the knowledge of the glory of God in the face of Christ" (2 Cor. 4:6).

Our Lord continued His teaching with this axiom: "There is nothing hidden which will not be revealed, nor has anything been kept secret but that it should come to light" (Mark 4:22). Here was a truism conveying the fact that every secret has its appropriate time to be told. The whole point of keeping a secret is that now is not the time for it to be known. In the disciples' case, they were not yet commissioned and sent into the world. But when that time came, they were to go, and speak boldly. This relates to our Lord's frequent command not to speak about Him or His miracles until after His death and resurrection (Matt. 8:4; 9:30; 12:16; 17:9; Mark 1:44; 3:12; 5:43; 7:36; 8:30; 9:9; Luke 4:41; 8:56; 9:21). One clear reason for such a restriction was to make clear that the message He wanted His followers to spread was not that He was a healer or a political liberator, but a Savior who died and rose from the dead.

A farmer's usefulness is connected to the amount of seed he sows. The more he sows, the more seed he scatters, and the more likely it is that some of the seed will land on good soil. To communicate this duty, Jesus followed the proverbs in Mark 4:21–22 with a clear promise: "With the same measure you use, it will be measured to you; and to you who hear, more will be given" (v. 24). That is the language of eternal rewards, and it provides great motivation to proclaim the gospel both actively and accurately. Though we cannot control the results, we are called to spread the message. And even if we are rejected by our hearers, our faithful efforts will one day be rewarded by the Lord.

There are false Christians, and there are false evangelists, and the Lord will judge both. But true believers are obedient to evangelize whenever they have opportunity, remembering that our obedience leads to divine blessing both here, and in the life to come.

Confidently

Knowing that our evangelism is energized by the power of God gives us confidence in divine results.

This is precisely why Mark concluded this extensive section on evangelism with a final parable describing the kingdom of God: "It is like a mustard seed which, when it is sown on the ground, is smaller than all the seeds on earth; but when it is sown, it grows up and becomes greater than all herbs, and shoots out large branches, so that the birds of the air may nest under its shade" (Mark 4:31–32).

Remember, the disciples were worried that the Old Testament promises of a kingdom might not happen with Jesus. He had been preaching for two years, and yet there seemed to be so few who had truly believed. The Twelve were on the verge of giving up hope. But Jesus told them that if the seed was scattered, the gospel would grow, and the kingdom would come. What Jesus meant is that the kingdom would start small but it would explode, and eventually the birds of the nations would be resting in its shade (Ezek. 31:6). The gospel would go global, and it would do so through these beleaguered disciples.

This is exactly what happened. After the resurrection there were but 120 followers of Jesus, and after the Day of Pentecost that number jumped to 3,000 (Acts 1:13; 2:41). This number quickly jumped to 5,000 (Acts 4:4). In a few months there were more than 20,000. The power of the gospel was turning the world upside down. Two thousand years later, countless people have been saved, and are now either in the church militant on earth or the church triumphant in heaven. One day, Christ will return and establish His millennial kingdom on this earth. Even then, the gospel will continue to call sinners to repentance.

The message of salvation keeps moving through those who are sowers, producing spiritual life and genuine fruit in good soil. It does so solely because it is empowered by God—which means that the popularity or persuasiveness of the human messenger has nothing to do with it.

Evangelism is a privileged calling. We do what we can to spread the gospel wherever we are able. Then we go home and go to sleep. If we have worked hard we can sleep well, knowing, as the farmer did, that the growth does not depend on us.

2

God's Global Goal: The Power of the Great Commission

Jesse Johnson

The Great Commission is certainly the most important command given to Christians. Some variation of it ends all four Gospels, and Jesus' last earthly words in the book of Acts are another form of this charge. Despite these repetitions, the radical nature of the command for global evangelism is often overlooked. As far back as Genesis 3 God indicated He was sending a savior to the world, but God did not allow believers to go throughout the world with that message until after the crucifixion and resurrection. Understanding the "why" of the Great Commission helps to unlock its power.

One of the most sober and chilling charges given to pastors concerning evangelism is found in Paul's final words to Timothy. In 2 Timothy, Paul had warned his disciple and fellow pastor to be ready for godless days. "The time will come," he wrote, "when they will not endure sound doctrine" (2 Tim. 4:3). Paul wanted Timothy to brace himself to experience rejection (v. 4), and even to endure the same suffering as Paul (v. 5).

The solution, Paul told Timothy, was found in embracing the sufficiency of Scripture. It alone can make the man of God "complete, thoroughly equipped for every good work" (2 Tim. 3:17). In light of this, Paul had a severe charge for his protégé: "I charge you therefore before God and the Lord Jesus Christ, who will judge the living and the dead at His appearing and His kingdom: Preach the word!" (2 Tim. 4:1-2a). Notice how serious this command is. Paul speaks these words (1) before God, (2) before the Lord Jesus Christ, and (3) in light of the judgment of the living and the dead. It is difficult to imagine how Paul could have made this charge appear more important.

Yet Paul was not done. Timothy was not only to preach, but Paul also wrote that he was to "be watchful in all things, endure afflictions, do the work of an evangelist, fulfill your ministry" (v. 5). Timothy could preach all he wanted, but if he neglected to do the work of an evangelist, he would not be accomplishing what God wanted him to do.

This truth—that the work of evangelism should be central to any ministry—is not limited to the office of a pastor. All Christians are called to be faithful to our Lord's command to bring the gospel to every person. But it is astonishing how often the command to evangelize gets relegated to the background of Christian life. Some even fall into a pattern of neglecting the command to evangelize for prolonged periods of time, and I have even heard people say that evangelism is something that God simply has not called them to do.

The reality is that evangelism is central to the mission of Christ, and in fact it is the focal point of God's work in creation. If a person fails to understand the importance of evangelism, he misses the entire point of Jesus' ministry, for "the Son of Man has come to seek and to save that which was lost" (Luke 19:10). Evangelism is not one thing that Christians are called to do; it is the primary task. All other tasks are intermediate.

For example, Christians pursue sanctification in all areas of life so that our testimony is believable to the outside world. When we proclaim the riches of Christ, we need to be able to show the unbelieving world that we personally value Christ above this world. We refuse to steal, because the pleasure of God is worth more than anything we could get our hands on. We refuse to lie, because we trust God's sovereignty more than any fiction we could invent. We pray, because we know that nothing of value is possible in this life without God's blessing. All of our sanctification has the effect of making believable our claim that Jesus has surpassing value.

Moreover, the pastoral ministry is not an end in itself. In a healthy church, pastors preach expository sermons; people listen and apply, while the church matures. But all of this is not of final importance. The goal is for a healthy church to understand the gospel more clearly, and be able to proclaim it more powerfully. Churches develop opportunities for fellowship and care for one another's needs so that the world will know the love of God by the way Christians love one another (John 13:34–35). It is all bound up in the goal of spreading God's glory to more and more people through evangelism (2 Cor. 4:15).

When evangelism is neglected, it indicates that there is a lack of understanding about the purpose of God in the world, and in the plan of salvation. Ever since the creation of man, global belief has always been God's plan. But it was not until after Jesus rose from the grave that God's followers were told to go into the world and spread the news about Him. In fact, one of the most effective ways to increase your passion for evangelism is to understand how evangelism fits into God's work in the world. It has always been His goal, but until the church began, God had not given His people marching orders (along with His Spirit) to take the gospel to every tribe, language, and nation.

George Peters explains that the call to evangelize is embedded in the very core of Scripture:

> The Great Commission is not an isolated command arbitrarily imposed upon Christianity. It is a logical summation and natural outflow of the character of God as He is revealed in the Scriptures, of the missionary purpose and thrust of God as unfolded in the Old Testament and historically incarnated in the calling of Israel, of the life, theology and saving work of the Christ as disclosed in the gospels, of the nature and work of the Holy Spirit as predicted by our Lord and manifested on and after Pentecost, and of the nature and design of the church of Jesus Christ as made known in the Acts of the apostles and the epistles.[1]

In other words, if our churches are to rediscover biblical evangelism, we must come to grips with God's priorities as laid out in Scripture. As Peters so aptly states, the Great Commission is not simply another command in Scripture to be obeyed, it is the command that gives life to all other commands given to the church.

Evangelism in the Old Testament

From the opening pages of Scripture, the stage is set for the drama of re-demption. God created people sinless, yet they sinned. Sin brought enmity be-tween God and his creation, but Genesis 3 shows that God was going to recon-cile people to Himself. While Adam and Eve were hiding from God, God had already ordained the means to bring humanity out of hiding and into a right relationship with Himself. This is the proto-evangel (gospel beforehand), and it reveals the evangelistic heart of God.

The promise itself is shrouded in mystery. God said that there would be a seed, an offspring of Adam, who would crush the head of Satan (Gen. 3:15; Rev. 12:9). While this seed will be bruised by Satan, hope nevertheless remains. Someone, sometime, somewhere in the future, will defeat Satan and restore peace between God and His creation.[2]

Who exactly this person would be remained a mystery. Eve apparently thought it was Abel, or even Seth (Gen. 4:25). Noah's father thought it could be Noah (Gen. 5:29). This mystery is compounded by the events of Genesis 11. Before Babel, it was conceivable for God to send this son of Adam into the world to defeat Satan, and everyone would know about it. But following the events at the tower of Babel, God separated nations and confused languages. By scattering the nations throughout the world and by confusing their tongues, God made certain two things: the nations would not be able to communicate with ease, and they would all go their own way (Acts 14:16).

After Genesis 11, the question ceased to be "who will be this promised re-deemer?" and became "how will others find out?" Theologians refer to this last question as the problem of God's universality.[3] If Yahweh is the God of all nations but He chooses to reveal Himself to only one nation, how would that nation bring the news of who the redeemer is to all the others?[4] This question of how to spread news of Yahweh is the foundation of the divine mandate for missions.[5] People were left wondering how the future Messiah would commu-nicate with people who did not speak His language, follow His laws, or expect His coming.

To further complicate matters, God chose and then promised one man, Abram, that he would be the start of another nation.[6] When the dust of the tower of Babel settled, God had already turned redemptive focus to this new nation that—unlike the others—was not from Babel, but from God's covenant with Abram. This future nation would have a unique purpose in the world, as its people were to show other nations the way back to God (Isa. 42:6; 51:4).[7] Through them, "all the families of the earth [would] be blessed" (Gen. 12:3).

Thus, evangelism was the foundation of the nation of Israel. God's ultimate goal and heart's desire in these promises—to Adam, Eve, Abram—was for the entire world to be the recipients of His blessing. This global theme is so pervasive throughout Genesis that the universal blessing is reiterated five times throughout the book (Gen. 12:3; 18:18; 22:18; 26:4; 28:14).

The identification of Israel as the nation that would produce the Messiah marked a new phase in God's mission to the world.

A LIGHT TO THE WORLD

Israel was God's chosen nation. While there were many reasons God chose a nation—that is, to produce the Messiah (Rom. 9:5), to be stewards of the Law (Rom. 9:4), and to reveal a New Covenant (Heb. 8:6)—one reason stands out in the context of evangelism: God chose one nation to become a beacon of light to the world. God spoke to Israel through Isaiah: "I, the LORD, have called You in righteousness, / And will hold Your hand; / I will keep You and give You as a covenant to the people, / As a light to the Gentiles" (Isa. 42:6). God's design has always been that the nations of the world should hear of his glory, and put their trust in Him. His plan for the nation of Israel was that they would carry out this plan by bearing His name and illustrating His glory as a testimony to the world.[8]

Abram's calling did not identify who precisely the promised redeemer would be. Instead, this promise passed down through the patriarchs in Egypt. Through their time in Egypt the Israelites grew into a separate nation, and God led them into the promised land in dramatic fashion that served as witness to Yahweh's power and superiority. But before they entered the land, they received their Law, and the Law explained to them how they were to bring the news of God's glory to the world.

It is in this sense that the Israelites were to be a light to the world. God gave them wisdom the form of the Torah, and they were to live it out.[9] Moses explained this to the Israelites before they crossed the Jordan:

"Surely I have taught you statutes and judgments, just as the LORD my God commanded me, that you should act according to them in the land which you go to possess. Therefore be careful to observe them; for this is your wisdom and your understanding in the sight of the peoples who will hear all these statutes, and say, 'Surely this great nation is a wise and understanding people.'

"For what great nation is there that has God so near to it, as the LORD our God is to us, for whatever reason we may call upon Him?" (Deut. 4:5–7)

The Law was so glorious that if the Israelites kept it, the nations of the world would hear about it and be astonished. Thus the nations that went their own way from Babel would learn about God and His infinite wisdom through witnessing how the Israelites kept the Torah.

Christopher Wright explains that: "Because God's ultimate mission is to bring about the blessing of the nations, as he promised Abraham," God chose to do that "by the existence in the world of a community that will be taught to live according to the way of the Lord in righteousness and justice (ethics)."[10] The Jews were to live differently from the other nations, and the goal of this distinction was evangelistic.[11]

This evangelistic function of Israel explains why, immediately before giving them the Law, Yahweh told Israel that He was going to make them "a kingdom of priests" (Exod. 19:6). This exclusivity does not mean that all the other nations of the earth were rejected, but rather that Israel was to be the means through which they would receive the way back to God.[12] Thus, "this concept of national priesthood has an essentially missional dimension, for it puts Israel in a dual role in relation to God and the nations, and gives them the priestly function of being the agent of blessing."[13] In other words, the nations would be blessed by having God revealed to them through the nation Israel.

Obviously much of the Mosaic Law served the function of differentiating the Israelites from the surrounding nations, which highlighted the uniqueness of His commands. The dietary laws, the Sabbath laws, land laws, circumcision, and even the laws banning idolatry, all intentionally differentiated Israel from its neighbors for the purpose of evangelism.[14]

For Israel, evangelism meant keeping the Torah. Thus the whole book of Deuteronomy can be seen as "an urgent call to covenant loyalty . . . worked out in practical ethical obedience . . . with a view to the affect this will have on the nations."[15]

Interestingly, the Israelites were never commanded to go into the world and preach the gospel.[16] They were not supposed to be missionaries in the New Testament sense.[17] Rather, they were to stay in Israel and bear witness to the world by keeping the Torah. Covenant obedience was their form of evangelism.

It can be said that the Israelites had their own Great Commission (Deut. 4), only it was a call to stay and obey rather than go and proclaim. Theologians refer to this as "centripetal missions."[18] That term conveys the idea that rather than scattering through the world, as modern missionaries would, they were to stay and attract the world to them. Instead of global scattering, the Israelites were to demonstrate global gathering, by acting as a light to the nations. The surrounding nations would hear of the greatness of the Israelite laws, and they would be drawn to Israel. When they came to investigate the source of the wisdom the Israelites possessed, they would see that this wisdom ultimately came from Yahweh. In short, Israel, as a kingdom of priests and a light to the nations, formed "the essence of the Old Testament."[19]

This is why, as Wright noted, "Obedience to the law was not for Israel's benefit alone. It is a marked feature of the Old Testament that Israel lived on a very public stage . . . and this visibility of Israel was part of its theological identity and role as the priesthood of YHWH among the nations."[20]

However, with the possible exception of the queen of Sheba (1 Kgs. 10), there is not an example in the Old Testament of Gentiles being attracted to Israel because of its covenant obedience. Instead, the Old Testament draws to a close with Israel displaced, the temple destroyed, and the mystery still unsolved—who would this redeemer be, and how would he draw the world to himself?

THE PROMISED MESSIAH

Only through the advent of the Messiah could Israel possibly fulfill its mission to the nations. In Isaiah 49:6 (ESV) God describes the Messiah's mission to earth as being "a light for the nations, that my salvation may reach to the end of the earth." In other words, God promised that the Messiah would come and be that light to the nations who were held in the darkness of sin, and John specifically called Jesus the prophesied "light of the world" (John 8:12; 9:5; see also John 1:9; 3:19; 12:46).

Jesus, of course, came as the fulfillment of that Messianic prophecy. Interestingly, he did not fulfill *all* prophecy. There are some promises that relate to Israel's current national and political identity that will be fulfilled (e.g., Ps. 72:8–14; Isa. 9:6–7; Jer. 23:5; Zech. 14:4–21). Nevertheless, Jesus did declare that he was the one of whom the Scriptures spoke (Matt. 11:3–5; Luke 4:2; John 4:26).

Yet amazingly, Jesus did not tell his followers to take this news into all the world. Instead, he told them the opposite. For example, after healing a leper, he told the man, "See that you tell no one" (Matt. 8:4). Even after the disciples finally realized that He was indeed the Son of God and the seed that would crush Satan and restore Israel, Jesus "strictly charged the disciples to tell no one that he was the Christ" (Matt. 16:20 ESV).

In some cases, this silence was commanded in the most impossible of circumstances. Consider the miracle in the Decapolis. There, a large crowd brought Jesus a man who was known to all as a deaf-mute. Jesus took the man aside, and healed both his hearing and his speech, then commanded the crowd that "they should tell no one" (Mark 7:36). Of course, Mark points out, "The more He commanded them, the more widely they proclaimed it" (v. 36*b*).

Another example, found in the book of Luke, is particularly staggering. Luke tells the story of a well-known synagogue leader, certainly an influential Jew whose family affairs would be public. He fell at Jesus' feet and begged him to heal his twelve-year-old daughter. Jesus began the walk to the man's house, and a large crowd gathered to follow. As they walked, word came that the daughter had died, and by the time Jesus and the veritable parade had arrived at the leader's home, there were already professional mourners wailing.

Jesus threw everyone out of the house except the parents. He then took Peter, James, and John inside, and raised the girl from the dead. He "charged them to tell no one what had happened" (Luke 8:56) and walked back out into the crowd. Jesus departed with his disciples, leaving the parents to figure out what to tell the funeral party outside. [21]

When astonished witnesses of impossible miracles were instructed to keep silent, the command seemed counterintuitive. After all, if Jesus was the Messiah, why did He not tell his disciples to take the message of His signs and wonders everywhere? Jesus did, however, explain why he wanted people not to spread the news of his miracles: the miracles were not the message. Even after something as profound as the transfiguration, Jesus commanded the disciples to remain silent because first, "The Son of Man must suffer many things, and be rejected by the elders and chief priests and scribes, and be killed, and be raised the third day" (Luke 9:22). Elsewhere, he told them not to tell others of the miracles he did "until the Son of Man had risen from the dead" (Mark 9:9 ESV).

THE GREAT COMMISSION

The gospel is not the fact that Jesus is the Messiah, or Jesus would have sent His disciples much earlier than He did. Rather, the gospel is the news that Jesus is the Messiah who was crucified in the place of sinners, and then raised from the dead on the third day. Thus, after the Crucifixion and resurrection, the restraints came off of the disciples. They were told to wait for the Holy Spirit to empower them, and then to start a global movement that would spread to every nation. It is impossible to overstate how radical of a concept this commission is in redemptive history.

Illustrating the importance of this command for evangelism, all four Gospels end with some variation of the Great Commission (Matt. 28:18–20; Mark 16:15; Luke 24:46–47; John 20:21).[22] In fact, Jesus' very last earthly words were yet another charge to the disciples to "be witnesses to Me in Jerusalem, and in all Judea and Samaria, and to the end of the earth" (Acts 1:8).

Never before had God commanded every one of His followers to live a life consumed by taking the news of redemption to the corners of the world. The disciples were expecting Jesus to restore the kingdom to Israel (Acts 1:6), and instead they were told to wait for that. However, in the meantime they were to take the kingdom of God to every creature.

Rather than building up a nation through covenant obedience for the sake of attracting the nations of the world to God through wisely following His law, the New Testament calls Christians to "go into all the world and proclaim the gospel to the whole creation" (Mark 16:15 ESV). In contradistinction to

God's command for the nation of Israel to stay and obey, Christ commanded the church to go and to proclaim for the sake of a new body, made up of people from every nation.

Rather than using one nation's obedience as a means of attracting the world to God, the church is called to attract people to God through the gospel. This is why Paul says that he was not sent to baptize, "but to preach the gospel" (1 Cor. 1:17). Paul did not take a message of obedience to a set of laws as a means of global transformation, as did Moses in Deuteronomy 4. Rather, he went preaching only Christ, and Him crucified (1 Cor. 1:23; 2:2).

Israel was to use obedience to the Torah to create a beautiful culture that would attract people to be saved by faith in Yahweh and His glory. The church, on the other hand, was to use sacrificial living to fund a global invasion of people proclaiming the beautiful gospel that attracts people to be saved by faith in the glorious God.[23] The end is the same; but the method of the mission is different.[24]

This was God's plan from the very beginning (1 Pet. 1:20). From the initial promise in the garden to Adam and Eve that they would have an offspring who would crush Satan, through the scattering of the nations at Babel, to the calling of Abraham, and through the odyssey of Israel, God was directing redemptive history to the point of sending His son into the world as the light of the world. And now His people are to take that light, and bring it to every unbeliever on the planet.

IMPLICATIONS OF THE GREAT COMMISSION ON EVANGELISM

Apathy about evangelism is unexplainable for this reason: the Great Commission is not just one of many commands, but it marks a change in redemptive history. To say that the death and resurrection of Jesus is the focal point of all of history is correct, but it is only half true. The corollary is that the purpose of life from that moment forward is to glorify God by telling as many people as possible the truth about His son.

This is exactly the passion that is described in the New Testament. As soon as the church is launched, the narrative of Acts tracks its growth and expansion. Believers everywhere grew in their faith and became eager to spread the gospel. After Paul was converted, he and Barnabas found themselves preaching in Antioch to almost the entire city, including both Gentiles and Jews. Luke writes that Paul and Barnabas grew bold and told the crowd, "the Lord has commanded us: 'I have set you as a light to the Gentiles, / That you should be for salvation to the ends of the earth'" (Acts 13:47). Paul saw himself as the recipient of the Great Commission and also saw its place in redemptive history. The result of his bold evangelism is striking: "Now when the Gentiles heard this, they were glad and glorified the word of the Lord. And as many as had been appointed to eternal life believed" (Acts 13:48).

Elsewhere, Paul describes a Christian as someone who is "compelled" by the love of Christ to urge others to come to faith in Jesus (2 Cor. 5:14, 20). Paul borrows language from Babel and likens himself to an ambassador, sent by God, for the purpose of reconciling alienated nations (2 Cor. 5:18–20). He lived his life enduring suffering and afflictions, all for the purpose of taking the name of Jesus to places where it had yet to go (Rom. 15:20).

The evangelistic drive evident in Paul was not unique to him, but is in fact a mark of any Christian who rightly understands his place in the redemptive work of God. This is why Peter explained that the purpose of sanctification is so that a believer is ready to evangelize at a moment's notice. He writes, "But sanctify the Lord God in your hearts, and always be ready to give a defense to everyone who asks you a reason for the hope that is in you, with meekness and fear" (1 Pet. 3:15).

Seeing that all of redemptive history built toward the Great Commission results in an understanding of the imperative of gospel proclamation and a rightful passion for evangelism. Only when believers are obedient to the commands to evangelize will they truly be imitators of God's heart for the world.

3

The Common Case of Unbelief: A Biblical Perspective on Unbelievers

Jonathan Rourke

Often, evangelistic training stresses the need for the Christian to find common ground with unbelievers in order to effectively witness. But because all unbelievers have a few characteristics in common, this quest for a shared starting point is often misguided. All unbelievers have a common deception, a common destiny, and a common deliverer. In short, they have a common case of unbelief. Understanding the implications of this will make the evangelist more compassionate, and will bring the glory of the gospel to the center of the conversation.

What comes to mind when you hear the word *pagan*? What about the word *heathen*? For many, these words might conjure up images of naked savages engaged in unrestrained debauchery. They are words used negatively, and they imply a complete lack of morality.

But these words did not always have religious or moral connotations. To be a heathen once meant someone who lived on the heath, or outside the limits of the urban center. The word *pagan* was actually a Latin word used by the Romans to describe an incompetent soldier. It did not take on a religious meaning until the second century AD when Tertullian adopted it to refer to anyone who was not a faithful soldier for Christ.[1] Now these words are often used by Christians to describe people whom the Bible simply refers to as *unbelievers* (Luke 12:46; 1 Cor. 6:6).

The way we speak about the lost influences our attitudes toward them. If we perceive unbelievers as a savage enemy, we are less likely to feel compassion for them. If we view them as lost souls in need of rescue, we are more likely to help.

The purpose of this chapter is to identify common characteristics of unbelievers. Rightly understood, these commonalities should drive Christians to be more faithful in evangelism. They apply to the atheist, the idolater, and even the agnostic. In short, those outside of Christ have a common case of unbelief marked by a common deception, a common destiny, and a common deliverer.

A COMMON DECEPTION

Sun Tzu, in *The Art of War*, said, "All war is deception,"[2] and Satan is an expert when it comes to disinformation. He is the father of lies (John 8:44), and the whole world is under his power (Eph 2:2). But when people fail to recognize his existence and his evil intent, his danger is masked. To some he is far more powerful than he actually is; to others he is far less evil than he actually is. Still others deny his existence entirely. In all of these cases, the result is the same. Satan has succeeded in amassing an army of deceived followers, distracted from the truth, and has empowered them to enlist others.

The Gospel of John records an intense exchange between Jesus and an unruly crowd. In the confrontation, Jesus traced the genealogy of every unbeliever back to the devil himself. When the crowd was ready to deny Jesus as the Christ, Jesus rightly diagnosed that their denial was based on this pedigree. The murderous intent of the unbelievers in the crowd matched the murdering nature of their spiritual father. These people were deceived by Satan, and turned away from the Christ (John 8:39–47).

Tragically, there are many who will hear the truth of the gospel and yet refuse to believe because they have been successfully swayed by the disinformation of atheism, false religion, or self-righteousness. The Bible makes clear that all of these represent a willful suppression of the truth (Rom. 1:18). Rejection of the gospel is the outward manifestation of the inward corruption of an understanding induced by Satan. No matter how clearly the gospel is presented, or how passionate the preacher, the one who hears it is not capable of knowing the truth. This is because, Paul said, "What may be known of God is manifest in them, for God has shown it to them" (Rom. 1:19). In other words, all people know the truth about God, and yet unbelievers simply choose to reject it.

They do so because they have been deceived by the world, themselves, and Satan (1 John 2:16). Thus, they willingly "suppress the truth in unrighteousness" (Rom. 1:18). Paul makes it clear that it is not a lack of evidence or reason that is keeping somebody from the gospel. Rather, "His invisible attributes are clearly seen, being understood by the things that are made, even His eternal power and Godhead, so that they are without excuse" (Rom. 1:20).

One of the great mysteries of human existence is not the existence of God, but the existence of those who reject Him. How is it possible that people can have a clear view of God's nature and attributes, and still refuse to worship Him? It is because they have been deceived by Satan. Elsewhere, Paul writes that "our gospel is veiled, it is veiled to those who are perishing, whose minds the god of this age has blinded, who do not believe" (2 Cor. 4:3–4).

Paul explains that as a result of their suppression of the truth about God, unbelievers are trapped in an endless cycle of confidence in their own wisdom. An unbeliever "does not receive the things of the Spirit of God, for they are foolishness to him" (1 Cor. 1:24). Rather than believe what they know to be true, sin and Satan have given the unbeliever confidence in his flesh to reject God, and replace Him with something else. It is not ignorance of God, but hatred of God stemming from a foolish carnal worldview that is set against Him.

Some people are deceived into thinking their religion is true. Paul's point in Romans 1 is that when people reject God, they not only replace Him with a lie, but with a world view that is logically untenable. People go so far as to worship idols, believing what is certainly foolish over and against the truth about God.

Others reject God and replace Him with their own standards, which they can't even obey. Loyalty to this system is not intellectual, but the product of deceit.

This deception is supernatural and demonic. At this moment Satan is the prince of the power of the air (Eph. 2:2), and he is at work in the sons of disobedience. This means that he has been given limited but direct access to the world and those who inhabit it, and he uses that access to inflict suffering and pain on humanity.

The New Testament shows how Satan afflicts people with illnesses and diseases (Mark 9:17–29), tests believers with trials (Luke 22:31), possesses unbelievers (Luke 22:3), and even works to lead people into a life of idle gossip and uselessness (1 Tim. 5:13–15). His work is not limited to unbelievers. Satan can gain a foothold into Christians' lives through promoting a lack of forgiveness (2 Cor. 2:10–11), and he can drive a wedge between spouses when they do not carry out their intimate responsibilities toward each other (1 Cor. 7:5). The power of his influence in the early church can be seen where he filled Ananias's heart to lie to the Holy Spirit (Acts 5:3). Satan hindered Paul somehow from getting to Thessalonica and will even empower the Antichrist during the Tribulation to perform miracles designed to convince lost humanity that he is the Messiah (1 Thess. 2:18). He comes as an angel of light (2 Cor. 11:14) determined to keep his true identity secret, his motives concealed, and his victims blinded.

Despite all of this activity, the brunt of Satan's power is seen in deceiving people so that they reject God.

The task of the evangelist is not to bind Satan, but to break the cycle of deception by introducing truth. The fruitfulness of the effort is left to the will of God. The Bible says that most will continue to reject the truth until the Final Judgment, and that God will often leave them to their own devices.

The gospel is God's gracious warning to the deceived human race concerning the global destruction that is coming. For many the message falls on deaf ears, and the truth is taken away from them as the devil takes the seed away in the parable of the soils (Mark 4:15). Others have an intellectual agreement with the facts, but when confronted with persecution, they go back to their old lives, withered like the plant in the shallow soil, scorched by persecution (Mark 4:16–17). Still others believe what they read, and know that judgment is coming, but when they consider leaving everything behind—home, possessions, family, and friends—to flee the judgment, the cost seems too high, and the lure of their world prevails. They are like the plant choked out by the cares of the world (Mark 4:18–19). Only a few are able to heed the warning, overcome the persecution, resist the temptations to stick with their beliefs, and flee their old lives. They are the few who believe and bear fruit to prove it (Mark 4:20).

Satan has blinded the eyes of unbelievers. He has stolen the seed of the gospel before it took root, persecuted those who showed a shallow acceptance of it, and tempted others with the trivial things of this world to abandon their artificial faith.

Genesis 19 tells the story of the destruction of Sodom. Angels arrived at the city to rescue Lot and his family, and they gave Lot the opportunity to warn those whom he loved of the coming destruction (Gen. 19:12-13). Yet when Lot went to his family and plead with them to take flight, they assumed Lot was joking with them (v. 14). Despite the supernatural events, the presence of angels, and the pleading of Lot, they chose to stay in Sodom, and as a result they were destroyed.

This is the portrait of the unconverted. Those who reject the gospel ignore the warning, take up permanent residence in the city of destruction, and bear the judgment for that decision.

A Common Destiny

Hebrews 9:27 is abundantly clear: "it is appointed for men to die once, but after this the judgment." It is as true as it is blunt. We have seen that all unbelievers are deceived by Satan and in need of the truth. These are the ones who "stumble, being disobedient to the word, to which they also were appointed" (1 Pet. 2:8). The end result of this stumbling and rejection of God is hell. Unbelievers are going there. They all have this common destiny.

Nobody in the New Testament talks more about Hell than Jesus. The word γέεννα (geenna, Gehenna) appears twelve times in the New Testament, and eleven of them were spoken by Jesus. Despite this, people still object to the existence of hell.

But the Bible is unequivocal. First Thessalonians 5:3 says that unbelievers will face "sudden destruction." This does not mean that hell will be brief, but rather that it will come upon them suddenly. The villain in the parable of the rich man and Lazarus is seen tormented by the flames and desperately seeking relief (Luke 16:23–24). Even in the eternal state, burning causes eternal smoke (Rev. 14:9–11) to rise, implying the burning of fuel forever.

The Bible simply does not speak of the cessation of existence after death. In fact, the Bible speaks specifically to the ongoing nature of the torment that will be inflicted, calling it "everlasting destruction" (2 Thess. 1:9). Furthermore, the term *destruction* is only one of no less than five pictures used to describe hell. They include darkness, fire, "weeping and gnashing of teeth," and punishment, all in addition to death and destruction (Matt. 8:12; 25:30; see also Matt. 13:42, 50).

In Revelation 19:20 (ESV) the beast and the false prophet, both satanically controlled human agents during the Tribulation, are thrown "alive into the lake of fire that burns with sulfur." Far from being annihilated in this act, Revelation 20:7–10 explains that they suffered for 1,000 years, and even then their time was not done. Instead of gaining release, the devil will join them and together "they will be tormented day and night forever and ever" (Rev. 20:10).

As appalling as hell is to imagine, God is just in sending unbelievers there. Humans are guilty of crimes against God. Hell is horrible not only because the punishment fits the crime, but because the punishment also fits the grandeur of the one who was offended by the crimes. It is not only what the sinner did, but against whom he did it. Since we have sinned against an infinitely holy God we are not unjustly punished to suffer eternally. If a hockey player fights with another hockey player he gets five minutes in the penalty box. If he fights with the referee, he gets a multi-game suspension, and God is infinitely more elevated than a referee.

The final sealing of the destiny for the unsaved will happen at death. Death is the passageway to judgment, and that Final Judgment is described in Revelation 20:11-15. This scene of Final Judgment opens with a stunning description of the sentencing of the wicked. The verdict will be passed upon them at this death, and those held in the terrible confinement of the sea, Death, and Hades will meet their ultimate sentencing.

When those who die in their unbelief are ushered into the presence of God, they will be confronted with the utterly disorienting lack of a material universe. The only fixed point of reference will be the ominous throne of judgment. This will constitute the end of the present world order, and all that will be left of the earth and the once seemingly infinite universe will be the doomed souls of dead unbelievers. They will be struck by the utter hopelessness of their situation, and overwhelmed by the certainty of their destination.

They will find Jesus sitting on a throne, wielding His authoritative power. The throne will be white, indicating the purity and righteousness of the judgments that proceed from it. The destiny of the unbeliever at this point will be certain. There will be nothing about the process of judgment or the outcome that in any way diminishes the fairness of the verdict.

God is a compassionate God. He shows mercy to those who ask for it in faith. He is quick to forgive, and has heaven reserved for His children so that He can display his compassion toward them for eternity. Yet His compassion does not mitigate hell. Love and wrath coexist in God, and this is part of His glory. It is impossible to take one of God's attributes and suggest that it diminishes another. Holiness and justice are mandatory and essential, existing to infinite degrees in a being with attributes that do not function independently. A human judge who let a convicted criminal go free out of compassion would certainly deserve to be removed from the bench. God, in His glory, will display both His compassion and His wrath. Those who die apart from His gospel will justly experience this punishment, and God's glory will be displayed. This is their common destiny.

But this destiny is not entirely reserved for the future. In fact, unbelievers are exposed to this wrath even in this life. They live every day in the crosshairs of His judgment, kept from hell every moment by nothing but the mercy of a patient, yet offended and angry God. For this, Christians should have compassion for unbelievers. They have a horrible destiny, and yet they live suppressing that truth, choosing to reject any hope of escape.

The evangelist must not only warn people of their destiny, but must offer them an escape. You do this not by minimizing the effects of their sin, and certainly not by telling them that if they believe the gospel their punishment is taken away. Rather, you explain to them that Jesus has borne that punishment in the place of those who believe.

In 1791 in the United States, a tax was put on distilled spirits to help pay down the national debt. Distillers protested by taking to the streets in western Pennsylvania. They quickly formed an armed rebellion, referred to as the Whiskey Rebellion, and President George Washington called in nearly 13,000 troops from various state militias to quell the opposition. Determined to emphasize the authority of a fledgling government, the "whiskey rebel" leaders were charged with treason.

In the coming months many were released or pardoned, but others stood to face judgment. Two men were convicted of treason, and were sentenced to death by hanging. However, for the first time in American history, George Washington pardoned those convicted criminals. In an act of unmerited kindness, those criminals had their just sentence removed.[3]

This is not what happens in the gospel. What God the Father does for sinners who repent is different. He does not offer clemency, commute a sentence, or simply pardon the offender. He still carries out the sentence of death in its entirety, but pours it out on someone else. The Lord Jesus suffered the full judgment for our sin and therefore the sentence was not commuted, but transferred. Most astonishing and outrageous is that Jesus then declares that those who believe the gospel are not just forgiven, but are in fact righteous.

To stretch the illustration slightly, it would be as if George Washington not only pardoned the whiskey rebels, but had himself been executed for their crimes after awarding them the Congressional Medal of Honor and commanding that a monument in the capital be built to honor them.

The compassion and forgiveness God shows to those who repent must not be misunderstood as a pardon. Clemency is leniency, and the gospel is not lenient. God did not show clemency toward those he would forgive, but rather poured out the wrath they deserved, in full strength, on the only substitute who could bear it. This wrath will be poured out for the judgment of sin, either on the person of Jesus Christ at the cross, or on the individual in hell forever.

A Common Deliverer

There is a painting by Ludolf Backhuysen hanging in the National Gallery of Art titled "Ships in Distress Off a Rocky Coast." It is a powerful seascape of three Dutch ships battling a terrible storm and nearing destruction on the rocky beach. The holds of the merchant ships were large enough to carry a sizable load of cargo acquired on their journey from distant lands. Three ships are battered, and the storm has destroyed a fourth ship.

This is a genre of art called *vanitas* because it represents the futility of human actions. In much the same way every unbeliever traverses this world with their cargo of sin and empty hopes, only to be dashed to pieces against the rock of God's judgment. Their only hope, like these ships, is a deliverer.

All unbelievers are under a common deception, and they all have a common destiny. But most importantly, they also all have a common deliverer.

There is only one name under heaven by which sinful men and women can be saved. This means that every person who is saved is saved by the same person. This is what Paul meant when he described Jesus as "the Savior of all men" (1 Tim. 4:10).

One of the most challenging concepts in the discussion of the non-Christian is this notion of elect unbelievers. By that I mean that there are those who have been chosen before the foundation of the world for salvation, their names are written in the book of life, and their place in heaven is secured, yet their lives at this moment show no evidence of that. Look back on your life before God saved you, and you will find such a person.

This is a massive evangelistic incentive. Nothing stimulates evangelism more effectively than the reality that the message of hope will be received by some. In Acts 18:9–10 Paul is given a promise: "Now the Lord spoke to Paul in the night by a vision, 'Do not be afraid, but speak, and do not keep silent; for I am with you, and no one will attack you to hurt you; for I have many people in this city.'" This is an amazing statement. The Lord had souls in the city of Corinth that he intended to save, and He desired to use Paul for just that purpose. Paul responded to this promise by settling there for a year and six months, time that he spent teaching the word of God (Acts 18:11).

There were no doubt people who were saved in the last month of Paul's ministry who had spent the previous seventeen months living in open rebellion against God. However, when the Lord was ready, He saved them. The perfect ransom of Christ was made effective in their lives.

It is important to understand that the common deliverer has paid a price for the sins of the elect that is sufficient to justify the wrath of God against them. There is a common deliverer for all who believe. When we read in 1 Timothy 2:6 that Jesus "gave Himself a ransom for all," it must be informed by the direct saying of Jesus in Matthew 20:28 where he says that his mission in the world was not to be served, but to serve, "and to give His life a ransom for many." In this case the many must clarify the all in 1 Timothy 2:6. He did not die to pay the penalty for the sins of those who would never believe, because then the punishment they suffer in hell forever would be unwarranted.

However, 1 Timothy 2:6 does offer hope for the evangelist. Because we do not know who the elect are, we can proclaim with boldness that if anyone turns from his sin and believes the gospel, Jesus is that person's ransom. In fact, after calling Jesus a ransom for all, Paul explains that this ransom "is the testimony given at the proper time" (1 Tim. 2:6 ESV). In other words, Jesus is a ransom for people in that the gospel can be preached to them. In God's appointed time, a testimony can be given to any person anywhere that Jesus is the person's ransom, if only he will turn from sin and believe the gospel.

The fact that there is only one name under heaven by which one must be saved should encourage Christians in evangelism. This means that every unbeliever, no matter what type of sin or rebellion he is in, or religion he follows, has the same solution. Those who qualify as religious will not be saved unless they fix their faith on the risen Savior. Likewise, the openly immoral person, regardless of the catalog of sin that crushes him with guilt, has the same hope. If he calls on the name of Jesus, he will be saved (Acts 2:21; Rom. 10:13). The resurrection of Christ offers the world hope of escaping eternal death (John 11:25). The gospel offers all people salvation (Rom. 10:13), and the Father bids them to come (1 Tim. 2:3–4).

The reality is that even believers have something profound in common with unbelievers. Every person ever born is born in the image of God. People were designed by God to display the glory of God through their lives in a way the angels, animals, and trees cannot. Had Satan not been permitted to lead the human race astray it would have continued in perfect obedience to God, enjoying fellowship with Him and magnifying His glory. But because of sin, that relationship is broken. This is yet another reason why the Christian should have compassion for unbelievers. They are living their lives without knowing that they were made with a purpose, namely, to magnify the glory of God with their lives. This is another way of saying that because of their deception, they do not even know why they are alive.

It is normal for a father to have a relationship with his children. In the spiritual world, it is the unbeliever who has broken with that relationship. Everyone—even the Christian—experiences the first death. But the unsaved also experience a second death. Yet because Jesus died in the place of sinners, they have hope. And through the gospel, they can have their relationship restored with God. "For Christ also suffered once for sins, the just for the unjust, that He might bring us to God, being put to death in the flesh but made alive by the Spirit" (1 Pet. 3:18).

In the top left corner of the painting mentioned above there is a golden hue on the outer edges of the storm clouds. This is meant to symbolize the end of the storm and the dawn of hope. What is left unsaid in the painting is whether or not the storm breaks before the ships do. In a similar fashion the believer has the privilege of sharing with the unbeliever the dawn of hope that exists in the Son. One of the greatest privileges a Christian has is the opportunity to share the radical truth of a divine Savior with a doomed world. The loving thing to do is accurately present the horrible consequences of rejecting the savior, and then plead with the unbeliever to turn while there is still time.

The Word of Truth in a World of Error: The Fundamentals of Practical Apologetics

Nathan Busenitz

Apologetics is not a form of philosophy reserved for professionals or academics. Rightly understood, apologetics is a tool for evangelists to help people see with clarity the truth about the gospel. Apologetics is not primarily concerned with winning arguments, but with winning souls. Therefore, the basis of apologetics is the Bible. It is an attempt to defend Scripture by using Scripture. These nine fundamentals will help the evangelist understand false worldviews, as well as utilize the Scriptures that point people to Christ.

Apologetics has been variously defined as "the Christian's answer to the world's attacks directed against the truth claims of Holy Scripture";[1] "that branch of Christian theology that seeks to provide rational warrant for Christianity's truth claims";[2] "the vindication of the Christian philosophy of life against the various forms of the non-Christian philosophy of life";[3] "the reasoned defense of the Christian religion";[4] and "the art of persuasion, the discipline which considers ways to commend and defend the living God to those without faith."[5]

Derived from the Greek root apolog- (ἀπολογ-), the word literally means "legal defense" or "response to a formal charge." For the earliest Christians, apologetics included a distinctly legal element, as church leaders made various appeals to hostile Roman emperors and other government authorities. Yet these ancient apologists were likewise concerned with "a philosophical, theological, and historical demonstration of the truthfulness of Christianity."[6] In this way, they resemble the apologists of today, as those wholeheartedly committed to "giving a defense for the Christian faith."[7]

Contemporary evangelical scholars generally agree on the basic definition of apologetics, yet they differ widely on its application. Thus, while universally affirming that the Christian is called to defend the faith, they disagree on how best to do so. As a result, a number of apologetic schools have arisen—from the classical to the evidential to the presuppositional.[8] Though different in their approaches, these systems share the same goal: to demonstrate and defend the truthfulness of the Christian message in the midst of an antagonistic world.

Nonetheless, believers must look to the Word of God as the final authority for evaluating the comparative merits of any apologetic approach. Such is the necessary implication of the Protestant principle of *sola scriptura*—namely, that Scripture alone is the final authority for faith and practice. Evangelicals share in that conviction with the Reformers and the church fathers, but we ultimately hold to it because it is the claim of Scripture itself.[9] As God's self-revelation, Scripture reflects His perfect character (John 17:17) and carries His full authority (Isa. 66:2). It is "the power of God" (1 Cor. 1:18), the "word of Christ" (Col. 3:16), and the "sword of the Spirit" (Eph. 6:17). To obey the Word is to obey its Author. Therefore, we seek to be biblical in all that we do (Ps. 119:105).

For the evangelist, the effort to understand apologetics is worthwhile because it is a valuable tool when witnessing to others about Christ. When apologetics is applied biblically, evangelism is strengthened. And if we are to be truly biblical in the application of apologetics, it follows that we must base our approach upon the Word of God. As Scott Oliphint observes:

> The Bible should be central to any discussion of apologetics. It is the Bible that we need, and must open, if we are going to think about

apologetics and begin to prepare to do it. To fight the Lord's battle without the Lord's sword is foolishness. To fail to use the only weapon that is able to pierce to the heart is to fight a losing battle.[10]

Elsewhere, Oliphint and Lane Tipton add this important point:

Christian apologetics is, at root, a biblical discipline. To some this may sound so obvious as to be redundant. To others, however, it is a hotly contested proposition. A Reformed apologetic is only Reformed to the extent that its tenets, principles, methodology and so forth are formed and re-formed by Scripture.[11]

When we look to God's Word for our apologetic method, we look to God Himself.

Nine Fundamentals for Practical Apologetics

With that in mind, the goal of this chapter is to develop nine fundamental, biblical principles concerning apologetics that will empower evangelism. These fundamentals are not intended to be exhaustive, but to provide an initial, Scripture-based framework for considering our evangelistic approach. Though an in-depth critique of the various apologetic systems is outside the limits of this study, it is hoped that these principles will further assist those who are thinking through such issues.

The Authorization: The Stand for Truth Is Mandated by God

In a world of postmodern tolerance and ambiguity, what right do Christians have to reject the claims of other worldviews while asserting the absolute truth of the gospel message? The authorization to do so comes from God Himself. We are those who affirm "the supremacy of Christ in truth in a postmodern, dying, rotting, decaying, and hurting world. Let us therefore embrace it and proclaim it passionately, confidently, and relentlessly, because, after all, that is why we are here."[12] The lordship of Christ compels and commissions us to confront the false ideologies of the culture.

All believers, and especially those in positions of spiritual oversight, are commanded to defend the faith, contend for right doctrine, and share the good news with others—no matter how unpopular the message might be. We are called to cast down that which raises itself against the truth (2 Cor. 10:5), to be ready to give an answer for the hope that is in us (1 Pet. 3:14–16), and to contend for the faith once for all delivered to the saints (Jude 3–4). When worldly philosophies threaten the church, the apologist exposes them for what they really are: expressions of foolishness (Rom. 1:22; 1 Cor. 1:20). When persecution arises, as it surely will at times (Mark 13:9; 2 Tim. 3:12), the apologist is ready with an unwavering defense (Luke 21:12–15). When false prophets introduce destructive heresies into the church, the apologist denounces the error (Titus 1:9–11) and guards the truth of the gospel (Acts 20:28; 1 Tim. 6:20; 2 Tim. 1:14).

By what right does he do these things? He is authorized to do so by God's express command. Though others may label him proud and judgmental— since he claims to know absolute truth and condemns alternative viewpoints as false—the faithful apologist understands that true arrogance would be to deny the mandate of God. Submission to God's Word is, in fact, the essence of genuine humility (Isa. 66:2).

In the New Testament era, apologists defended Christianity against opposing worldviews such as Greek philosophy (Acts 17:16–31; Col. 2:8), the early cult of Gnosticism that sought hidden knowledge (1 Tim. 6:20; 1 John 4:2–3), legalism (Gal. 2:15–21; Col. 2:20–23), and the teachings of various heretics (2 Pet. 2; Jude 1:4). They did so in an age of intense persecution (2 Tim. 1:8; cf. Rev. 2:2–3), when temptations to abandon the faith were heightened by the threat of violence (Heb. 10:32–39).

Today, Christians similarly defend the faith against opposing worldviews such as naturalistic atheism, secular humanism, other world religions, and Christian cult groups. Though we do not face the same threat of persecution (at least in Western societies), we live in a world that is nonetheless still hostile to the gospel. The spirit of postmodern tolerance may tempt us to be silent or at least to soften the message.[13] But we can be neither silent nor soft. We have been authorized to proclaim that which is antithetical to the wisdom of our age. As David Wells observes, "Biblical truth contradicts [postmodern] cultural spirituality. . . . Biblical truth displaces it, refuses to allow its operating assumptions, declares to it its bankruptcy."[14] The gospel has never been popular. But we take our marching orders from a higher authority than popular opinion. As the apostles told the religious leaders of their day, "We must obey God rather than men" (Acts 5:29 ESV).

The Aim: The Goal Is to Glorify God by Reaching the Lost

The ultimate goal of apologetics is to bring glory to God (1 Cor. 10:31; 2 Cor. 5:9) by guarding the truth and contending for the faith. But apologetics is not simply defensive. As Robert Reymond explains:

> In the fullest sense, [apologetics] is the defense and vindication of the Christian faith against all attacks of doubters and unbelievers that will include the positive presentation of the reasonableness of Christianity's truth claims and its more than ample sufficiency to meet the spiritual needs of humankind. Apologetics in this last sense then is not only a defensive but also an offensive discipline, to be employed not only in defense of the gospel but also in its propagation.[15]

In "presenting positive arguments for Christian truth claims,"[16] apologetics should be decidedly evangelistic. In the words of Francis Schaeffer, "The positive side of apologetics is the communication of the Gospel to the present generation in terms they can understand."[17] The aim is not simply to renounce error, but to bring sinners to repentance (2 Tim. 2:25). Though the truth can always triumph over error in a debate, the apologist's goal is not just to win arguments, but more importantly to win souls. Thus, "the apologist must always be ready to present the gospel. He must not get so tangled up in arguments, proofs, defenses, and critiques that he neglects to give the unbeliever what he needs most."[18]

Though apologetics and evangelism are distinct concepts, the two cannot be divorced from each other. Christians are commanded to engage in both: to proclaim the gospel and to defend the faith. The Lord instructed His followers to "make disciples of all the nations" (Matt. 28:19a), but also warned them to be on guard against false teachers (Matt. 7:15). Paul reminded Timothy to "do the work of an evangelist" (2 Tim. 4:5), but also explained to Titus that church leaders must "be able, by sound doctrine, both to exhort and convict those who contradict" (Titus 1:9). Peter encouraged the wives of unbelievers to win their husbands to Christ through their godly behavior (1 Pet. 3:1). A few verses later, he coupled that evangelistic instruction with this command: "But sanctify the

Lord God in your hearts, and always be ready to give a defense to everyone who asks you a reason for the hope that is in you, with meekness and fear" (1 Pet. 3:15). Jude's charge to "contend earnestly for the faith" (Jude 1:3) was similarly balanced with this hopeful exhortation, "And on some have compassion, making a distinction; but others save with fear, pulling them out of the fire, hating even the garment defiled by the flesh" (Jude 1:22–23).

Such passages underscore the twofold responsibility of every Christian with respect to reaching the world around us. We are called to be both apologists and evangelists. We are to be protectors and proclaimers, defenders and disseminators, advocates and ambassadors. These roles are not exactly the same, and yet they cannot be separated. To confront error is to proclaim the truth. And vice versa; to preach the gospel is to simultaneously destroy "arguments and every high thing that exalts itself against the knowledge of God," as we take "every thought into captivity to the obedience of Christ" (2 Cor. 10:5).

If the glory of God is our ultimate aim, we cannot be content with merely winning a debate. Our desire is to win the lost (1 Cor. 9:20–23). As John Piper rightly observes, "Missions is not the ultimate goal of the church. Worship is. Missions exists because worship doesn't."[19] Our efforts in both apologetics and evangelism are fueled by a desire to see God worshipped and glorified by those who currently reject Him. "Worship, therefore, is the fuel and goal in missions. It's the goal of missions because in missions we simply aim to bring the nations into the white-hot enjoyment of God's glory."[20] Because apologetics is an intrinsic part of the missionary endeavor, it shares that same goal.

The Answer: Our Apologetic Must Point to Christ

Insofar as the aim of apologetics is evangelistic, its message must center on the person and work of Jesus Christ. He is the answer to every social ill and for every searching heart. "We preach Christ crucified," Paul explained to the Corinthians. "To the Jews a stumbling block and to the Greeks foolishness" (1 Cor. 1:23). He similarly told the Colossians, "Him we preach, warning every man and teaching every man in all wisdom, that we may present every man perfect in Christ Jesus" (Col. 1:28). Armed with the motto "To live is Christ" (Phil. 1:21), Paul confronted the world as His ambassador, begging his hearers, "On Christ's behalf, be reconciled to God" (2 Cor. 5:20). He never made an apologetic stand that did not point to Christ. Whether on Mars Hill

(Acts 17 KJV) or on trial before the Roman governor (Acts 26), Paul's defense of the faith always centered on the gospel (1 Cor. 15:3–4).

An apologetic that falls short of presenting the whole gospel leaves sinners in the same place: still lost. Until sinners confess Jesus as Lord and believe that God raised Him from the grave, they remain dead in their sins (Rom. 10:9). Their eternity is dependent on what they do with Jesus Christ. To the question, "What must I do to be saved?" Jesus is the only answer (Acts 16:30–31). For the problem of sin, He is the only solution. As John the Baptist said of Jesus, "He who believes in the Son has everlasting life; but he who does not believe the Son shall not see life, but the wrath of God abides on him" (John 3:36).

We must not become content with an apologetic approach that minimizes or neglects the gospel. After all, our ultimate goal is not only to convert atheists to theism or evolutionists to creationism but instead to call unbelievers (whether atheists or theists, whether evolutionists or creationists) to embrace Jesus Christ. Arguments for theism and creationism are important, yet a Christian apologetic is incomplete if it culminates there and stops short of the gospel.

By way of illustration, some evangelicals took great stock in the conversion from atheism to theism of renowned British atheist Antony Flew. Flew documented his change of mind in the book *There Is a God*, where he admitted that arguments from design led him "to accept the existence of an infinitely intelligent Mind." [21] At the end of the book, Flew notes that he might be open to Christianity, but stops short of acknowledging any personal commitment to Christ. Flew for his part has identified himself as a deist. [22]

How are we to assess such a conversion? On the one hand, we can be glad that a renowned atheist publicly renounced his former errors. We can be thankful for the efforts of those who, through their influence, helped him to see the philosophical bankruptcy of the atheistic system. At the same time, however, we cannot be fully satisfied with the outcome, since Professor Flew did not become a Christian.

When the apostle Paul stood before opposition, whether on Mars Hill or before Felix and Festus, he was not content to simply convince his hearers of the existence of God. In fact, they were already theists. Even so, they desperately needed to be reconciled to God, which is why Paul's message centered on the gospel of Jesus Christ. In a day when naturalistic atheism is gaining popular approval, it may be tempting to think that defending God's existence should be our primary goal. But if we leave out the Christ-centered message of the gospel, our apologetic task is left incomplete.[23] We have been commissioned to make disciples of our Lord (Matt. 28:18–20), not just to make theists. Thus, we must preach Christ and Him crucified to all people, whether or not they claim to believe in God.

The Authority: The Word Is the Ultimate Standard of Truth

Because the Bible is God's Word, it comes with His very authority, and there is no standard of truth higher than God Himself. Our approach and our arguments should be established in the authority of the Scripture, even if extrabiblical evidences are used as secondary affirmation. Such stems from the conviction that Jesus is Lord, and that His Word is our final standard. John Frame notes:

> The lordship of Jesus is our ultimate presupposition. An ultimate presupposition is a basic heart commitment, an ultimate trust. Since we believe him more certainly than we believe anything else, he (and hence his Word) is the very criterion, the ultimate standard of truth. What higher standard could there possibly be? What standard is more authoritative? What standard is more clearly known to us (see Romans 1:19–21)? What authority ultimately validates all other authorities?[24]

Elsewhere, Frame reiterates this point:

> When he [God] speaks, we are to hear with the profoundest respect. What he says is more important than any other words we may hear. Indeed, his words judge all the affairs of human beings (John 12:48). The truth of his words, then, must be our most fundamental conviction, our most basic commitment. We may also describe that commitment as our most ultimate *presupposition*, for we bring that commitment into all our thought, seeking to bring all our ideas in conformity to it. That presupposition is therefore our ultimate criterion of truth. We measure and evaluate all other sources of knowledge by it. We bring every thought captive to the obedience of Christ (2 Cor. 10:5).[25]

Thus, the Word of God is central to the apologetic task. If He is to be front and center in our apologetic, His self-revelation must have the place of prominence.

This is not to say that evidences from general revelation and human experience have no legitimate place in apologetics. Jesus pointed His critics to His miracles (John 5:36; 10:38); Paul appealed to creation (Acts 14:15–17; Rom. 1:20), the conscience (Rom. 2:15), and even cultural confusion (Acts 17:22–30); Peter observed the apologetic power of Christian behavior (1 Pet. 3:1, 14–16). Yet appeals to general revelation and human experience can only go so far in the apologetic task. Special revelation is needed to explain and interpret general revelation and experience (Ps. 19:1–10; 2 Pet. 1:19–21).[26]

Priority, then, is to be given to the Word of God—the authoritative source of absolute truth. "Your law is truth," wrote the psalmist. "The entirety of Your word is truth, / And every one of Your righteous judgments endures forever" (Ps. 119:142, 160). The Lord Himself prayed, "Sanctify them in the truth; Your word is truth" (John 17:17 NASB). The apostles likewise understood the Scriptures to be "the word of truth" (2 Tim. 2:15; Jas. 1:18), and the gospel of salvation to be "the message of truth" (Eph. 1:13; see also Col. 1:5). As the inspired word of the living God, Scripture is "profitable for doctrine, for reproof, for correction, for instruction in righteousness, that the man of God may be complete, thoroughly equipped for every good work" (2 Tim. 3:16–17). The true knowledge of God revealed in its pages, through His divine power, "has granted to us everything pertaining to life and godliness" (2 Pet. 1:3 NASB).

The authority and sufficiency of Scripture make it an essential apologetic tool. Only "the word of God is living and powerful, and sharper than any two-edged sword, piercing even to the division of soul and spirit, and of joints and marrow, and is a discerner of the thoughts and intents of the heart" (Heb. 4:12). Insofar as our goal is to truly change the hearts of others, we must employ the Scriptures in our efforts.

The Agency: The Message Is Empowered by the Holy Spirit

The reason Scripture is such a critical component in the Christian apologetic is that it is empowered by the Spirit of God. It is His Word (1 Pet. 1:11; 2 Pet. 1:21; cf. Zech. 7:12; Acts 1:16) and His sword (Eph. 6:17; cf. Heb. 4:12). Only the Holy Spirit can convict the unbeliever of sin (John 16:6–15), open blind eyes to the truth (1 Cor. 2:6–16), regenerate the heart (John 3:5–8; Titus 3:3–7), and subsequently produce the fruits of righteousness (Gal. 5:22–23). The Spirit empowered the witness of those in the early church (Acts 1:8), enabling them "to speak the word of God with boldness" (Acts 4:31 NASB). As Paul told the Thessalonians, "Our gospel did not come to you in word only, but also in power, and in the Holy Spirit and in much assurance" (1 Thess. 1:5).

Unless the Spirit blesses the use of His Word to convict the sinner's heart, no amount of arguing can convince anyone to truly embrace Christ.[27] Thus, we concur with the words of Francis Schaeffer: "It is important to remember, first of all, that we cannot separate true apologetics from the work of the Holy Spirit, nor from a living relationship in prayer to the Lord on the part of the Christian. We must understand that eventually the battle is not just against flesh and blood."[28]

The Christian apologist must constantly and prayerfully depend on the Spirit of God, trusting Him to use His Word to do His work. To be sure, we do our best to present the message in a way that is clear and accurate; but we ultimately rest in the reality that God alone can transform the heart. His Spirit is the divine agent of change.

Understanding this truth liberates the apologist to remain focused on presenting the gospel message (and trusting God with the results) rather than get sidetracked by petty arguments about secondary issues. The story is told of an evangelist on a college campus who was witnessing to a young man in the dorms. Upon meeting the evangelist, the student immediately raised what he thought would be an insurmountable objection, demanding that the evangelist provide proof that Jonah could have been swallowed by a giant fish and survive. But the evangelist was undeterred, and wisely responded by saying, "You know, we can talk about that later but first let me tell you about Christ." As the evangelist shared the gospel, the Spirit moved the young man's heart. He was convicted, repented of his sin, and committed his life to the Savior. Afterward the evangelist asked him if he still wanted to talk about Jonah. The young man, his heart now transformed, replied with words of simple faith, "No, there's no need. If that's what the Bible says, I believe it." The Spirit had opened his eyes to the truth, shattering any objections he had previously held.

We can win arguments because the truth can always triumph over error. But even if we answer every question and every objection, we cannot force belief. Only the Holy Spirit can impart saving faith to the sin-enslaved heart. A biblical apologetic reflects that reality.

The Attitude: We Ought to Be Marked by Confident Humility

Knowing that the Word of God is true gives us certain confidence. Knowing that only the Holy Spirit can change the heart keeps us humble.[29] Remembering that were it not for His grace (Eph. 2:4–9) we would still be dead in our sins (Eph. 2:1–3) enables us to confront the lost with love and care. Thus, we proclaim the truth without compromise, but not without compassion. Though the message itself is an offense (1 Cor. 1:23), the apologist must take care not to be a stumbling block through his own cockiness or contentiousness. "After all, though the gospel can be offensive in some respects (because, for one thing, it assumes that all human beings are sinners), those who preach and defend the gospel ought not to be offensive."[30]

In showing love toward lost people, we emulate the example of Christ who "when He saw the multitudes, He was moved with compassion for them, because they were weary and scattered, like sheep having no shepherd" (Matt. 9:36; see also Mark 6:34). Jesus' immediate response was evangelistic. "Then He said to His disciples, 'The harvest truly is plentiful, but the laborers are few. Therefore pray the Lord of the harvest to send out laborers into His harvest'" (Matt. 9:37–38).

The apostle Paul gave similar instruction to Timothy regarding the confrontation of error in the church:

> And a servant of the Lord must not quarrel but be gentle to all, able to teach, patient, in humility correcting those who are in opposition, if God perhaps will grant them repentance, so that they may know the truth, and that they may come to their senses and escape the snare of the devil, having been taken captive by him to do his will. (2 Tim. 2:24–26)

The apostle Peter similarly instructed his readers to always be ready with their defense, "with meekness and fear" (1 Pet. 3:15). In both passages, the apologetic approach is marked by a gracious, respectful, and patient disposition, with a view toward heart change in the life of the unbeliever.

At the same time, it must be noted that there is a biblical distinction between those who are merely deceived (and should be treated with compassion) and those who are actively deceiving others (and should be denounced with conviction). The authors of the New Testament openly condemned false teachers, admonishing believers to stay away from the purveyors of error. Jesus warned His disciples with these words, "Beware of false prophets, who come to you in sheep's clothing, but inwardly they are ravenous wolves" (Matt. 7:15). Paul told the Galatians, "But even if we, or an angel from heaven, preach any other gospel to you than what we have preached to you, let him be accursed" (Gal. 1:8). Peter described false teachers this way: "It has happened to them according to the true proverb, 'A dog returns to his own vomit,' and, 'a sow, having washed, to her wallowing in the mire" (2 Pet. 2:22). Jude similarly described them as those who "speak evil of whatever they do not know; and whatever they know naturally, like brute beasts, in these things they corrupt themselves" (Jude 1:10). John warned his readers to avoid any association with false teachers. "If anyone comes to you and does not bring this doctrine, do not receive him into your house nor greet him; for he who greets him shares in his evil deeds" (2 John 1:10–11).

In this way, the New Testament draws a clear distinction between compassion and compromise. Though we seek to win sinners by presenting the truth to them in love, we must avoid any accommodation toward false teachers—even in an effort to be nice. The New Testament never equates true love with the postmodern notion of tolerance. Biblical love rejoices in the truth (1 Cor. 13:6), abhors that which is evil (Rom. 12:9), and walks in the commandments of Christ (2 John 6). Thus, the Christian apologist aspires to balance a biblical compassion toward those who are lost with a righteous indignation toward those who are leading others astray.

The Assumption: Unbelievers Already Know God Exists

The Bible teaches that unbelievers already know certain spiritual realities, though they "suppress the truth in unrighteousness" (Rom. 1:18). The Christian apologist is right to assume that unbelievers are already aware of certain truths, even if they deny them. For example, unbelievers innately know that there is a God, "because that which is known about God is evident within them; for God made it evident to them" (Rom. 1:19; cf. 1:21 NASB). Thus, while atheists claim that they do not believe in God, the Bible claims that God does not believe in atheists. He has revealed Himself to them such that, in denying Him, "they are without excuse" (Rom. 1:20).

God has given unbelievers an external witness to His glory in creation (Rom. 1:20). Thus, "the heavens declare the glory of God" (Ps. 19:1), "the world and all things in it" point to the Creator (Acts 17:24 NASB), the seasons give testimony to His providential care (Acts 14:15–17), and even the human body is a marvelous reminder of His creative genius (Ps. 139:13–14). The order and design of the natural world, including its very existence, lead the unbeliever to the inescapable conclusion that there is a God. Only "the fool has said in his heart, 'There is no God'" (Ps. 14:1; cf. Rom. 1:22), yet his reasons for doing so are moral, not logical (as the rest of Ps. 14 makes clear).

God has also given unbelievers an internal witness to His moral law through the conscience. The apostle Paul calls this "the work of the law written in their hearts" (Rom. 2:15), because they know "the righteous judgment of God" (Rom. 1:32), even though they disobey it. Along with the created world around them (revealing the truth that God is Creator, Sustainer, Provider, and Designer), the conscience within people bears witness to the truth of a transcendent moral order, of which God is the supreme Standard and Judge (Eccl. 12:14). Human beings, additionally, have been given a sense of the eternal, because God "has also set eternity in their heart" (Eccl. 3:11 NASB).

The evangelist is greatly aided in his mission by these witnesses to God. The unbeliever is innately aware of the fact that God exists—the Creator, Sustainer, and Judge of the universe. Unbelievers are already mindful of eternity and feel the guilt of having violated their consciences. The testimony of God's general revelation has made these truths evident to them.

To be sure, the special revelation of Scripture is needed to explain the specifics of who the Creator is and what He expects. The gospel message is essential if the unbeliever is to fully understand his condemnation before God and his need for the saving work of Christ. Moreover, the effects of sin and depravity cause unbelievers to reason wrongly and to stifle the truth (Rom. 1:18–22). Nonetheless, the evangelist can rightly assume that unbelievers are already aware of certain fundamental truths about God, because God has made those truths evident to them.[31]

On a practical level, this means we do not need to get sidetracked with intricate arguments about that which unbelievers already know (like whether or not there is a God). Rather, we can build upon what God has already made evident to them, trusting the Holy Spirit to use His Word to do His work.[32]

The Anticipation: We Will Not Be Popular

In spite of the fact that the faith we are defending is absolutely true, and the gospel we are proclaiming is the good news of reconciliation, the reality is that our message will often be rejected and scorned. We live in a world antagonistic to Christianity. Popular movies and television shows mock biblical history and deride evangelical values. Best-selling books proudly promote atheism while openly scorning those who believe in God. Even public education—especially at the university level—has made itself the outspoken enemy of a biblical worldview. Though our currency still reads "In God We Trust," everything about American popular culture suggests that our nation is anything but truly Christian.

Such hostilities should come as no surprise. Jesus Himself warned His followers, "If the world hates you, you know that it hated Me before it hated you. … If they persecuted Me, they will also persecute you" (John 15:18, 20). The apostle Paul echoed this warning to Timothy: "all who desire to live godly in Christ Jesus will suffer persecution" (2 Tim. 3:12). He told the Corinthians that "the message of the cross is foolishness to those who are perishing" (1 Cor. 1:18), noting that the "natural man does not receive the things of the Spirit of God, for they are foolishness to him; nor can he know them" (1 Cor. 2:14). For his part, Paul was glad to be regarded as a fool for Christ's sake (1 Cor. 4:10). After preaching the gospel on Mars Hill, some of Paul's hearers "mocked [him]" (Acts 17:32). At his defense before Festus, the apostle was met with these words: "Paul, you are beside yourself! Much learning is driving you mad!" (Acts 26:24).

If the ministry of Christ and the apostles were met with resistance and rejection, we should expect to be treated no differently. Jesus taught that not every soil would receive the seed of the Word of God (Mark 4:3–20). His ministry was rebuffed by many in His day (John 12:37–40), to the point that His enemies sought His death (John 11:53). As the apostle John explains, "He came to His own, and His own did not receive Him" (John 1:11). The apostles too would suffer greatly for the gospel. Most of them would be martyred, including the apostle Paul who, at the end of his life, found himself abandoned in a Roman dungeon (2 Tim. 4:9–14). Yet in spite of the many difficulties he faced (2 Cor. 11:23–28), Paul remained faithful to the gospel he had been charged to defend (2 Tim. 4:7).

The message of the gospel is antithetical to the fallen philosophies of men, meaning that faithful Christians have seldom been popular. Evangelical apologists must avoid the trap of desiring intellectual respectability at the expense of biblical fidelity. Believing in the God of the Bible and in His Son Jesus Christ has social consequences, as we daily take up our cross, deny ourselves, and follow Him (Mark 8:34). But there is joy in the persecution (Acts 5:40–41; cf. Luke 6:22–24), and we should embrace the ridicule and rejection for His sake (Col. 1:24; cf. 2 Cor. 4:17). Such does not mean we promote anti-intellectualism or stick our heads in the sand; as representatives of Christ, we should pursue excellence in any field of study. However, we must also remember that the gospel we cling to is an inherently unpopular message, and we cannot compromise the truth simply to gain a false respect.

The Assessment: Apologetic Success Is Defined by Christ

A final question to consider is this: how are we to evaluate the relative success of our apologetic efforts? In asking this question, we might wonder if apologetic effectiveness is best measured in terms of debates won, arguments articulated, converts made, or accolades received. Such criteria may indicate something of our philosophical credibility or rhetorical flair. Yet they tell us very little about whether or not we have been successful in the only sense that truly matters.

Like everything else in the Christian life, apologetic success is assessed by a higher standard than anything on this earth. Numbers of opponents confounded or unbelievers converted is no real measure of how well we have done. If it were, the prophet Jonah would be a runaway sensation (with the entire city of Nineveh responding to his preaching), while the prophet Jeremiah would be a dismal failure (with his ministry bearing virtually no visible fruit). Yet from God's perspective, Jeremiah's faithful obedience made his ministry the true success, while Jonah's rebellious resistance rendered him a disappointing failure.

To Jeremiah's name, we could add many of the other Old Testament prophets—men of whom the author of Hebrews wrote:

> Others were tortured, not accepting their release, so that they might obtain a better resurrection; and others experienced mockings and

scourgings, yes, also chains and imprisonment. They were stoned, they were sawn in two, they were tempted, they were put to death with the sword; they went about in sheepskins, in goatskins, being destitute, afflicted, ill-treated (men of whom the world was not worthy), wandering in deserts and mountains and caves and holes in the ground. (Heb. 11:35–38; cf. Matt. 23:29–37)

These courageous servants of God—men like Elijah, Elisha, Isaiah, and Ezekiel—persevered in the midst of rejection, persecution, and affliction because they were far more concerned with being faithful than with being popular. In their own day, they were often viewed as eccentric outcasts and failures. But from heaven's perspective, they epitomize true success.

As noted in the previous section, the New Testament expectation is that the gospel message—rightly proclaimed—will often be met with rejection and scorn. It follows, then, that popularity and acclaim are false measures of success. When the apostle Paul lay in that Roman dungeon at the end of his life, his circumstances looked exceedingly bleak. He was abandoned and alone, falsely accused and awaiting execution, without fame, fortune, or even his coat (2 Tim. 4:13). Like the Old Testament prophets, Paul was seen as a failure by the society of his day. After decades of hardship-laden ministry, his life was about to end in tragedy and obscurity. Yet from God's vantage point, Paul was a success. Though he had faced repeated trials and temptations, he had remained faithful. His life had been lived for the honor of his Lord (2 Cor. 5:9; Phil. 1:21). He had diligently completed his ministry (2 Tim. 4:7); even in his final hours, he had proclaimed the gospel without compromise (2 Tim. 4:17); soon he would see Christ and receive his reward (2 Tim. 4:8).

When we stand before Christ to give an account of our lives (Rom. 14:9–12; 2 Cor. 5:10), the accolades and recognition of this world will be meaningless. In that moment, the apparent value of wood, hay, and stubble accomplishments will quickly fade away (1 Cor. 3:11–15). The only words we will care about are these: "Well done, good and faithful servant. . . . Enter into the joy of your lord" (Matt. 25:21, 23). Faithfulness, not temporal fame or visible fruitfulness, is His measure of success; and in the end, His assessment is the only one that matters.

Knowing this, the Christian apologist is primarily concerned with being faithful to the Master (whom he loves and serves), faithful to the message (which he defends and proclaims), and faithful to the ministry (to which he has been called). Our success is not determined by how the world responds to us in this life—whether with animosity, ambivalence, or applause—but by how Christ will evaluate us in the next. Thus we say with the apostle Paul, "We make it our aim to please him. For we must all appear before the judgment seat of Christ" (2 Cor. 5:9*b*–10*a* ESV).

5

Christ, the Savior: Evangelism as a Person, Not a Plan

Rick Holland

Much of modern evangelism has become institutionalized. Systems, steps, and summaries of how to share the gospel have replaced simply introducing people to Jesus. While biblical evangelism should have a theological gravitas to it, it is essential not to allow the plan to eclipse the person. The evangelist must always remember that the message's essence is the person of Jesus Christ.

The flight was overbooked so every seat was supposed to be taken. As I sat in my window seat on the British Airways 747, I was surprised the two seats next to me remained vacant. Selfishly, I relished the thought of those two empty seats and already made plans for how I would turn that section of airborne real estate into a king-size bed.

That hope evaporated when an elderly British couple made their way to the two seats just as the doors closed. We exchanged polite greetings and turned our attention to the all-too-familiar clinic on fastening seat belts. When the video presentation was finished, I was instantly pierced with a convicting burden to share the gospel with them.

With a couple of decades of pastoral ministry experience preaching and studying Scripture weekly, I should have had no trouble starting a gospel conversation. But the truth is, I had a hard time steering the conversation to spiritual realities.

After an hour or so of small talk and trying to turn the conversation to the gospel, I finally and awkwardly blurted out, "Are you believers?"

"Believers in what?" the woman responded.

I spent the next three minutes presenting the plan of salvation. As I finished, I silently congratulated myself for my clarity, brevity, and evangelistic courage. However, my celebration was short lived. To my disappointment, they had no interest in talking about going to heaven or being forgiven of sin. In fact, the man finally shut the conversation down with an offended response, "Sir, we are not interested in talking about religion with you." The next eleven hours were very awkward as I sat trapped by the window.

I thought a lot about that encounter over the next weeks and months. In fact, I still think about it. Why would anyone not be interested in the forgiveness of sins, the presence of hope in this life, assurance of heaven, and a thousand other benefits of salvation? The more I thought about it, the more that man's response actually indicated the answer. I was asking why anyone would decline the benefits of salvation; I was not asking why anyone would reject the Savior of salvation. I think he was right. My gospel presentation sounded more like a sales pitch for a new religion than an introduction to the living, risen Savior, Jesus Christ.

Is Salvation a Plan?

From childhood I have heard the phrase "the plan of salvation." Books, evangelistic tracts, and preachers have organized the facts of and response to the gospel into a plan. Systematizing the essential elements of the gospel into a logical progression is certainly helpful. Believers who desire to see others saved typically learn some sort of presentation like *The Four Spiritual Laws* or attend a class such as *Evangelism Explosion*.[1] Such approaches can provide excellent guidance for learning how to explain the gospel. They ensure that the essential facts and necessary theology are included when explaining how a sinner can be justified before God. However, left to themselves they can create an unintentional misunderstanding. I think this explains the response from the couple on the plane. Looking back at how I explained the gospel, I can see where the emphasis fell on the biblical truthfulness of the gospel, the theological implications of God's plan to save sinners, and the benefits of salvation. But there was something in the background that should have been center stage, something marginal that should have been central, something mentioned that should have been foremost. That something was Someone—Jesus.

Every evangelical presentation of the gospel explains Jesus. Who He is, what He did on the cross, how to seek Him as Savior; these are hallmarks of all true gospel plans. But when the gospel is explained and understood as a plan, the response can be philosophical and sterile. However, when the gospel is explained and understood as Someone to know, the response is relational. Please do not overreact to the shift in emphasis. Telling a sinner the plan of salvation is not wrong, but I am convinced that a careful examination of Scripture will reorient our gospel appeals away from data to be believed and toward a Savior to behold. Salvation is about the Person of Jesus Christ, not merely a plan.

Co-Laboring with God

At His final gathering with His disciples, Jesus told them that when the Holy Spirit comes, He will glorify the Son by pointing people to the Messiah (John 16:14). The Holy Spirit convicts hearts, opens spiritual eyes, affirms the veracity of Scripture, and regenerates souls, so they turn to Christ for salvation. The end goal is to have people bow before Jesus Christ as their Lord and Savior in this life to avoid unwilling submission in eternity.

God the Father is consumed with the same occupation as the Holy Spirit—glorifying His Son. He expressed His pleasure with Jesus when He was baptized (Matt. 3:13–17). He declared His affirmation to Peter, James, and John on the Mount of Transfiguration (Matt. 17:1–13; Luke 9:35). Do not miss the fact that the miracles Jesus performed—that for which He was most known during His ministry—were expressions of the Father's desire to glorify His Son. In one instance, when Jesus heard that Lazarus was sick, He said, "This sickness is not unto death, but for the glory of God, that the Son of God may be glorified through it" (John 11:4). The same occurred at the wedding in Cana after Jesus turned water into wine and "manifested His glory" (John 2:11).

The Holy Spirit glorifies the Son by directing people's gaze toward Jesus; God the Father glorifies the Son by affirming Him to be the only Redeemer who experienced death, resurrection, ascension, and coronation. And when we proclaim the glories of Jesus, we are joining God the Father and the Holy Spirit in their preoccupation. They are unwavering in their devotion to glorify Jesus and we are privileged and mandated to do the same.

A Critical Text

The foundation of evangelism is concisely described in 1 Peter 2:9. This verse is the bedrock that supports our evangelistic endeavors.

Peter wrote this brief letter shortly before the first wave of severe persecutions overtook Christians in Rome. A few years later, the Roman emperor Nero would go insane, and merely watched while half of his capital city burned to the ground. When the Romans responded in anger over the burning of their beloved city, Nero found the perfect scapegoat for his crime: Christians.[2] But the church in the Roman Empire was not ready to face Nero's rage. They were not deserving of it and they had no way of anticipating it.

With a pastor's heart, Peter longed to help these Christians think appropriately about the impending trials. Some of the suffering they were about to endure would be so severe that many would be taken to heaven. Peter is determined to encourage the believers who would soon be scared for their lives. So as the flames were closing in on the Christians under Rome's rule, Peter calmly reminded them of their great salvation (1 Peter 1:1–12).

You might expect this epistle to be full of comfort and encouragement about trials. And while Peter does give such encouragement (1 Peter 2:21–25; 4:12–19), he emphasized that they were saved so "that you may proclaim the praises of Him who called you out of darkness into His marvelous light" (1 Peter 2:9).

In the face of unprecedented persecution, Peter called them to the task of evangelism. He reminded them of their salvation, their savior, and their need to represent Jesus no matter what happens in life (1 Peter 1:17). We are not only promoting the gospel of Jesus, but Jesus Himself. We are not merely explaining the Word of Christ but the Person of Christ. We are engaging people with conversations about what God has done for us through His Son. We are calling people to commit to a new relationship with the living God incarnated in Jesus. We exist to glorify Christ and when we do this, we are imitating the Holy Spirit and God the Father.

THE EXCELLENCIES WE PROCLAIM

Peter reminded the church in the Roman Empire that part of being a Christian is to live a life that figuratively waves banners to the world, and those banners are inscribed with the virtues of Jesus. Christians are not to be intimidated or troubled (1 Peter 3:14), but instead they are to gently and reverently proclaim the hope that they have in Jesus Christ. As these young believers were determined to fulfill Peter's teaching, he handed them the banners that they are to fly.

Jesus: The human cornerstone (1 Peter 2:6–7)

The analogy of the cornerstone is intriguing. This stone functioned as the meeting place of the two walls that joined at the corner, hence the term *cornerstone*. It was the starting point of a building project and the most pivotal stone in any house. If it was inappropriately positioned, the entire structure would be affected. Peter used this as a picture of the proclamation of the gospel, by showing that the way Christians live requires Jesus to be their cornerstone. By living in this way, a person is eternally stable and there will be no shifting. In evangelism, believers proclaim the excellencies of this cornerstone to anyone who would listen.

Jesus: A living stone (1 Peter 2:4–5)

For Peter, evangelism was simple: preach Jesus Christ. This is exactly what he does by presenting Jesus as the living stone. For example, Peter writes about the "word of God which lives and abides forever" (1 Peter 1:23) and then describes Jesus as the "living stone" (1 Peter 2:4). There is a wonderful parallel between the written Word of God and the incarnate Word of Jesus. Because Jesus Himself is the author and substance of Scripture, He is also the object of its revelation.

Shortly after His resurrection, Jesus took a walk from Jerusalem to Emmaus (a little village approximately seven miles from Jerusalem), and on the way he met two of his disciples. As the discussion developed around the events of the weekend, Jesus quickly turned the conversation toward Himself, explaining his suffering, resurrection, and exultation from "all the Scriptures" (Luke 24:27). Peter learned this lesson, and it is clear that he saw Jesus as the target of the Scriptures. As such, he reminded his fellow Christians that Jesus is the object, the goal, the prize, the attraction, the source, the desire, and the sweetness of their faith that is rooted in the Scriptures.

To call Jesus a living stone would bring bittersweet memories to Peter. Only thirty years earlier, Jesus asked his disciples, "Who do men say that I, the Son of Man, am?" (Matt 16:13). After a few popular answers, Peter was bold enough to articulate the opinion of the disciples: "You are the Christ, the Son of the living God" (16:16). In response, Jesus called him "the rock" (see 16:18). This marked his name change from Simon to Peter.

Yet when writing to Christians who were scared for their lives Peter instead called Jesus the Rock—not himself. Jesus, however, is not just any mere stone. Because of the resurrection, he is the "living stone." He alone offers hope for death, having conquered it Himself. He is the all-defining stone, critical to the foundation of the Christian life that we are called to live and proclaim.

Jesus: A rejected stone (1 Peter 2:7)

Along with being the living stone, Christ endured the tragedy of being the rejected stone. Peter went on to say that he is a "stone, rejected indeed by men" (1 Peter 2:4). In the low point of human history, people rejected that Jesus Christ was the Messiah, denied that he was the Savior, and attacked His claims of deity.

The rejection of Jesus was prophesied in the Old Testament (Isa. 8:14), predetermined by God (Ps. 118:22–23), and witnessed by Peter (Acts 4:1–12). This rejection occurred throughout His life but found its ultimate expression in the Crucifixion. The Cross was the climax of man's rejection of Jesus. And yet as Peter wrote these words, he realized that this rejection was ongoing.[3] In fact, even today as we proclaim the excellencies of Christ, some will consider it foolishness. To these people He will still be a stumbling block.

Isaiah prophesied the rejection of Jesus nearly 700 years before He was even born (Isa. 8:14). Citing Isaiah, Peter explains that there will always be some who are "disobedient" (1 Peter 2:7, 8; 3:20) and who choose not to build their lives around the cornerstone. Because of this refusal, they look at Jesus as "a stone of stumbling and a rock of offense" (1 Peter 2:8). Even in this, the beauties of Jesus are seen; He is the cornerstone around which no one passes. No one can go around him.

The gospel message is the determinative fact in every person's life. Evangelism confronts people with the excellencies of Christ, and invites them to see that at the center of their eternal destiny is the gospel, and at the center of the gospel is Jesus Christ. Christ is the Great Unavoidable. We either meet Him now in His grace, or we will meet Him at the end of life's journey. Then, He will not be a stone, but an impenetrable wall with no way around Him. Pastor Leonhard Goppelt said it this way:

> Christ is laid across the path of humanity on its course into the future. In the encounter with him each person is changed: one for salvation, another for destruction.... One cannot simply step over Jesus or go on about the daily routine and pass him by to build a future. Whoever encounters him is inescapably changed through the encounter: Either one sees and becomes "a living stone," or one stumbles as a blind person over Christ and comes to ruin.[4]

To those who refuse to believe that Jesus is in the way, He is an inconvenience, obtrusive, frustrating, disdainful, and even a cause of anger. People reject Christ by disobeying the Word that points to Jesus as Lord and Savior. They fall on the stumbling stone.

The rejection that Christ endured is a pattern to follow for those despised for their faith, rejected by people, but who will eventually be vindicated by their resurrection through His power. Only those who do not reject Jesus will experience Christ's resurrection promise and will qualify to become "living stones."

Jesus: An elect and precious stone (1 Peter 2:6)

After showing how the world rejects Jesus, Peter contrasts that with how God views His own Son. While people reject Jesus, He remains an elect and precious stone to God. By calling Jesus an elect stone, Peter indicates that God selected and marked Jesus specifically to bring salvation to sinners. By calling Him precious, Peter shows that Jesus was indeed dear and precious to His

Father, more loved by God than any saved sinner, yet God sacrificed His Son for the redemption of sinful people—something we can never understand.

I have three sons, and I love each of them immeasurably, but the Father holds Jesus precious to an infinite degree. Despite the conflicting response the world has to Jesus, God sent His precious son to die on behalf of those who reject Him.

Peter encourages us to hold Jesus as precious, to value Christ because our faith in Him will not result in disappointment. He refers to the prophet Isaiah to reinforce this promise. Isaiah writes: "Therefore thus says the Lord GOD: 'Behold, I lay in Zion a stone for a foundation, / A tried stone, a precious cornerstone, a sure foundation; / Whoever believes will not act hastily'" (Isa. 28:16). Peter applied this promise to the first-century believers, thus guaranteeing that we will never be disappointed.[5] The implication is that Christians should be bold and fearless when it comes to the proclamation of Christ's excellencies. We are not to be ashamed now or in the future. In our death, our faith will be vindicated.

It is possible to love the things that surround Christ, without loving Jesus Himself. A person can love doctrine, theological systems, even ministry, without loving Christ. But to those who are truly His, to them He is precious. This is why the evangelist proclaims Christ and not behavior modification. This is why our sanctification hinges on our love of Christ, not our own righteousness.

Jesus Our Resurrection

Jesus and believers have something in common: Peter calls us "living stones" who are actively being built up for the worship of Christ. Peter describes our new nature with the same word He used to describe the nature of Christ; we are both "living." Jesus is "living" because He rose from the grave, and our nature—though once dead in sin—is also now alive through the life of Christ.

The life that Peter attributes to believers comes from Jesus' resurrection. Because He rose from the grave, He paved the way for the resurrection of those who would believe in Him. Death is conquered. For us, death is not the end, but is instead our corridor into eternity with our Savior. This is what makes Jesus so attractive: though He was murdered, He still lives. His resurrection is a constant source of hope for our greatest fear: death. And if this fear has been removed, we are to live life as He lived it: without fear. This changes everything: our values, decisions, goals, relationships, meaning, and evangelism. We are awaiting the redemption of our bodies, not maximizing the pleasure of these bodies. Jim Elliot was right when he said, "He is no fool who gives what he cannot keep to gain that which he cannot lose."[6] I vividly remember being asked many years ago, "What do you have that money can't buy and death can't take away?" The answer is Jesus and the resurrection He offers. Our resurrection is guaranteed, so we should evangelize like we believe that.

Christ died and was raised from the dead. This becomes the foundation of our evangelism. The entire gospel rests on whether or not Jesus was raised from the dead. Paul develops this theology in his letter to the struggling church in Corinth, a city full of philosophical ideas that found the resurrection too fantastical. In 1 Corinthians 15 Paul established that if resurrections are impossible, then Christ is still dead. If that is true, our preaching is futile, our faith is worthless, our repentance is invalid, our God is a liar, dead believers have perished forever, our future is pitiable, and spiritual death is certain. Yet "Christ is risen from the dead, and has become the firstfruits of those who have fallen asleep" (1 Cor. 15:20). He was raised and this is what we preach. We proclaim that death is not the end. We are personal, confident, and holy witnesses that Christ has been raised, conquering death and delivering us from sin. The greatest fear that has ensnared all men has been destroyed, and now every believer can say "O Death, where is your sting? / O Hades, where is your victory?" (1 Cor. 15:55).

The venom of death is neutralized by the resurrection of Christ. This is the essence of Christ's excellence.

A PRIESTHOOD OF WORSHIPPERS

Anyone living in Israel during the life of Jesus would have known about the Herodian temple in Jerusalem, which served as the central location for Jewish prayers, sacrifices, and communion with God.

Everyone knew of its beauty and splendor, and everyone understood its meaning and significance, so Peter used this vivid imagery to make a metaphor for Christ, the church, and the role of believers.

The temple always had a priesthood whose responsibility was simple: represent God to the people and people to God. But in the New Covenant, believers are the holy priesthood. We represent God to people through evangelism, and we represent people to God through prayer. We are the locus of the presence of God and we are the priests of God. We are indwelt by the Spirit of God. Our daily spiritual activity is "to offer up spiritual sacrifices acceptable to God through Jesus Christ" (1 Peter 2:5). The spiritual sacrifices we offer are our service of worship, which is the worship of Christ (Rom. 12:1). The greatest need of any human heart is to be accepted before a holy, almighty, and wrathful God. We are accepted when we offer our sacrifices for and through the Savior.

The gospel message we proclaim is dominated by this thinking. We are made for worship, and in our evangelism we offer people a new object to worship. We are calling people to turn from their idols, which can only offer temporary satisfaction, and replace them with worship of the Triune God, whose presence is filled with joy and pleasures forever (Ps. 16:11). People try so hard to make life on earth like heaven, but it will never be heaven. No idol will bring heaven to earth. Evangelism gives us the opportunity to enter the world of the unbeliever and offer him a glimpse of heaven through a relationship with Jesus. The Cross is what makes this glimpse possible for anyone who would believe. We are holy priests offering holy worship through the Cross for the pleasure of Jesus.

Martin Luther highlighted the doctrine of the priesthood of believers from this text. He rightly believed that all believers have equal access to God as priests.[7] But with the privilege of priestly access comes the responsibility to be evangelists and intercessors. We are proclaiming our God to the people around us. We are joining two hostile parties and begging the rebels to accept the terms of peace from the king against whom they committed treason. We demonstrate the attraction of this peace offer by highlighting the beauty of the Author of Peace, Christ Himself. He is the Prince of Peace (Isa. 9:6) who has become our personal peace (Eph. 2:14). By His Cross we have been adopted into the holy race. These are His excellencies and this is our message. He is our message.

ADOPTED FOR LIFE

Adoption is one of the kindest and most compassionate acts a person is capable of. Parents who adopt are admirable, and people respect them for their sacrifice. In fact, in the Roman Empire, Christians would often adopt children who were "exposed." Unwanted children, primarily girls, were left by their parents on hillsides or door steps, and whoever wished could pick them up. Most were adopted by prostitutes, slave owners, or gladiator trainers, in each case for financial gain.[8] Christians began to rescue these children, and by adopting them they reared them in the knowledge of the Lord. To this day this tradition continues, and it is rooted in the gospel message that we have been adopted by God.

Paul says that we have been "predestined … to adoption as sons" (Eph. 1:5), and John writes that "as many as received Him, to them He gave the right to become children of God, to those who believe in His name" (John 1:12). This is the imagery Peter wants to instill in his readers' minds. He is intending to comfort and encourage Christians who are scared, who feel like their rights as Romans have been stripped from them after their conversion, and Peter reminds them that they have been chosen by God for eternity even if their lives right now are filled with heartache and suffering.

Christians are God's chosen people. Remember that Peter wrote to a mixed group of believers, both Jews and Gentiles. Yet he uses incredible language about God's relationship with them that he borrows from the intimacy God had for Israel. This is a loud echo of Isaiah 43 where God announced that He Himself is Israel's savior, and He declared that He would deliver the Israelites from their Babylonian captivity. God says, "I have called you by your name; / You are Mine (43:1).

But more than this, the language Peter used transports us back in Israel's history to the time of the exodus. More specifically, this language transports us to the time God made a covenant with Israel, calling the Israelites His covenant people if they would continually obey Him. In Exodus 19:5–6 Moses recorded God's promise to Israel:

> "Now therefore, if you will indeed obey My voice and keep My covenant, then you shall be a special treasure to Me above all people; for all the earth is Mine. And you shall be to Me a kingdom of priests and a holy nation." These are the words which you shall speak to the children of Israel.

Peter imported this promise and applied it to his audience, reminding them they are included in God's chosen people. As such, they are a holy nation, ordained to function as a royal priesthood mediating God in Christ to the nations.

Owned by God

We are not merely priests and chosen people; we are a "holy nation" (1 Peter 2:9) as well. The church consists of God's holy people who are set up as lights in this world. Christians are citizens of another world, a world of righteousness and holiness, and our King calls us to obedience and allegiance. Paul motivates the Philippians to this mind-set when he reminds them that "our citizenship is in heaven, from which we also eagerly wait for the Savior, the Lord Jesus Christ" (Phil. 3:20).

Our proclamation includes a call to holiness and lays out the process of sanctification. Sanctified living is the sole proof of saved souls. We are to work out our salvation with fear and trembling (Phil. 3:12), pursuing conformity to the image of Christ for which we were predestined (Rom. 8:29). We are to die to sin and live in righteousness. This was a vivid purpose for the suffering of Jesus on the cross (1 Peter 2:24). Our message is simple: God has granted to us everything we need for life and godliness (2 Peter 1:3), and this kind of life naturally results in every person who belongs to God (1 Peter 2:9).

What beautiful imagery—owned by God! Again Peter transports us back to the Old Testament, to the time of Hosea when God promised, "I will have mercy on her who had not obtained mercy; / Then I will say to those who were not My people, 'You are My people!' / And they shall say, 'You are my God!'" (Hos. 2:23).

Do not misunderstand how precious you are to God as a believer in His Son. You are now God's child. If He gave up the most precious possession for you, He will certainly provide anything else you need as His son or daughter (Rom. 8:32). God is not ashamed to be called your God (Heb. 11:16), and Jesus is not ashamed to call us brothers and sisters (Heb. 2:11), all because we are His possession. This is what we need to preach to a world seeking companionship and acceptance. What better friend is there than Jesus?

Vessels of Mercy

Discipline is a part of most households. It should be no surprise that my sons often require discipline. But once in a while, instead of showing them justice through discipline, I extend mercy. They enjoy mercy more than they do discipline, to the extent that when the moment of discipline comes, they usually plead, "Please, Dad, give us mercy!" In a small way, that's a picture of the cry of every heart before a Holy God. The good news of salvation is that, because of Jesus, God shows mercy instead of justice.

Mercy is the opposite of grace. Grace gives us what we do not deserve, while mercy does not give us what we do deserve. All the benefits described above are only made possible because of the mercy we have received. Peter began his letter by blessing God for the mercy he extends to sinners (1 Peter 1:3). He continued by referring to the kindness of the Lord and used this as an invitation to come to Jesus (1 Peter 2:3).

When Paul decided to highlight the mercy of God, he said that He was rich in His mercy (Eph. 2:4). God was not stingy when He poured out mercy on those who needed it. In fact, Paul called God "the Father of mercies" (2 Cor. 1:3). This mercy does not stop at salvation but continues throughout our Christian lives. This is why the author of Hebrews encourages us to "come boldly to the throne of grace, that we may obtain mercy and find grace to help in time of need" (4:16). God is a God of mercies to such an extent that His locale radiates mercy. And this is the mercy that we proclaim because it has radically affected our identities.

There is a massive identity change in the person who has given his life to Christ. Our destination changes, from hell to heaven. Our nature changes, from children of wrath to children of God. Our purpose changes, from living for self to living for the Lord. We recognize that by mere mercy we have been called out of darkness into His marvelous light. We were snatched away from sin, Satan, and hell and placed into a kingdom of peace, light, and righteousness. And we are on our way to heaven. This forms both the motivation and content for our evangelism. We get to tell others what God did in our lives. God's mercy extends to individuals; it is personal. He chose me; He sanctified me; He saved me. The gospel is a personal message because God's mercy is personal. And everything about the Cross shouts mercy. It transforms us into redeemed vessels of God's mercy.

The Gospel Is a Person

It all comes down to one thing: our message is a person. We proclaim a person, not a dogma, a rule, or even a religion. Our message is a conversation that has an individual at its core. We are talking about Jesus. We are praising Jesus. We are exalting Jesus.

In Colossians 1:28 Paul summarized the purpose of his ministry in this simple statement: "Him we preach." Emphatically, he moved the personal pronoun to the very front of his profession stressing the importance of Jesus in his evangelistic message. If you are not proclaiming the beauty of Christ in your gospel presentation you are missing the point of the gospel. The gospel is about a person and a relationship with that person. And rejecting the gospel is rejecting a person (Matt. 7:21–23).

Every time we start an evangelistic conversation, we are asking people to "consider Jesus" (see Heb. 3:1). When properly understood, this simplifies evangelism. It is not an oversimplification to say that faithful evangelism is nothing more than explaining all that is excellent about who Jesus is and what He has done for those who believe. The plan of salvation is the person of Jesus Christ. We must introduce sinners to the one who died to save them from their sins. The only hope we have to offer is the gospel. And Jesus Christ is the gospel.

6

Giving Up to Gain: All Things to All People

John MacArthur

Paul's instruction to evangelists in 1 Corinthians 9 calls on Christians to give up freedoms for the sake of their testimony to the world. While the mantra of contextualization calls Christians to conform to the world so the gospel can seem relevant, real evangelism requires disciplined separation. Rooted in love, Christians are to give up their own desires for the purpose of gaining souls.

Much of modern evangelism training focuses wrongly on technique. There is a trend toward a reductionist gospel, as if the gospel was little more than a small set of basic propositions, as though evangelism was prompting people to assent to whichever of those propositions are acceptable. Classes are offered, books are written, and courses are developed that consist of little more than conversational methods and memorized monologues. The underlying notion is that a person can become a better evangelist by learning a certain technique or remembering a set formula.

Of course, the most obvious abuse of this wrong approach to evangelism is seen in those who think that the evangelist needs to live like the culture in order to win the culture. This is the worst kind of reductionism, because it not only assumes too much for the messenger, but invariably slants the message. Those who believe that the key to successful evangelism is familiarity with the world will inevitably reduce the message or muddle its clarity in order to make it more palatable to the very world they are trying to emulate.

On the contrary, evangelists in the Bible were countercultural. They did not become part of the culture; rather, they did the opposite of what the culture demanded. John the Baptist is, of course, the most salient example of being radically different, but other prophets exemplify this tradition as well. They dressed differently, often ate differently, behaved bizarrely, and were absolutely different from the world around them. In fact, the model in the New Testament is that Christians should be marked by holiness, which in every way would make them different from the culture, not identical to it (2 Cor. 6:7).

PAUL: THE MODEL EVANGELIST

The stellar example of an evangelist in the New Testament is the apostle Paul. Evangelism was the heartbeat of his life. By the end of his ministry, the gospel had launched Gentile churches throughout the Roman Empire, and practically every Gentile convert could trace the gospel message back to the preaching of Paul. What made him so effective in evangelizing the lost? There are at least seven explanations for his effectiveness.

The Right Message

Paul was an effective evangelist because he held fast to the right message. In fact, 2 Timothy 4:17 says that the Lord strengthened Paul so that in his evangelism the gospel was "fully" proclaimed. Paul clearly held fast to the truth, and did not tolerate any variations of the gospel message (2 Cor. 11:4; Gal. 1:7). One of the reasons people are not effective in evangelism is because they are not sure about the content of the gospel.

A Compelling Motive

Paul knew that everyone would eventually appear before the judgment seat of Christ to give an account of the things done in this life. Paul understood that people would be rewarded for how faithful they were in their Christian lives (2 Cor. 5:10). In other words, he knew he was going to be accountable for the record of his life and his service. This is why he said that the love of Christ compelled him to spend his life seeking the lost (2 Cor. 5:14). Notice that immediately after he described this rewards judgment, he wrote that in light of that judgment he would make it his aim in life to "persuade men" of the truth about Jesus (2 Cor. 5:11). He was motivated to be an evangelist by understanding that he would be rewarded for how he lived.

A Divine Call

Paul exclaimed, "Woe is me if I do not preach the gospel!" (1 Cor. 9:16). He knew that God had called him to proclaim the gospel to others and because of this, necessity was laid upon him. God had commissioned Paul to bring the gospel to the Gentiles, and Paul then had a sense of the divine call to evangelize.

An Eager Boldness

When he examined himself, Paul concluded, "I am not ashamed of the gospel of Christ, for it is the power of God to salvation for everyone who believes" (Rom. 1:16). This tremendous boldness enabled him to proclaim, "For to me, to live is Christ, and to die is gain" (Phil. 1:21). He had confidence in his Savior, and this confidence produced boldness in his evangelism.

A Walk in the Spirit

Paul was dependent on the Holy Spirit's power and guiding. He knew what it was to be continually filled with the Spirit (Eph. 5:18). He experienced the reality of having his mind filled with the knowledge of God's will (Col. 1:9). There was no consistent pattern of unrepentant sin in Paul's life that could quench or grieve the Spirit because he was submitted to God's will (1 Thess. 5:19). Because he was walking in the Spirit, he experienced the power of God in his life. Beginning in Acts 13:2 where the Holy Spirit said, "Separate to Me Barnabas and Saul for the work to which I have called them," all the way through his eventual martyrdom, Paul consistently experienced the power of the Holy Spirit.

A Deliberate Strategy

Paul's strategy can be seen in Acts 18, which describes his arrival in Corinth. He first went to the synagogue because he was a Jew and would thus be accepted. Under his preaching there, some were converted to Christ, which gave him a team of co-evangelists to reach the Gentile community. He used that same Jew-then-Gentile pattern commonly and effectively. Some people think that being dependent upon the Spirit means not having any strategy or plan. But Paul approached his evangelism deliberately and strategically.

An Unwavering Desire

Paul lived like he was in debt to all unbelievers; he felt like he owed them something because he knew what they so desperately needed. He saw unbelievers as people on a path that leads to destruction, and he knew the message that could change their destination. He owed them, at the very least, the proclamation of salvation. Paul evangelized like a man in debt.

These seven brief explanations capture the broad scope of what made Paul an effective evangelist. But behind these reasons is a vitally important principle that the apostle taught the Corinthians. This principle is what governed his method. Paul decided to sacrifice anything and everything in his life if it meant he could win more people to Christ. In short, Paul was willing to give up everything for the sake of reaching the lost.

First Corinthians 9 is a type of apologetic for why Paul was so passionate about evangelism, and he expressed his evangelistic intentions in four specific phrases. He declared that he would make sacrifices "in order to win more people" (v. 19 HCSB), "that I might win Jews [and] that I might win those who are under the law" (v. 20), and "that I might win the weak" (v. 22).

In the midst of discipling Christians, building churches, and training leaders, at the heart of everything was his goal of seeing people converted to Christ. And this goal was governed by the principle of sacrificing anything in this life that would hinder true gospel impact.

This is the issue Paul addressed in 1 Corinthians, where the apostle explained that he was willing to make whatever sacrifices were needed to reach different types of people with the gospel. Thus he writes:

> For although I am free from all people, I have made myself a slave to all, in order to win more people. To the Jews I became like a Jew, to win Jews; to those under the law, like one under the law—though I myself am not under the law—to win those under the law. To those who are outside the law, like one outside the law—not being outside God's law, but under the law of Christ—to win those outside the law. To the weak I became weak, in order to win the weak. I have become all things to all people, so that I may by all means save some. (1 Cor. 9:19–22 HCSB)

These verses are sometimes used to defend an evangelistic approach that appeals to unbelievers through morally questionable methods. I have heard this principle abused by people who use it to justify becoming like the world in order to see people come to Christ. Music leaders have said that their music needs to sound like the world's music so that they can win people. Pastors have said that their sermons need to use illustrations from popular culture so that the gospel seems relevant to those in the culture. Some people even use this passage to justify adopting whatever pagan worldview is held by the culture that they are trying to reach.

Ironically, these practices are the exact opposite of the principle Paul puts forward in 1 Corinthians 9. Paul believed that love limits our liberty, not that it expands it. The apostle was not teaching that the end justifies the means, as though fleshly methods (or an abuse of Christian liberties) should ever be used to create a common ground with unbelievers. Rather, his point was that he restricted the use of his Christian liberties, if necessary, in order to reach those whose consciences were overly strict (and therefore weaker than his own). As one commentator observes, Paul "refused to allow his own freedoms to prevent others from following the ways of Christ."[1] In so doing, "he avoids becoming antinomian and is careful not to transgress God's timeless moral principles."[2]

From both the context of this passage and the apostle's other teachings, it is unmistakably clear that Paul would never sanction the use of carnal conduct (1 Thess. 4:3–7), imagery (Phil. 4:8), humor (Eph. 5:3–5), or speech (Col. 3:8; Titus 2:6–8) to build bridges to the lost. Along with the other New Testament authors (James 1:27; 4:4; 2 Peter 1:4; 2:20; 1 John 2:15–17), Paul consistently exhorted his hearers not to embrace the corruption of the culture, but rather to distance themselves from it (e.g., Rom. 8:13; 1 Cor. 6:9, 18; Gal. 5:19–20; Col. 3:5; 2 Tim. 2:22; Titus 2:12). Paul was advocating self-denial, not self-indulgence.

He explained this clearly in 1 Corinthians 9:19 (HCSB): "although I am free from all people, I have made myself a slave to all, in order to win more people." He would make absolutely any sacrifice necessary to win people to Christ.

The Corinthians were wondering whether a Christian was free to simply do whatever he felt he had the freedom to do, and Paul told them no. They may have had the freedom to do some debatable things, but they risked making others stumble. So Paul simply said that an evangelist ought to limit his freedom because of his love for people.

In fact, 1 Corinthians 9:19–22 is an example of how much Paul sacrificed his Christian freedom to reach out to those who have not experienced it. Much of the chapter shows specific examples of Paul limiting his liberty. He may have had the right to marry, but he refused (1 Cor. 9:5). He had the right to be paid by churches, but instead kept working so that he could support his own ministry (1 Cor. 9:6–16). In fact, in chapter 8 Paul said that a Christian even has the freedom to eat meat offered to idols, but that often it is wise to abstain (1 Cor. 8:4–5).

Paul was free to do whatever he wanted, but he made himself a slave to everyone in order to win them. In what can be described as premeditative sacrifice, he decided to set aside his liberty in order to win others to Christ. The lesson is not to become like the world by doing what they do, but instead to limit your freedom to avoid unnecessarily turning people away from following Jesus.

This approach to evangelism is not popular because it invariably involves self-denial. This would not be an issue if we were called to abstain from things we do not desire anyway. But, instead, Paul is actually asking Christians to limit their liberty, to exercise self-denial, and be willing to give up their freedom for the sake of the gospel.

Paul willingly made himself a slave to all (ἐδούλωσα edoulōsa [v. 19]).[3] This may seem paradoxical. After all, if he was "free from all men" how could he be a slave again? An illustration of this paradox comes from Exodus 21:1–6 where Moses gave regulations concerning slavery in Israel. After serving six years, a Hebrew slave was to be freed from his master and had the right to go his way. But he also had the right to come back and say, "But I don't want to be free. I love you, and my service to you is not an act of obedience nearly as much as it is an act of love. Could I stay?" If the slave stays, the master takes him to the doorpost, puts his ear against the door, and then takes an awl and pounds a hole through his ear. Once the hole is in his ear, the slave has a sign for all to see that he serves out of love. In other words, he would be a slave out of his own volition, not obligation. He had his freedom, and he rejected it for the joy of being a slave again.

Christians likewise have spiritual holes in their ears. They have the freedom to live as they please, but they choose to become slaves of the unsaved, so that they might win some of them to Christ. Again, this does not mean they live like unbelievers, but rather that they refrain from doing things that are offensive to unbelievers. It is giving up freedom in order to protect the gospel.

This principle is not unique to Paul. It was Jesus who taught, "Whoever of you desires to be first shall be slave of all" (Mark 10:44). And that's precisely what Jesus was, as it says in the next verse: "For even the Son of Man did not come to be served, but to serve, and to give His life a ransom for many" (v. 45). Paul applied this principle to his own life, and made himself a slave of all people with whom he came in contact.

But why would he do this? He lived like this so that he might win more people to Christ. Paul wrote:

> Remember that Jesus Christ, of the seed of David, was raised from the dead according to my gospel, for which I suffer trouble as an evildoer, even to the point of chains; but the word of God is not chained. Therefore I endure all things for the sake of the elect, that they also may obtain the salvation which is in Christ Jesus with eternal glory. (2 Tim. 2:8–10)

Paul regularly became a prisoner by making sacrifices that might gain a hearing for the gospel.

Starting in verse 20 of 1 Corinthians 9, Paul gave some practical illustrations of this attitude and how they apply to evangelism. He reminded them that he adapted to the customs of the Jews in order to win the Jews. Whatever their ceremonial law dictated, Paul did. If it was important to them to have a certain meal in a certain way, he did it. If it was important for them to celebrate a certain day in a certain way, he did that too. If it was important for them to follow a certain custom, he did that as well. Why? So that he might win a hearing for the gospel among them.

Paul was not saying that Christians should win people to Christ by accommodating their false religion, but rather he was saying that one gains the right to speak the truth by giving up freedoms to avoid offense in matters of custom and tradition. If a Christian unnecessarily offends somebody else, he or she may forfeit the right to be heard.

GIVING UP TO GAIN IN ACTS 15

This principle actually did not originate with Paul, but with the apostles in Acts 15. The Jerusalem Council was meeting to try to determine what they should do with Gentile converts. There were some new converts who still upheld Jewish tradition and wanted Gentile believers to become Jewish in the way they lived. When the Jerusalem Council discussed the issue, it decided not to trouble the Gentiles who had turned to God by demanding that they live by Jewish regulations (Acts 15:19).

These Gentiles were now saved. They had turned to God and received the Holy Spirit. Therefore, there was nothing else to accomplish through ceremony. But the apostles went on to say, "We [should] write to them to abstain from things" that would give offense to Jews (Acts 15:20). This is a subtle point, but one with profound implications. The way Gentile believers applied this principle was not by participating in certain ceremonies, but instead by abstaining from certain freedoms. They were not to live like Jews to win Jews. They were to refrain from offending Jews to win Jews. They were to limit their freedom for the sake of the gospel. This is giving up to gain.

First of all, they were to abstain from the pollutions of idols (Acts 15:20). That meant that they were to stay away from meat offered to idols. This meat was not only a hindrance to Gentile converts but it was also offensive to Jewish people (1 Cor. 8:4–7). This is an obvious example of a freedom, because "an idol is nothing" (v. 4) so eating food offered to the idol is—in isolation—a completely indifferent act (1 Cor. 8:4, 7). But the apostles asked the Gentile believers to give up this freedom because the Jews despised pagan idolatry and believed eating meat sacrificed to such idols was egregiously wrong. So the goal was to avoid offending both new Gentile believers and Jewish unbelievers.

Second, they were to stay away from fornication. Most would think this is obvious, but in this context fornication has a broad meaning. It refers to any kind of sexual sin, and Gentile pagan worship was usually connected to sexual sin. The apostles wanted Gentile believers to have nothing to do with idolatrous offerings or with Gentile worship where these sins were taking place.

The Jerusalem Council also advised these Gentile Christians to stay away from meat that had been strangled. The Gentiles often killed their animals that way, while the Jews would slaughter their animals by cutting their throats, because Jewish law prohibited eating animals that did not have the blood drained out of them.

Finally, for the sake of the Jews they were to stay away from blood. This would be the most difficult of all the requests because many Gentile ceremonies included the drinking of blood. Now why did they lay these restrictions on these Christians? The reason given was "For Moses has had throughout many generations those who preach him in every city" (Acts 15:21). In other words, there were strong Jewish communities in these Gentile cities. If the Jews saw the Christians doing things that were deeply offensive to them (though neutral to Gentiles), it would have solidified in their minds that Christianity was not for the Jews. It would cost the Gentiles nothing other than preference to abstain from these liberties, but if they ever insisted on exercising those freedoms the Jews would refuse to listen to their evangelistic efforts. They were to avoid these freedoms so as to do nothing to detract from an opportunity to gain a hearing for the gospel.

GIVING UP TO GAIN IN 1 CORINTHIANS 9

Perhaps Paul learned the lesson about giving up freedoms for the sake of the gospel from the Jerusalem Council in Acts 15. Regardless of where he learned it, he lived by it and wanted the Corinthians to do the same. In 1 Corinthians 9 he said that he came "to those who are under the law, as under the law, that I might win those who are under the law" (v. 20). In other words, when he was with people under the law (Jews), even though he was no longer under the law, he put himself under some of their customs.

Paul was not compromising truth. He was maintaining certain things that were ceremonial in nature, indifferent to God in the same way the meat offered to idols was indifferent. He did this to gain entrance into the hearts and minds of the Jews so that he could bring them the gospel.

An example of this sort of thing would be the Sabbath. Paul wrote:

One person esteems one day above another; another esteems every day alike. Let each be fully convinced in his own mind. He who observes the day, observes it to the Lord; and he who does not observe the day, to the Lord he does not observe it. He who eats, eats to the Lord, for

he gives God thanks; and he who does not eat, to the Lord he does not
eat, and gives God thanks. (Rom. 14:5–6)

Some people thought that the Jewish dietary laws were important, and some
did not. Some thought the Sabbath should still be observed, and some did
not.[4] Paul's point was that ultimately it should not be an issue. It is not a question of right or wrong, and if a Christian can accommodate the preference of
others for the sake of gaining a hearing for the gospel, then Paul would say that
love triumphs over liberty.

This limiting of freedom was not just for the sake of the Jews. There are also
cases where for the sake of Gentiles Paul would abstain from freedom that he
had in Christ. He wrote, "To those who are without law, as without law (not
being without law toward God, but under law toward Christ), that I might
win those who are without law" (1 Cor. 9:21). When Paul was with the Gentiles he preferred not to do those things that would offend the Gentiles. He
likely avoided some Jewish observances that he otherwise normally would have
observed. For example, when he was in Jerusalem he would follow the Jewish
customs, but when he went to Antioch, he ate with the Gentiles and ate the
way the Gentiles ate (Gal. 2:1–14).

There is a third group that required limiting their freedom as well: "To
the weak I became as weak, that I might win the weak" (1 Cor. 9:22a). The
weak were overscrupulous Christians who were immature in their faith. They
were baby Christians who did not understand their liberty in Christ. For example, in the Jewish community there were new Christians who still wanted
to keep the Sabbath, continue to go to the temple, maintain some connection
with the rabbis, and maintain certain customs and feasts in the home. They
had not really understood their liberties. Among the Gentiles there would be
those saved out of idolatry who would want nothing to do with meat offered
to idols, nothing to do with activities in their community that were in any way
related to pagan gods.

These new believers easily developed into a group of ultrasensitive Christians who became legalistic. When Paul was with them he became like them—
he did not become legalistic, but he set aside his freedoms to avoid unnecessary
strife. He was sensitive to people who were easily offended, so that he might
gain the weak by ultimately strengthening their standing in Christ.

So to the Jew, Paul was as a Jew and to the Gentile, Paul acted as a Gentile. To the weak brother, Paul was as a weak brother. He did all this because "I have become all things to all men, that I might by all means save some" (1 Cor. 9:22). But was Paul just compromising? No, because there is a great difference between compromising and limiting liberty. The difference here is between what is optional and what is not optional. Limiting a freedom is meeting somebody at his own level and setting aside an action that is optional to begin with. Compromising is setting aside truth or accepting false teaching.

Paul was not a man pleaser (Gal. 1:10). He did not alter the message to make it more palatable. If a person Paul was evangelizing was offended by the Cross or the truths of Scripture, then that was not a concern to him. But if a person was offended by some behavior that a Christian did (especially one that was not necessary to begin with), then that became Paul's problem. This is why the faithful evangelist follows Paul's model and gives up liberty to gain listeners.

It needs to be noted that Paul's principle of giving up to gain applies to cultural situations and not propositional truths. He would act one way around Jews, another around Gentiles, and still another way around weaker believers. This was not hypocrisy, because his motives were from a pure and loving heart. It also was not carelessness, as these changes were not in relation to biblical truths, but to cultural issues.

Should the Audience Affect the Message?

The question is raised concerning how the culture should affect the message. Should the evangelist alter his message depending on what group he is talking to? While making every effort to present the message with excellence and effectiveness to the world around us, we must be careful to do so in a way that both stays true to the biblical gospel and stays within the biblical boundaries of moral propriety. "Relevance" is no excuse for diluting the gospel in an attempt to reach the unchurched. Nor is "contextualization" a valid justification for condoning sinful speech or conduct in order to identify with certain cultures or subcultures. Even in some Reformed circles,[5] it has become popular to flaunt Christian liberties, emphasize crass humor, and showcase sexual themes—all in the name of reaching the lost.

Such a mind-set is as spiritually dangerous as it is ultimately ineffective. We should never stoop to tempting people to sin, no matter the culture or the context. To dilute or distort the gospel is to preach another gospel altogether (Gal. 1:6–8). To use fleshly methods to reach the lost is self-defeating, bringing a reproach on the pure name of the Savior we proclaim (cf. 2 Cor. 10:3–5; 1 Tim. 3:7; 4:12; Titus 2:8). Christian evangelism is not about cleverness (1 Cor. 1:17), but faithfulness as we expose the culture around us to the unchanging truth of Christ (Eph. 5:6–14). The command to "be holy" applies to all evangelistic efforts (1 Pet. 1:15).

How then should the audience affect our message? The example of the apostle Paul is particularly instructive in this regard. Two of Paul's greatest sermons were apologetic in nature. In one, to the Gentile philosophers on Mars Hill in Acts 17, Paul started by pointing to creation (vv. 22–29). In the other, to King Agrippa in Acts 26, a man familiar with the Jewish faith, Paul started with Old Testament promises (vv. 7–8) and his own personal testimony (vv. 8–23). Although his starting points were different for these two audiences, the essence of Paul's message was identical. In both instances, he quickly transitioned to speak of Christ (17:31; 26:15), the resurrection (17:31; 26:23), and mankind's need to repent (17:30; 26:20). Though the apostle's context changed, his gospel message did not. We might also point out that Paul did not use cheap theatrics to establish common ground with either audience. Nor did he resort to scandalous behavior in order to arrest attention. Instead, he clearly, accurately, and reverently explained the truth in a way appropriate to each of them. No other "contextualization" was necessary.

The Role of Self-Control

The kind of self-denial that Paul exemplified for the evangelist will always involve self-control. Paul explains that if one is really going to limit his liberty, it will require discipline. The evangelist will have to forgo some freedoms that he otherwise would not want to give up, and live a life that is going to be circumscribed by the wishes of others. This is not easy, and this is why Paul used an athletic metaphor to illustrate this point: "Do you not know that those who run in a race all run, but one receives the prize? Run in such a way that you may obtain it (1 Cor. 9:24).

The Corinthians would have been familiar with this illustration. Ever since the days of Alexander the Great, athletics had dominated Greek society. Two of the most famous athletic competitions were the Olympic Games and the Isthmian Games, which were held in Corinth every other year. The Corinthians understood that those who competed in those games ran to win. In order to get into the finals, contestants at the Isthmian Games had to give proof of extensive training, and for the last thirty days before the event they all had to come into the city and train daily in the gymnasium.[6] Only when all of those conditions were fulfilled were they able to run. When they ran and finished, these athletes were immortalized. The highest honor and praise were given to the one who won those games.

Paul's point is that an athlete has the freedom to eat dessert, but he sets it aside while he is training. It is not that it would be wrong for him to eat recklessly before he runs, it just would not be smart. A Christian has the right to eat food offered to idols, but he sets it aside to win the Jews or the weaker believers.

The Corinthians were so busy grasping at their rights, they began losing the prize. Instead of obtaining the goal, which was to win souls, they were running the race while clinging to their rights, and as a result they were in danger of being disqualified. They were hurting their testimony and alienating their mission field for the sake of freedoms that were inconsequential.

This is not to make light of the sacrifices evangelists are required to make. Because the goal is worthy, the sacrifice required is immense. Evangelism is not unique in this regard. Success is impossible academically, spiritually, or athletically without discipline and self-denial commensurate to the grandeur of the goal. Paul's point is that people cannot succeed at anything unless they pay a high price, and the goal of evangelism is certainly worth that sacrifice.

We should be able to cut out anything in our lives that stands in the way of reaching people with the gospel. Athletes deny themselves many lawful pleasures in order to compete, and they do so for a perishable prize (1 Cor. 9:25). How much more worthy are the sacrifices that Christians make for the sake of winning others to Jesus?

Once you understand that your life will be filled with sacrifices for the sake of evangelism, then your goal will be clarified and your resolve strengthened. This produces confidence and clarity. That is why Paul declared, "I do not run aimlessly" (1 Cor. 9:26 ESV). An individual with no goal is not really running a race, and this aimlessness requires no effort. But the mature Christian knows his goal and runs with confidence and clarity.

Athletes have mental toughness and physical discipline. They are in control of their desires, and they desire to win. Paul evangelized in a similar way. He knew what his goal was and he was willing to make the sacrifices to get there, so he subjected his body to spiritual disciplines. Worldly lusts, passion, the flesh, whatever the spiritual battle might be that would rob him of the crown—he subdued those desires so that he could be a slave to the unsaved.

Why should anyone submit his body and will to such strict discipline? Paul's answer is this: "lest, when I have preached to others, I myself should become disqualified" (1 Cor. 9:27). This is a metaphor straight out of the Isthmian Games. When the Isthmian Games began, a herald came out and a trumpet was blown to capture everyone's attention. The herald would then announce the event, introduce the contestants, and define the rules. An athlete who violated any of those rules was immediately disqualified.[7] Paul was the herald in this analogy, spreading the gospel to others. How humiliating would it have been if the herald became disqualified? Paul feared that he might disqualify himself by refusing to give up liberties for the sake of reaching others.

There is a modern trend of using 1 Corinthians 9 to justify outrageous cultural indulgences, in the name of "becoming all things to all people" (see v. 22). As has been said already, this could not be farther from Paul's point. Paul described evangelists as those ready to give up freedoms, not exploit them. Athletes do not eat hot dogs to fit in with the fans, and Christians do not indulge the flesh to mesh with the world. They exercise self-control for the sake of their gospel testimony.

Sadly, there are many in Christian service who started out serving the Lord but failed to subdue the flesh, and they have been disqualified. The reckless and undisciplined Corinthians thought they could indulge their liberties to the hilt, while the devoted apostle was engaged in a life of self-denial and self-control to gain entrance for the gospel into the hearts of others. Paul corrected them, calling them to let go of their freedom on the basis of love, for the sake of others. This is a model of how we ought to live.

Effective evangelists do not appear accidentally. They are those who have made the sacrifices to be used by God.

7

Evangelism in the Hands of Sinners: Lessons from the Book of Acts

John MacArthur

The book of Acts not only shows the birth of the church but also describes the early church's evangelism. Contrary to the modern notion that churches should strive to make unbelievers comfortable, the church in Acts stressed purity. In fact, the biggest threat to evangelism in the early church was not persecution, but toleration of sin. While the church's first recorded sin (Ananias's hypocrisy) may have temporarily scared unbelievers away, the Lord used it to return the church to its focus: outreach based on a testimony of holiness, spurred on by persecution.

The New Testament presents a simple truism: those who love Jesus Christ care about evangelism. Christians are called to continually communicate the gospel to the world. When Jesus ascended into heaven, He left his disciples behind in Jerusalem. His saving work on the cross was complete, and the penalty for sin was paid. But there was still work to be done, and the disciples were left on earth to do it. Jesus commissioned His followers to go into all the world and preach the gospel to every creature, and to be His witnesses not only in Jerusalem but also in the uttermost parts of the earth.

There would be much opposition. The Jewish leaders, thwarted by Jesus' resurrection, were nevertheless going to oppose Christianity. The apostles would be arrested, Stephen and James martyred, and converts ostracized. Beyond that, Gentiles would treat the message as foolishness, and Christians were going to find themselves relegated to the second class of society.

But the fact of the matter is, none of those obstacles halted evangelism. On the contrary, the more opposition there was, the more the gospel went forth. However, there was and is today one danger potent enough to actually curtail evangelism: sin tolerated inside the church.

The book of Acts describes one of the most remarkable cultural revolutions in history. Jesus left his ragtag group of followers bewildered and confused, gazing into heaven. He gave them what could only be seen as an impossible task: to take the news of His death and resurrection to the entire world. And yet by the end of Acts, that initial group had been transformed and expanded. Churches were established in Ethiopia, Rome, Asia, and everywhere in between. By the end of Acts 2 the church was meeting in Solomon's Portico, outside of the temple. The center of opposition to Christ became a gathering place for thousands of Christians.

This is why no book in Scripture illustrates the power of evangelism as clearly as Acts. When the Holy Spirit inaugurated the church and gave power to the disciples, its members were changed into compelling preachers, evangelists, and even martyrs. While they gave their lives for the new church, it grew and flourished. At the end of Acts 1 there were 120 followers of Jesus. But by the end of Acts 2, the church added 3,000 converts in one day, and its growth had just begun. In fact, more people were being saved every day (Acts 2:47).

The first opposition to this growth came from the outside. The Jewish leaders did not look favorably on the Christians. After all, they had gone to extraordinary measures to eliminate Jesus and his teachings, and now the public gatherings of the church provided clear evidence that their efforts had failed. They retaliated by arresting and beating some of the apostles, with the hope of silencing them. But despite their attacks, the church kept growing. If anything, persecution from the outside caused the apostles' testimony to be more powerful, and it ended up promoting evangelism, rather than squelching it.

Sin's Power to Stop Evangelism

If persecution from outside the church propelled evangelism, Acts 5 describes the opposite effect: sin inside the church had the power to destroy evangelism. The church leadership had just endured arrests, beatings, and prohibitions—none of which slowed the movement. But the moment sin entered the church, the Lord turned His attention to the reality that the church's biggest danger is not external persecution, but internal iniquity.

The story of Ananias and Sapphira (Acts 5:1–11) is both well known and tragic. The details are straightforward: a husband and wife sold their land for the purpose of giving the proceeds to the church in order to help the poor in the church. They publically committed to give the whole amount to the apostles, and they made that commitment voluntarily, not under compulsion. However, when the sale occurred, they kept half of the proceeds for themselves. In front of the church, they laid the money at the apostles' feet in a dramatic fashion, while publicly declaring that they had donated the entire proceeds from the sale. It was lying pride cloaked in sinful and self-serving humility. For the first time, the focus of the church shifted from outside evangelism to inside hypocrisy.

Despite the sinful nature of this transaction, it actually began well enough. The church was compassionate, and Christians were demonstrating the love of Christ by taking care of one another. This selfless sacrifice was preparatory for evangelism. In addition to loving one another, they knew they could not expect to have an effective witness for Christ to those in need outside the church if those in need inside the church were being ignored.

So the early church made a practice of sharing its wealth as a means to meet its members' needs. The result was that "the multitude of those who believed were of one heart and one soul; neither did anyone say that any of the things he possessed was his own, but they had all things in common" (Acts 4:32). This was illustrated vividly by the sacrifice of Joses, who sold his home and publicly gave the money to the church, so that it could be used to alleviate the needs of other Christians (Acts 4:36–37). Because of this generosity, it was "with great power the apostles gave witness to the resurrection of the Lord Jesus" (Acts 4:33). The members of the church were generous to one another, and so their evangelism was particularly powerful.

It was in this context that Ananias sold a piece of property and pretended to place all the money at the apostles' feet. He was clearly emulating Joses, but unlike Joses, Ananias lied and kept back some of the proceeds for himself and he did this with his wife's full knowledge. Their sin was not that they did not give everything to the church. God never commanded anyone to sell or to give everything from a sale. Ananias was not commanded to give anything at all. The sin was deceit, rooted in pride. He wanted people to think that he gave everything.

In a word, this was hypocrisy. There was an explosive love in the early church, and people were not merely offering petty cash but were offering the proceeds from the sale of their homes and lands. Joy and spiritual devotion were apparent to everyone, and Ananias and Sapphira wanted a little of that prestige. Wanting to cash in on the opportunity to be admired, they paraded in front of the church, giving a pretense that they were giving everything they had received for the sale of their home. They sought to gain reputations of being godly, sacrificial, and generous. They wanted the applause for their sacrifice and to hang on to some of the cash at the same time.

Since the demonically inspired persecution of the church had clearly failed (Acts 3), Satan had shifted his approach. Rather than only attack the church from the outside, he assaulted it from the inside. Hypocrisy became Satan's weapon of choice to corrupt the church. Because the church was growing in large part based on the way Christians were meeting one another's needs, Satan moved in to twist that sacrificial behavior.

Ananias's actions are the first sin that the Bible chronicles in the life of the church. The initial internal demonic attack on the church of Jesus Christ was hypocrisy—the use of religion to puff oneself up rather than to serve the church. Not much has changed in the past 2,000 years. To this day this is Satan's chief weapon against the gospel. It is the best way to douse the flame of evangelism. God hates all sin, but no sin is as ugly as the one that attempts to paint pride so that it looks like spiritual beauty. When such people get into the church, they corrupt it. When they get into the leadership of the church, they can even kill it.

Sin's Exposure

True to what we would expect from a God who hates sin, the deception of Ananias's hypocrisy gave way to the spiritual perception of Peter's leadership

(Acts 5:3). Peter, who could only have known the truth behind Ananias's actions by direct revelation from God, confronted him. "Ananias, why has Satan filled your heart to lie to the Holy Spirit?" Peter recognized that Satan was behind this sin, and he also recognized that an attack on the church of Jesus was also an attack on the Holy Spirit.

God publicly confirmed the truth of Peter's accusation by striking Ananias dead. It is impossible to overstate how shocking this must have been to the early church. They were moving from one spiritual victory to another, and had grown from 120 in Acts 1 to many thousands by Acts 5. The Lord was strengthening them by persecution and blessing their evangelism. It must have seemed like nothing could stop the growth. But then Ananias fell down and breathed his last in front of the entire congregation. God had shocked the church by killing him.

Luke describes the fallout from this judgment with his typical understatement: "So great fear came upon all those who heard these things" (Acts 5:5). Fear stretched beyond the congregation to those outside the church who had heard the news. If there were any illusions about the nature of the Christian church, they were shattered. The church was not going to be about fun and games, because the God of the church is serious about sin. This was not exactly what you could call a seeker-friendly environment, and it certainly was not a sin-friendly environment. There is one true "seeker" in the church—the Lord who seeks to save—and He is not friendly to the presence of sin.

The message that Christians should be sending to the world is not that the church tolerates sin and sinners, but that God hates sin. When the world understands that God will judge sin, people are prepared to appreciate that God also has provided a means for complete forgiveness through His grace. That's the gospel message. The world needs to know that sin kills, but that God forgives.

Jews did not practice embalming, so they carried Ananias away and quickly buried him. Three hours later, his wife came and had no idea what had just transpired (Acts 5:7). Peter asked her if she and her husband had sold the land for the price her husband had claimed, and she—perhaps thinking this was her moment to be commended for her generosity—replied, "Yes, for so much" (v. 8).

"Peter said to her, 'How is it that you have agreed together to test the Spirit of the Lord? Look, the feet of those who have buried your husband are at the door, and they will carry you out'" (v. 9). Then immediately she fell down at his feet and breathed her last. And the young men came in and found her dead, and carried her out, and buried her by her husband (Acts 5:10).

God does not play church. Sapphira's death is a further powerful illustration that God hates the sins of His saints, no matter how trivial those sins might seem. The sins of Christians are the most heinous aspect of the church because they subtly allow Satan to destroy credibility and stifle evangelism. If someone comes in and teaches false doctrine, that is easy to deal with. If someone comes in and discounts the reality of the Trinity or attacks the person of Jesus Christ, he or she is easily combated because any of those errors are recognizable. It is the devious deceptions that reign in people's hearts that become an unseen cancer in the church until exposed and removed.

Because the sin was exposed, the Lord used this event to return the church's focus to its task of evangelism. After the burials, the church was again "all with one accord in Solomon's Porch" (Acts 5:12). This is in contrast to just a few moments earlier when sin caused disunity in the church. Ananias and Sapphira had lied to the Holy Spirit and polluted the fellowship, but God purified the church by rooting out the sinners, so that the testimony of the church was restored.

EVANGELISM FROM PURITY

Effective evangelism is empowered by a pure church. People might imagine that a church that deals with sin seriously would drive people away, not attract them. And to some extent this is true. Luke explains that despite the fact that the apostles were performing signs and wonders publicly, "none of the rest dared join them, but the people esteemed them highly" (Acts 5:13). The believers were meeting publicly, and nobody was impulsively joining them because they knew that they should not become Christians unless they were willing to have their lives exposed. The world knew that people who were not genuine in church ran the risk of being struck dead by God, so no one joined them who was not ready for that kind of commitment.

A church that refuses to deal with sin, like so many churches today, becomes a breeding ground for both sinful believers and false converts. People make false professions of faith and are even allowed to live the lie because there is never any exposure of their sin. I have been told countless times that a church that practices church discipline will destroy evangelism or that preaching on holiness will drive people away. The mantra of the seeker-sensitive movement is that unbelievers should feel comfortable in church, otherwise evangelism will be unsuccessful. But in the early church the public knew about the spectacle of Ananias and Sapphira, and twice Luke wrote, "great fear came upon all … who heard these things" (Acts 5:5, 11). The world was aware that the church dealt with sin, and people did not join it unless they were sincere. There was a short-term barrier to those who were only curious.

This reluctance, however, did not stifle evangelism long-term. The most shocking part of this entire story is that while the punitive deaths of Ananias and Sapphira kept sinners from joining the church for the wrong reasons, the end result of the whole event was that "believers were increasingly added to the Lord, multitudes of both men and women" (Acts 5:14). The world knew the church was pure, the world knew that God dealt with sin, and the world knew that sin was exposed and judged. They also knew the gospel offered forgiveness for sin. As a result of purity, the church that takes sin seriously will be effective in its witness to the world.

This is because with purity comes power from God to be used in reaching the lost. After the sin was dealt with, Luke writes that "through the hands of the apostles many signs and wonders were done among the people" (Acts 5:12). In order to confirm their evangelism, they performed miracles. Later Luke elaborates on these signs:

> They brought the sick out into the streets and laid them on beds and couches, that at least the shadow of Peter passing by might fall on some of them. Also a multitude gathered from the surrounding cities to Jerusalem, bringing sick people and those who were tormented by unclean spirits, and they were all healed. (Acts 5:15)

People believed in the power of the apostle and were drawn to the church. This power drew people because the purity of the church was consistent with its message. God was moving in the church. While the gifts of healing and miracles that Peter possessed are not performed in the same way in the church today, the principle that God blesses a pure church with evangelistic power still stands.[1] God is still doing miracles through the pure church, and the most powerful miracle of all is the new birth.

EVANGELISM, PURITY, AND PERSECUTION

Inevitably, a pure church active in evangelism will draw the ire of the world system. Because the ruler of this age is Satan (John 14:30), anybody who flees the world for refuge in Christ becomes an enemy of Satan, and will be opposed by those of the world.

The world operates by principles of lust, sin, and rebellion, so when a church begins to grow it disrupts this system. When people are saved, Satan reacts, and persecution begins. The world does not like it when churches make waves in the culture. By their testimony of holiness, pure churches confront the sins in their culture. Ironically, persecution results in the growth of the church. But a church that tolerates sin will undercut its own evangelism. After all, why would the world persecute a church that tolerates the sin that the world loves?

Immediately after Ananias and Sapphira were dealt with, a revival broke out in the Jerusalem church. The result of their purity was an increased witness, and the world system responded by attacking the church. Luke records that as the gospel moved forward, the High Priest and the Sadducees "were filled with indignation" (Acts 5:17).

The Sadducees were religious leaders who collaborated with the Roman occupiers to keep peace in Judea. Though they were a small minority of Jews, they were wealthy and influential. They viewed Christianity as a threat to their control. Thousands upon thousands of people were proclaiming the name of Jesus Christ, healing miracles were being performed, and no one could deny the power of God was active in the church.

In response, the Sadducees were filled with rage and seized the church leaders and threw them in jail (Acts 5:18). But God—as is typical—turned what Satan desired for evil into good. He sent an angel who "opened the prison doors and brought them out" (v. 19). God's sense of humor is seen in this defiant kind of miracle. The Sadducees had two theological doctrines that set them apart. They did not believe in a resurrection, and they did not believe in angels. Ironically, when they arrested the disciples for preaching about the resurrection, God used an angel to free them.

Again, God took the persecution leveled at the pure church and used it to actually encourage evangelism. The angel told the apostles, "Go, stand in the temple and speak to the people all the words of this life" (Acts 5:20).

Jesus came into this world to give life to spiritually dead people (John 5:21; Rom. 4:17). Because people are dead in their sins, they are slaves to the principles of this world. The gospel the disciples declared showed them how to obtain freedom from sin and inherit eternal life.

Of course the Sadducees did not relent, but by the time they learned of the jailbreak, the apostles were already back at the temple preaching. The Sadducees summoned the apostles (again) and interrogated them. Peter, undeterred by his night in jail, said, "We ought to obey God rather than men" (Acts 5:29). Amazingly, Peter saw this second arrest in twenty-four hours not as a setback, but as a further opportunity to preach the gospel. He told the leaders: "The God of our fathers raised up Jesus whom you murdered by hanging on a tree. Him God has exalted to His right hand to be Prince and Savior, to give repentance to Israel and forgiveness of sins" (Acts 5:30–31).

Note that Peter told them about the resurrection—the very topic they had just prohibited him from preaching.

Peter did not take no for an answer when it came to evangelism. He was not intimidated by the Jewish leaders' rejection of the gospel, but persisted in proclaiming the good news of Jesus Christ. Persecution did not produce timidity but persistence. He offered you, Peter says, "repentance to Israel and forgiveness of sins" (Acts 5:31). Despite persecution and threats of beatings and imprisonment, Peter and the apostles still confidently said, "We are His witnesses to these things" (Acts 5:32).

THE RESULT OF A PURE WITNESS

The witness of a pure, powerful, persecuted, and persistent church will produce conviction of sin in the hearts of unbelieving hearers. This would not have been possible with Ananias and Sapphira as evangelists. A person who is living in sin cannot credibly call others to flee from the wrath to come and be transformed into a righteous person by Jesus Christ.

But in Acts 5, after having dealt with the sin of hypocrisy, the church experienced growth, persecution, and more growth. Luke records how the Sadducees reacted to the preaching of the gospel—they were "furious and plotted to kill them" (Acts 5:33). The testimony of God will have a similar effect on people. Hebrews 4:12 says, "For the word of God is living and powerful, and sharper than any two-edged sword, piercing even to the division of soul and spirit, and of joints and marrow, and is a discerner of the thoughts and intents of the heart." It is a sword, and it rips people open. It convicted the Jewish leaders, and they reacted by conspiring to murder the apostles.

While Peter's evangelism in the temple produced converts, his evangelism to the Sadducees did not. Salvation is not guaranteed, but conviction is. When the gospel is clearly proclaimed and accompanied by the testimony of a pure church, then people will be confronted by the reality of sin in their own lives. This is what conviction means. People will realize that they love sin, and then they will either repent or continue in their sin while suppressing their conviction. The gospel is for some an aroma of "life unto life" and for others "death unto death" (2 Cor. 2:16). Not all conviction leads to salvation, but conviction is necessary for salvation. And in order to produce any conviction, the message must be backed by a pure testimony.

True conviction is mental, not merely emotional. Peter did not evangelize by telling tear-jerking stories that would generate superficial sadness and temporary guilt. That kind of conviction is shallow and unhelpful. Instead, Peter preached clearly about a Christ who was sent by God to forgive sin—a Christ whom the people crucified. He told those whom he evangelized that they were living in rebellion against God, then he offered those people salvation if only they would repent. Rather than repent, those to whom Peter spoke were enraged because their sin was exposed, showing that the gospel message had produced conviction of sin.

The entire narrative of Ananias and Sapphira is interwoven with lessons about evangelism. A church that tolerates sin corrupts its own testimony and makes evangelism ineffective. But when sin is purged, it empowers the church to preach the gospel with authority. Persecution will follow but even this will aid in spreading the message of the gospel.

Though the apostles were beaten, arrested, and commanded not to speak the name of Jesus, they departed both rejoicing and witnessing (Acts 5:41–42). Like Paul in Galatians 6:17, they bore in their body the marks of Jesus. Those blows had been meant for Jesus. They stood in His place, taking the blows meant for Him.

Many Christians who are veterans of a few evangelistic skirmishes seek an honorable discharge. Others seek to increase evangelism by designing a church that makes nonbelievers feel comfortable and welcome. But the pattern of the early church provides a different model. Its members love one another sacrificially, but refuse to tolerate sin in the fellowship, and boldly face persecution if necessary for the sake of the gospel. That kind of church continues to turn the world upside down (Acts 17:6).

Section 2

Evangelism from the Pulpit

8

Sunday Morning: Evangelism's Role Within the Service

Rick Holland

A preacher's primary duty is to call people to faith in the gospel. The truth that mankind is sinful and God is glorious in His providing salvation needs to be central to any Cross-centered sermon. As Christians, we beg people on behalf of Christ to be reconciled to God. Failure to make the truths of the gospel apply to the preacher's heart effectively nullifies gospel preaching.

On the anniversary of his conversion to Christ, Charles Wesley wrote his beloved hymn *O for a Thousand Tongues to Sing*. This is one of my favorite hymns because of the rich gospel truth it bellows. The second verse resounds: "My gracious Master and my God, assist me to proclaim, to spread through all the earth abroad the honors of thy name."

If preachers listened to iPods before they preach in the same way that athletes do to prepare themselves for their competitions, this would be on the pre-sermon playlist. What a great lyric—a plea for divine assistance to proclaim the honors of God's name throughout the whole earth. In these four lines, Wesley expresses his dependence on God by seeking the power of God to spread the gospel of God for the honor of God to people who do not know God. Whether stated in written form or not, such should be a part of every church's mission statement. This is evangelism.

What role does evangelism play in a Sunday service? Ask most preachers and they will likely answer, "A big role!" However, close examination of sermonic praxis might not reflect that same conviction. For those committed to expository preaching, especially consecutive exposition, there is a potential pitfall in evangelistic preaching.

Anyone concerned about the salvation of souls ought to be concerned about evangelistic preaching. I am not so much talking about evangelistic sermons—that is, sermons that are, from beginning to end, an explanation and appeal to unbelievers to repent and believe the gospel—but rather preaching that always reveals the connective tissue of the passage or topic to the gospel. Preachers should certainly preach evangelistic sermons. But I want to suggest that all preaching should have an evangelistic note in its melody.

Church history offers us this lesson: where the gospel was preached, and preached often, people were converted, communities were transformed, and nations were shaken. God's omnipotent power resides in the good news that Jesus is Lord and Savior (Rom. 1:16; 1 Cor. 1:18, 24). Conversely, find the pulpits of history that strayed from a faithful witness to the gospel and you will find dying churches and societal decline.

Evangelism is the responsibility and privilege of every believer. However, preachers have a higher accountability to the mission of evangelism. In fact, trace the word *preach* (κηρύσσω kēryssō) in the New Testament, and you will discover that it most often refers to a public-speaking event for the purpose of evangelism.[1] Actually, what we have come to know as preaching is more akin to the New Testament's description of teaching and exhortation (1 Tim. 4:13). Faithful preachers are not only to be expositors of Holy Scripture, they are to be evangelists as well.

Because God has gifted some especially for the purpose of evangelism (Acts 21:8; Eph. 4:11–13), it is easy for preachers to think that evangelism is for a gifted specialist. However, Paul instructed Timothy to "do the work of an evangelist" (2 Tim. 4:5). This is quite different from saying, "Become a gifted evangelist." The work of evangelism should not be confused with the gift of evangelism.[2] For the pastor, evangelism is a mandate to obey, a work to do, a responsibility to fulfill, and a joy to employ. Evangelism should not only have a seat at the table on Sundays; it should sit at the head.

Evangelism and Preaching

When properly understood and delivered, preaching simply cannot avoid being evangelistic in tone and nature. Christian preaching is the proclamation of Jesus, and it inherently reminds people that Jesus is the only Savior from sin. He is what integrates evangelism with all of our preaching. To preach Jesus is to be evangelistic and to be evangelistic is to preach Jesus.

Paul provides his most definitive description of his own preaching in 1 Corinthians 2:1–5 (NASB). The apostle had been criticized for his preaching style and foolish logic. His five-verse retort shows that the person of Jesus was the integrating centrality of his proclamation:

> And when I came to you, brethren, I did not come with superiority of speech or of wisdom, proclaiming to you the testimony of God. For I determined to know nothing among you except Jesus Christ, and Him crucified. I was with you in weakness and in fear and in much trembling, and my message and my preaching were not in persuasive words of wisdom, but in demonstration of the Spirit and of power, so that your faith would not rest on the wisdom of men, but on the power of God.

This does not mean that Paul only preached sermons about the life and crucifixion of Jesus, nor that he only preached sermons that were expositions of one of the four Gospels. Any reading of Paul's letters quickly shows that he preached and provided instruction on the full spectrum of Christian living. However, every subject he considered was anchored in Christ and gospel truth. D. A. Carson explains that Paul "cannot long talk about Christian joy, or Christian ethics, or Christian fellowship, or the Christian doctrine of God, or anything else without finally tying it to the cross."[3]

J. C. Ryle extends the centrality of Christ beyond Paul to the whole Bible:

> I charge every reader ... to ask himself frequently what the Bible is to him. Is it a Bible in which you have found nothing more than good moral precepts and sound advice? Or is it a Bible in which 'Christ

is all'? If not, I tell you plainly, you have hitherto used your Bible to very little purpose. You are like a man who studies the solar system and leaves out his studies of the sun, which is the center of all. It is no wonder you find the Bible a dull book![4]

Even more to the point, John Jennings challenges:

Let Christ be the matter of our preaching. Let us display the divine dignity and loveliness of His person as "God manifest in the flesh,"—unfold his mediatorial office, the occasion, the design, and purport of his great undertaking,—remind our hearers of the particulars of his incarnation, life, death, resurrection, ascension, and intercession,—set forth the characteristics he bears as a prophet, priest, and king; as a shepherd, captain, advocate and judge. Let us demonstrate the sufficiency of his satisfaction, the tenor and excellence of the covenant confirmed with and by him, our justification by his righteousness, adoption through our relation to him, sanctification by his spirit, our union with him as our head, and safe conduct by his providence; [let us show] how pardon, grace, and glory accrue to the elect through his suretyship and sacrifice, and are dispensed by his hand. Let us declare and explain his most holy laws in his name, and teach the people whatever duties he has commanded to God, our neighbor, and ourselves,—quicken the saints to duty, raise their hopes, establish and comfort their souls by the exceedingly great and precious promises of the gospel, which in Him are "yea and amen."[5]

Jennings is right. Jesus is to be the matter of our preaching. There is enough value in the person of Jesus to fill every sermon of every Sunday of every preacher for all eternity.

But this raises a question with which every preacher has struggled: how do you accent Jesus if He is not in the text you are preaching? Obviously, this is not a problem if you are preaching one of the four Gospels or a christological text. But what if the passage you are preaching does not have Jesus and the good news of salvation as its topic?

Some solve this dilemma by creatively materializing Jesus in such texts. Hypertypology, allegory, spiritualization, and analogy are used to reveal that Jesus is really there if you look hard enough. Yes, the Scriptures speak of Jesus

(Luke 24:27; John 5:39). Yes, He is the focus and aim of all of the written Word of God. But interpreting every verse, paragraph, and pericope to be specifically about Christ and the gospel swims in the water of Origen's hermeneutic. Origen saw multiple layers of meaning beyond the plain reading of Scripture.[6] And most often, he tied everything to an allegorical connection with Jesus. However, not every passage is about Jesus. To find Him in places where He is not in the author's mind disregards the authorial intent of both the human author and divine Author.

So how should we preach Jesus from texts where He is not the direct referent? Simply, Jesus should be in every sermon though He is not in every text. There is a massive difference in transitioning from a text to gospel truth and finding the gospel in a text where it is not explicitly referenced. Most are aware of C. H. Spurgeon's famous line, "I take my text and make a beeline to the cross."[7] In this I find hearty agreement with the Prince of Preachers. Finding a route to the gospel from the preaching text is far different from playing hide-and-seek with the gospel in a text that does not contain it. The good news that God has provided a Savior should be an integrating centrality in our sermons without tampering with the authorial intent of a given passage.

There are different approaches to connecting a sermon to the gospel, depending on the text. For example, some texts have themes that fairly clearly lead to the gospel, but which a layperson might miss. For example, in 1 Samuel 14 Jonathan is sentenced to death for breaking one of Saul's commands. However, the soldiers of Israel ransomed Jonathan from Saul, which they could do because they had kept the law perfectly (v. 45). The idea is that a person can have sin forgiven by someone standing in for them, and that this only works if the one paying the ransom is sinless in the eyes of the Law. It is a short walk from this passage to the gospel, and these kinds of examples abound in the Old Testament.

Other texts have broader gospel implications. For example, if you find yourself teaching through 1 and 2 Kings, a common motif is that sin brings judgment, while repentance brings forgiveness. Another theme is how the line of David refuses to live up to the Davidic promises, yet God is nevertheless faithful to that promise. Examples of this are legion, and they provide an easy connection to the gospel message.[8]

The bottom line is that every passage/text/topic eventually comes around to the sinfulness of man and the glory of God. As these issues arise in the sermon, it is not difficult to explain and offer the gospel in short or longer presentations. In fact, it is imperative.

WOE IS ME

Nowhere is the imperative of preaching the gospel personified better than in 1 Corinthians 9:16. With soul searching and eternally consequential accountability, Paul exclaims, "Woe is me if I do not preach the gospel!" In other words, Paul says, "Let me be accursed, condemned, damned if I don't proclaim the good news that Jesus is the Savior." With even stronger language, the apostle tells the Romans that he would rather be accursed himself than see his fellow Jews perish without Christ:

> I tell the truth in Christ, I am not lying, my conscience also bearing me witness in the Holy Spirit, that I have great sorrow and continual grief in my heart. For I could wish myself were accursed from Christ for my brethren, my countrymen according to the flesh, who are Israelites, to whom pertain the adoption, the glory, the covenants, the giving of the law, the service of God, and the promises; of whom are the fathers and from whom, according to the flesh, Christ came, who is over all, the eternally blessed God. Amen. (Rom. 9:1–5)

There is no stronger, no more passionate, no more personal passion for the souls of others than to be willing to sacrifice your own soul for their eternal salvation. Did Paul really consider leveraging his salvation for others? No, he was merely using the most hyperbolic illustration to express the most intense desire for others to come to faith in Christ.

As preachers, this is the kind of longing we are to have for the salvation of souls. Evangelism should be a driving, passionate, personal goal every time a preacher opens his mouth. Puritan Thomas Brooks wrote: "The salvation of souls is that which should be first and most in a minister's eye, and that which should always lie closest and warmest upon a minister's heart."[9] Too many preachers find it easier to focus on whether or not the hearers appreciate their sermons than to focus on whether or not the souls of the hearers embrace salvation.

Preachers need to come to terms with the fact that the sermon is not an end. It is a means to a few ends, such as strengthening faith, encouraging the saints, and confronting sins. But certainly one of the main ends is the salvation of souls. Pastors should embrace the fact that Sunday is not just an opportunity to deliver a sermon, but, more important, to see souls converted.

Too Proud to Beg?

Besides the Lord Himself, it is difficult to imagine a more gifted, faithful, and fearless evangelist than the apostle Paul. Because his letters are so theologically heavy, one might be tempted to conclude that he was a theological, esoteric intellectual who ministered in a fabled ivory tower. Nothing could be farther from the truth. Paul employed his divine gifting and theological genius in evangelistic persuasion. He explained to the Corinthians: "Now then, we are ambassadors for Christ, as though God were pleading through us: we implore you on Christ's behalf, be reconciled to God. For He made Him who knew no sin to be sin for us, that we might become the righteousness of God in Him" (2 Cor. 5:20–21).

There is much for preachers in this verse.

First, notice how Paul identifies himself and his team as "ambassadors for Christ." He viewed himself as promoting Christ, not himself. He wanted the praise of his preaching to be directed to Jesus, not to himself. Faithful representation of Christ flies against the strong headwind of self-promotion in the pulpit. A. E. Garvie unmasks this temptation with these penetrating words for the preacher about his preaching:

> The calling itself brings with it a secret and subtle peril to the preacher in the desire for the praise of men. Human applause may mean more than divine approval. Popularity may appear to him his heaven, and obscurity his hell. A false estimate of the value of preaching prevails. Does the preacher draw? Does he please? Do his hearers praise? These are the questions asked; and not such as these: Did he utter the truth fully and fearlessly? Did he offer the grace of God tenderly and earnestly? Did he call men to repentance, faith, holiness effectively? Even

if the preacher escapes the degradation of trimming his sails to catch the breeze of popularity; even if the content and purpose of his sermons remain right, yet he may very easily in preaching think rather of the ability he is displaying, and the reputation he is acquiring, than of the glory of God and the gain of men.[10]

Desiring the praise of men over divine approval is a ministerial riptide and the undertow is deadly for the preacher (James 4:6). While attempting to direct the congregation's focus on God, there is an ever-present whisper of pride that audaciously attempts to steal His glory (Isa. 42:8). This is the epitome of ministerial hypocrisy, and it is combated by making the goal of preaching the salvation of souls rather than the applause of people.

Second, Paul continues his metaphor by identifying the referent of his representation—God Himself. He reminds the Corinthians that "God [was] pleading through us." God dispatches His representatives with the terms of peace contained in the gospel. It is the ambassador's duty and privilege to faithfully represent his king with perspicuity and passion.

Third, Paul reveals his attitude in evangelistic preaching: begging. He writes, "We implore you on Christ's behalf, be reconciled to God." This is Paul's passionate care and concern on behalf of the lost. The Greek word for "implore" (δέομαι deomai) has a range of meaning that includes strong desire, passionate entreating, and even emotional begging.[11] Are we too proud to beg, to weep, and to plead? Are we too proud to entreat the unbeliever to consider Jesus (Heb. 3:1)? Spurgeon's famous words regularly ring in my ears: "Oh, my brothers and sisters in Christ, if sinners will be damned, at least let them leap to hell over our bodies; and if they will perish, let them perish with our arms about their knees, imploring them to stay, and not madly to destroy themselves."[12]

May it never be said or even perceived that we are too proud to beg people to approach the cross to have their sins forgiven.

Hindrances to Gospel Preaching

Luke 11 describes an afternoon where Jesus was eating lunch at a Pharisee's house. While there, Jesus rebuked the hypocrisy of the Pharisees and the lawyers, and the outcome was predictable: "And as He said these things to them, the scribes and the Pharisees began to assail Him vehemently, and to cross-examine Him about many things, lying in wait for Him, and seeking to catch Him in something He might say, that they might accuse Him" (Luke 11:53–54). In the middle of this hostility, while thousands were stepping on one another in an attempt to hear Jesus' every word, He turned to his disciples and encouraged them to be fearless evangelists.

His disciples had seen their Master provoked and heard Him badgered. They found themselves surrounded by a crowd whose hearts were set on murder. It was inevitable then that these men would be terrified. If the crowds did not like Jesus and what He said, what hope did the disciples have in their preaching?

The fact that rejection seems so certain is one of the main reasons we are reluctant to share the life-giving message of Jesus Christ. If we boil all our reasons and excuses down to the lowest common denominator, it is fear. This is exactly the same paralyzing hindrance that the disciples faced. We are afraid, afraid of being rejected, ridiculed, labeled, persecuted, fired, demoted, passed by, ignored, left out, looked down upon, challenged with questions we cannot answer, or simply embarrassed. Strangely, fear keeps us from proclaiming the truth that the gospel dissolves all fears.

As Jesus looked into the fear-filled eyes of his disciples, he provided a map to navigate through their fears as they were to preach His gospel. These insights are encouragement for us in our evangelistic preaching. Rather than fearing the threat of man, we should fear the threat of God. In that moment of tension, Luke records Jesus' words: "And I say to you, My friends, do not be afraid of those who kill the body, and after that have no more that they can do. But I will show you whom you should fear: Fear Him who, after He has killed, has power to cast into hell; yes, I say to you, fear Him!" (Luke 12:4–5).

Jesus never guaranteed his disciples protection of their physical life. In fact, the majority of them followed in the footsteps of John the Baptist and died also. And still, Jesus called them to the same level of commitment and reminded them that the preacher's boldness in preaching the gospel is rooted in his understanding of the reality of hell. God is the author of life, the sovereign over death, and the judge of all. He alone has the authority to determine who the inhabitants of hell will be.

Hell is described as a place of fiery torment where the "worm does not die / And the fire is not quenched" (Mark 9:44), as an "eternal fire" (Matt. 18:8 NASB), as "fire and brimstone" (Rev. 14:10; 20:10; 21:8), and a "furnace of fire" (Matt. 13:42, 50). Jesus preached about hell more than any other individual in the Bible. Still, theologians have tried to extinguish hell's fire. Clark Pinnock succinctly expresses the liberal perspective on the doctrine of hell when he says:

> Let me say at the outset that I consider the concept of hell as endless torment of body and mind an outrageous doctrine. . . . How can Christians possibly project a deity of such cruelty and vindictiveness whose ways include inflicting everlasting torture upon his creatures, however sinful they may have been? Surely, a God who would do such a thing is more nearly like Satan than like God.[13]

This is precisely why ministers are called to preach the gospel, so they can participate in God's grace to keep people out of hell. Compare Pinnock's quote with the words of William Nichols, and ask which one of these theologies leads to earnest evangelism: "The heat of the fire will everlastingly torment them, and the stench of the brimstone will offend their senses, while the blackness of darkness will horrify them. . . . For the damned who inhabit that place of eternal wrath, Hell is truth learned too late."[14]

In Sunday sermons, preachers must not neglect preaching on the horrors of hell and the catastrophic consequence of rejecting Christ. When you abandon preaching on hell, you ignore the accent in the Epistles on the coming judgment, you will need to skip large portions of Jesus' teaching in the Gospels, and you might as well rip Revelation out of your Bible.

Some neglect to teach on hell, while others minimize the torments of hell. Underestimating the reality of hell leads to a belief in a kind of purgatory where a second chance after death is expected, thereby making people think that there is plenty of time to "get right with God." Hell is physical pain, loneliness, darkness that accentuates fear, regret, separation from God, and the absence of a second chance. God sends us as His ambassadors to beg people to be reconciled to Him. Do not be misled; the reality of hell is essential to preaching the gospel message.

While fear is one hindrance to evangelism, so is familiarity. Familiarity can dull the evangelistic zeal. Casualness with the sacred leads to complacency.

A careless attitude toward God's Word and His Great Commission will shift your focus from the glory of God in salvation of souls to behavior modification and legalistic teaching.

Irresponsible Calvinistic convictions may also hinder evangelistic preaching. An imbalanced understanding of the sovereignty of God, accenting his sovereign will in election while diminishing the means by which God brings the lost into His kingdom, can foster a diminishing fervor for evangelistic preaching. John Frame describes this temptation unique to Calvinistic preachers and the cure this way:

> I have heard Calvinists say that our goal in preaching should be only to spread the word, not to bring conversion, since that is God's work. The result is often a kind of preaching that covers biblical content, but unbiblically fails to plead with sinners to repent and believe. Let us be clear on this point: the goal of evangelistic preaching is conversion. And the goal of all preaching is a sincere response of repentance and faith. Hyper-Calvinism actually dishonors God's sovereignty, because it suggests (1) that vigorous, goal-directed human effort negates God's sovereign grace, and (2) that such vigorous efforts cannot be God's chosen means of bringing people to salvation. God's sovereign purpose is to save people through the witness of other people.[15]

Remembering that we are the means God has sovereignly chosen to bring salvation to the world is the antidote to using God's sovereignty as an excuse to limit evangelism (cf. Rom. 10:14-15).

Finally, presuming that all the attendees in our Sunday congregations are saved may hinder gospel sermons. Paul calls every believer to regularly examine his stance in the faith. He commands the Corinthians to "examine yourselves as to whether you are in the faith. Test yourselves. Do you not know yourselves, that Jesus Christ is in you?—unless indeed you are disqualified. But I trust that you will know that we are not disqualified" (2 Cor. 13:5–6; see also 1 Cor. 11:28–31).

There is to be a regular self-assessment of our faith in Christ. It is the preacher's responsibility to preach the gospel against which the congregation may examine themselves. The apostle John echoes the same principle: "Now by this we know that we know Him, if we keep His commandments.... He who says he abides in Him ought himself also to walk just as He walked" (1 John 2:3, 6). The preacher must never assume faith in his audience. Instead, the standard of biblical expectations and the message of the gospel is to be weekly presented for the sake of examination and salvation.

Preaching the gospel glorifies the Savior, sanctifies the preacher, brings sinners to salvation, refreshes believers, focuses the church, and fuels missionary efforts. In short, gospel preaching upsets the world (Acts 17:6). We have one mission and one mandate: make disciples (Matt. 18:18–20). And we have the weekly reminder of the gospel that functions as the catalyst to convert the unsaved. Why would any preacher neglect preaching the gospel?

Horatius Bonar said, "Men lived, and it was never asked of them by their minister whether they were born again!"[16] Let that never be said of the people in our congregations.

9

Equipping the Saints: Training Believers to Win the Lost

Brian Biedebach

Pastors bear the ultimate responsibility for training their people how to evangelize. This can seem overwhelming and intimidating, which often means it is neglected. However, the task is actually simpler than might be imagined. The New Testament shows that evangelism—rightly understood—is intimately connected to the normal work of the local church. As the church in Acts 6 shows, the pastor who focuses on teaching and prayer will best equip his congregation to be passionate about bringing the gospel to the lost.

One of the pastor's primary goals is to equip his congregation to bring the gospel to the world. If it is true that evangelism is the primary task of believers, and if it is true that a pastor's primary task is to equip the saints to do the work of the ministry, then it follows that teaching a congregation how to evangelize is one of a pastor's biggest priorities.

But in a world that is antagonistic toward the gospel, and in a church that often seems hesitant toward the task, this can seem like a daunting challenge. How can a pastor equip his flock to bring the good news to a world that hates Christ, is apathetic about the afterlife, and is ready to reject divine revelation?

The truth is that most pastors probably wish they did a better job at training their members to win the lost, and often they themselves feel inadequate when it comes to evangelism.

Highlighting this weakness, there is no shortage of programs that offer to help a pastor in this task. It is common for churches to run weekend seminars, after-church courses, conferences, and Sunday school classes, all with the goal of equipping the saints for the work of evangelism. But while some training programs are helpful, it may surprise you to know that these are not the primary resources given by God to the pastor for his task. Actually, the best way a pastor can make his people passionate about evangelism is for the pastor himself to be passionate about the ministry.

A pastor is responsible for studying, discipling, preaching, counseling, witnessing, visiting, leading, and just about everything else that happens in the church. If a pastor devotes himself to the right responsibilities, then training others in evangelism should be a natural by-product of what he already does. This is accomplished by remembering these three principles: evangelism involves more than witnessing, evangelism is modeled through preaching, and evangelism is motivated through prayer and the ministry of the Word.

Evangelism Involves More Than Witnessing

Because I grew up in the church, short-term mission trips were a normal part of my teenage years. It was on those trips that I first learned about evangelism. I had memorized key Scripture passages relating to salvation, and learned how to share the gospel by sharing passages in Romans:

1. A person must recognize his or her sin (Rom. 3:23).
2. Because God is holy, sinners deserve eternal punishment for breaking His law (Rom. 6:23).
3. To solve the dilemma of God's holiness and mankind's sinfulness, Jesus was crucified so that those who would trust in His sacrificial work could be saved (Rom. 5:8; 6:23).
4. If a person believes this, he should repent of his or her sin and trust in Christ as Lord (Rom. 10:9–10).

Armed with some underlined passages in a Bible, the verses I had memorized, and those key steps to salvation, I spent many days speaking to others about the gospel. I would knock on doors or go up to people in a park and ask if I could tell them about Jesus Christ. Most of the time, these were people I had never met before and would probably never see again.

While dozens of doors were literally slammed in my face, I was overjoyed that many people listened. Some even followed the steps I gave them and committed their lives to Jesus Christ. While I am grateful for those experiences and believe that God may have used those conversations to draw people to Himself, the entire endeavor was not "evangelism" in the fullest sense of the word. At best, they were times of "witnessing," but "witnessing" is only one part of "evangelism."

In the New Testament, evangelism involved more than merely witnessing. The concept of witnessing comes from the Greek word μαρτυρέω (martureō), which simply means to "testify." It is a legal term that can refer to someone testifying in a courtroom about what he has seen or experienced. For example, in John 5:33, John the Baptist gave "witness" to the truth about Jesus. All Christians can give a similar witness to others about Jesus when they simply describe how they themselves came to know the gospel (1 John 1:2).

Witnessing is a responsibility of every genuine believer—especially those who are gifted in evangelism. But biblical evangelism is more than a testimony. *Evangelism* is a broader term that can be better understood by what "evangelists" did in the Scriptures.

Ephesians 4:11–12 gives an example. Paul wrote that God "gave some to be apostles, some prophets, some evangelists, and some pastors and teachers, for the equipping of the saints for the work of ministry." In the context of Ephesians 4, Paul was explaining how God was going to not only build the church, but how He was going to maintain unity in the church through various gifts provided by God (4:7–16). Among the gifts that God has given the church for growth and guidance are evangelists and pastors.

This is an indicator that evangelists, like pastors, are connected to the local church. While pastors may be those who teach regularly (1 Tim. 5:17), evangelists are those who proclaim the good news regularly. Evangelists focus particularly on areas that have not yet heard the gospel, but in so doing they are focused on church planting and church strengthening. For example, in Acts

21:8 Philip is called an evangelist. But to say that proclamation (or witnessing) is the only responsibility of an evangelist is not accurate.

New Testament evangelists are more like today's missionaries and church planters than what we normally think of when we hear the word *evangelist*. Crusades and revival meetings may have their place, but the biblical picture of an evangelist is someone involved in church planting and church strengthening. John MacArthur says the same when he writes:

> The evangelist is not a man with ten suits and ten sermons who runs a road show. New Testament evangelists were missionaries and church planters ... who went where Christ was not named and led people to faith in the Savior. They then taught the new believers the Word, built them up, and moved on to new territory.[1]

The New Testament's clearest connection of pastoral ministry and evangelism is certainly 2 Timothy 4:5. There Timothy is told to "do the work of an evangelist." The context of this charge is pastoral; Timothy knew that the Bible is God's Word (2 Tim. 3:16), and that he should devote himself to it (3:17). In fact, in the presence of God, Christ Jesus, and in light of the coming kingdom, Timothy was to "preach the word" (4:2). He was to "convince, rebuke, exhort" with patience, because he was a minister of God's Word. This lengthy description of pastoral ministry ends with a resounding charge to Timothy to "do the work of an evangelist" so that he can fulfill his ministry (4:5).

Paul's instructions to Timothy make Timothy the perfect example of what a biblical evangelist is. It is obvious that for Paul and Timothy, the work of evangelism was inextricably connected to a prolonged preaching ministry in the local church. This means that if a pastor is faithful to his ministry by preaching, correcting, counseling, and opposing errors, he will be an example of evangelism to his church. Thus, the preaching of the Word is able to equip a congregation to evangelize.

This is critical for a pastor to understand. Perhaps the best thing he can do to strengthen his congregation's evangelism is to do with excellence the tasks that God has given him. The stronger he preaches, the more people he disciples, and the more devoted he is to the church, the more his church's evangelism will prosper.

Evangelism Is Modeled Through Preaching

I remember clearly the moment when I fell in love with evangelism. It was 1987 and I spent the summer in London with other teenagers, telling people about Jesus Christ.

On that trip, I met a man who said he was a satanic priest. When I first saw him, he had upside-down crosses sewn on the front of his jacket and the numbers 666 on the back. We spoke on the streets of London one day and when I began to share Scripture verses with him, he told me that the Bible contradicted itself. He quoted some Bible passages that seemed to contradict one another, and declared that there was no way Scripture could be true. When I looked them up with him, I was stumped and could not answer his objections. But I told him that if he met me that evening I would have found out how to reconcile those passages by then.

I spent the afternoon with my fellow travelers poring over those passages and praying for the man's salvation. That evening I was surprised that he showed up, and even more surprised that he had red flames painted on his face. He was convinced that hell was going to be a big party and that Satan would reward him for his evil deeds. The group and I shared with the man all that we had learned that afternoon about the passages he brought up, and it was enough for him to say that he wanted to talk with us more.

On many occasions that summer the man visited us. He read Scripture with us, argued with us, and even prayed with us. Eventually he repented of his rebellion against Christ and committed himself to the Lordship of Jesus Christ. I remember the night he began to pull the upside-down crosses off of his jacket. During those short weeks we saw him transform inside and out. His attitude was different; his friends were different; his entire appearance had changed.

That August I returned to my parents' home in California, but I have been back to London a number of times. I have even been back to the London City Mission in Croydon and visited the staff member who hosted us. But I have never spoken to the man since that summer trip in 1987, and I do not know anyone else who has. My prayer is that he is faithfully serving the Lord somewhere, but I just do not know if he is. What I do know is that on that summer mission trip I was not able to do the work of an "evangelist" in the complete sense of the word. What that man needed most after verbally committing his life to Jesus Christ was to be shepherded with the Word.

In Ephesians 4:11–12 Paul describes the instrumental role that pastors play in building up believers for works of service. This passage describes different offices in the church, and by implication makes the point that pastors and evangelists are different people. Homer Kent noted, "The pastor-teacher describes the person whose responsibilities are usually localized, in contrast to the evangelist."[2] In other words, evangelists and pastors have many responsibilities that are the same, but the main difference is that generally the evangelist has an ongoing preaching ministry in places where Christ is not known, while the pastor has an ongoing preaching ministry where a church is already established. In both cases, preaching is the method of proclamation that dominates their ministry.

Preaching is the primary tool used by a pastor to shepherd his flock, and the early church shows us that preaching is also the primary way a pastor evangelizes. The first example of church-based evangelism was Peter's sermon in Acts 2, and this sermon served as the foundation of the church. In Acts 7 Stephen preached on several Old Testament passages in order to proclaim Christ to the Jews. Paul also followed this pattern, and the first thing he did when he entered a new town was to preach to the Jews in the synagogue and then to the Gentiles.

Because God gives pastors to the church for the purpose of equipping the saints for the work of service (Eph. 4:11–12), and because the pastor's primary ministry is to expose the Scriptures to his congregation, expository preaching will therefore equip a congregation for the work of service. That work includes evangelism. Obviously evangelism is different from merely preaching, but proper preaching is a key component to modeling evangelism. As members of a congregation gain a deeper understanding of God's Word, they are better equipped to witness, disciple, and minister to others who do not know Jesus Christ. A pulpit that expounds God's Word diligently, passionately, and accurately will naturally help to motivate its members to do the work they have been equipped to do.

Evangelism Is Motivated by Prayer and the Ministry of the Word

A number of years ago, while I was pastoring a church in South Africa, a new believer asked me a question that led me to evaluate what truly motivates people to share Christ with the lost. "Pastor," he asked me, "what is a missionary?" At first, I thought it seemed like the answer was pretty obvious, but I asked him why he wanted to know. He replied, "Because I have met all kinds of people in Africa who call themselves missionaries and I can't figure out what they all have in common."

It was apparent to that young South African that many people who call themselves missionaries are not directly involved in the proclamation of the gospel. A missionary is someone who has been sent out to help fulfill the Great Commission (Matt. 28:19–20). The main active phrase in Matthew 28:19–20 is "make disciples." That is at the heart of what it means to be a missionary. In Matthew 28:19–20 the participles "baptizing" (βαπτίζοντες baptizontes) and "teaching" (διδάσκοντες didaskontes) help describe how one "makes disciples." Ultimately, unless someone is involved in baptizing new believers and teaching them all that Christ has commanded, they are not involved in all that the Great Commission commands.

Many people who call themselves "missionaries" are sidetracked with social issues like working with AIDS orphans, feeding the hungry, providing job training, and other mercy ministries. While these are all important tasks, the clear model in Scripture is that these good works should not be separated from local church ministry. Furthermore, local churches need to keep a proper focus on making disciples by baptizing and teaching, and this focus motivates congregations to influence the world for Jesus Christ.

The question is how can a pastor keep his church (and his missionaries) from being sidetracked with social issues, while keeping them prepared and motivated to influence their world for Christ? This is the same question faced by the early church in Acts 6. There, the church was dealing with a social issue (hungry widows), and yet it remained focused on evangelism. This ordeal is enlightening because it represents the first instance of the church potentially losing focus on the Great Commission to turn aside to social ministry. How the pastors of that church responded not only teaches us about the priority of preaching and prayer but also how a church can stay focused on evangelism while being faithful to one another. There are three marks of that early church that teach us about their motivation for evangelism: they were eager to serve one another, the leadership was focused on the right things, and their testifying followed naturally.

A Congregation That Served One Another

Acts 6 began with a problem. At the very time when the church was experiencing exponential growth, there were some in the church who had physical needs and those needs were being neglected. The Greek-speaking widows were being overlooked, and they were not properly cared for by the leadership.

It was no secret that many Palestinian Jews looked down upon those who were Greek-speaking Jews. While the Greek-speaking Jews were from places scattered around the empire (Acts 2:9–11), the Aramaic-speaking Jews were from Palestine. According to Jewish tradition, there was a weekly dole for the Hebrew needy (given every Friday and consisted of enough money for fourteen meals).[3] There was also a daily distribution for nonresidents and transients (that consisted of food and drink). It seems that in all the growth of the church, a division was being created between these two groups, and Greek-speaking Jewish believers were being overlooked in the daily distribution of food, and evidently the native widows were not.

Note how the apostles dealt with this issue: they did not stop the distribution altogether, or respond in any way that showed neglect for the care of the poor in the church. Rather, the apostles tapped into what apparently was an eagerness in church members to care for one another. What the apostles said was: "Brethren, seek out from among you seven men of good reputation, full of the Holy Spirit and wisdom, whom we may appoint over this business" (Acts 6:3).

Acts 6:5 (NAS) says, "The statement found approval with the whole congregation," and they chose men who loved the church. This was not done out of a desire for political correctness, but was motivated by the apostles' desire to see the gospel as a means to continue forward. Because the church was eager to care for one another, the church could remain focused on outreach. By refusing to get bogged down in a political turf war, the widows—as well as the men—chose to respond in humility. The result was that the church could remain focused on evangelism.

Thus the leadership of the early church (both the apostles and these first deacons) was actually promoting evangelism by their eagerness to love and serve one another. This is a critical reminder to pastors who are tempted to see any inward focus of the church as a distraction from evangelism. If the church is not harmonious on the inside, evangelism becomes impossible. By serving one another, the church kept on its evangelistic mission.

A LEADERSHIP FOCUSED ON THEIR PRIORITIES

Earlier in this chapter, I wrote about the pastor's responsibility to do the work of an evangelist by being faithful in his preaching. Because preaching and prayer are the best means a pastor has to shepherd his flock, the best way he can demonstrate his love for his flock is to pray for them and minister the Word to them. This was the priority of the early church leaders. They said, "We will give ourselves continually to prayer and to the ministry of the word" (Acts 6:4).[4]

This leadership from the early church becomes our standard. In order to remain focused on evangelism, the pastors devoted themselves to prayer and preaching. This may seem counterintuitive, but consider the following five ways that a pastor's preaching can motivate his congregation to witness and evangelize:

1. Gospel Preaching

   If he clearly and consistently articulates the gospel message in every sermon, his congregation will learn the basics of the salvation message and how to explain it.

2. Admonition

   By instructing his congregation to go out and share with unbelievers what they are learning each week, he will challenge those who are growing in their understanding of God's truth to proclaim the gospel. This motivates his congregation to be active in witnessing because it is the response to what they hear from the pulpit.

3. Evangelistic Illustrations

If a pastor speaks about times he has witnessed and responses he himself has heard, by way of illustration, it will encourage his congregation to also witness to others. A pastor can share the testimonies of those who have come to salvation in Christ because they have understood certain passages, and this can encourage others to use the same passages when sharing with their loved ones.

4. Gospel Depth

Since the word *gospel* (εὐαγγέλλιον euangellion) is found in the New Testament more than ninety times, a pastor will have many opportunities in the normal course of expositional preaching to go deeper into its meaning. It would be appropriate at times to preach an entire sermon on a single element of the gospel, such as the crucifixion or resurrection of Christ. A pastor could focus on particular themes inherent to the gospel, such as substitution, atonement, or justification. Especially while preaching through the Gospels, many sermons could have applications that relate to evangelism. The more the pastor's people see the gospel in the Bible, the better they will understand it. The goal is that the more they understand it, the more they will love it, and the more eager they will be to tell others about it.

5. Contagious Enthusiasm

A pastor who is excited about people coming to Christ will naturally encourage his congregation to evangelize. It is hard for a believer to keep from sharing the gospel when those around him are so passionate about its importance. As Paul cried out, "Woe is me if I do not preach the gospel!" (1 Cor. 9:16). By highlighting baptisms, allowing others to give their testimonies, and dwelling on radical conversions in the Scriptures, the pastor can continually remind people of the wonder of salvation that is brought to others through evangelism.

Those are just five examples of how a pastor can better equip his people for evangelism by improving something he already does: preaching the Word.

Ultimately, believers who are excited about what they are learning from the Word will naturally share those truths with others.

A Church That Testified to the Lost

The result of having a church where the congregation genuinely serves one another and where the pastors are focused on their priorities is that the congregation will naturally testify to the lost. If the church leadership has the right focus, then the members of the congregation cannot keep themselves from sharing with neighbors and family members about the changes that are taking place in their lives.

There is a peculiar expression in Acts 6:7 (NAS) that captures this. Luke writes that the word of God "kept on spreading." It is not just that the Word of God "spread," but it "kept on spreading" (continuously, actively). Luke is communicating that the proclaimed Word was being preached in wider and wider areas of the Jerusalem community as a result of the apostles' decision to focus on prayer and preaching. When the word of God is clearly proclaimed, and the seeds of the gospel fall on fertile soil, then it cannot help growing and spreading.

What is amazing about this gospel growth is that it happens through the God-ordained means of preaching and prayer. It is a growth that cannot be faked or falsely stimulated, and often yields unexpected results. For example, in Jerusalem "a great many of the priests were obedient to the faith" (Acts 6:7). This was certainly the least likely group in Israel to be converted, and yet astonishingly many of them were saved.

This kind of unexpected salvation is the by-product of the faithful preaching of God's Word, and these salvations continue even today. As genuine believers grow in their understanding of the Bible and the gospel, they will naturally grow in their love for one another and in their desire to reach the lost with the good news of salvation from the wrath of God.

If a pastor desires to better equip his congregation in evangelism, his primary effort should be put into expositing better the treasures of God's truth. Prayer-bathed biblical preaching will model evangelism and equip new converts. Biblical preaching will motivate your congregation to evangelize just like that early congregation in Acts—whose leaders' focus was on "prayer and the ministry of the Word."

10

False Assurance: A Biblical Look at the Sinner's Prayer

Kurt Gebhards

Much of modern evangelism is marked by use of the familiar sinner's prayer: "Lord, I love you and know that I am a sinner. I ask that you come into my heart, and make me whole …." Contrary to popular belief, the language in most sinner's prayers is simply not biblical. Beyond that, the result of using the sinner's prayer is that churches are weakened, people are deceived, and false converts are encouraged. This chapter explains why, and offers a better approach.

In June 1988, I was a typical American sixteen-year-old kid finishing my sophomore year of high school. I had gone to church three times in my entire life, and it was always because I was taken there by someone else. But for some reason, in the summer before my junior year I decided to go on my own. I joined up with the youth group to visit an amusement park and got to ride in the front seat with the youth pastor. As he drove the church van, he taught me about Jesus and the gospel.

Needless to say, I opted not to ride in the front on the way home. I appreciated his gracious boldness, but it was just a little too much for me as a spiritual novice.

Christianity was brand-new to me in those days, but despite my initial hesitation, I now realize that God was drawing me powerfully to Himself. I began attending church and the youth group every week. In November of that year I was approached by one of the church's senior saints, who asked if I had become a Christian. My response reflected so much ignorance that it embarrasses me to this day: "No," I said. "I'm waiting until New Year's, and it's going to be really big."

In my mind, I had planned the moment of my conversion with a strategically placed sinner's prayer. However, New Year's came and went—and I forgot. On January 3, it dawned on me that I had missed my "appointment" with God. So I hastily knelt by my bed, apologized to God, and walked through the standard prayer that I had heard so many times before.

There was a problem with my empty and formulaic attempt at prayer: I was not committed to God in any way at all. Despite my prayer and church attendance, I was diving deeper and deeper into sin and its pleasures. It was not until months later that God mercifully put an end to my hypocrisy, delivering me from my sin and shallowness. I repented from my sin, and submitted my life to God, and He transferred me from the kingdom of darkness to the kingdom of His beloved Son (see Col. 1:13). In other words, I was born again.

My story is common. Many people pray the sinner's prayer without being converted. Yet in much of the evangelical community, the sinner's prayer is almost universally accepted as the way to become a Christian. Furthermore, too many Christians consider their evangelism encounters to be fruitful only if they lead the unbeliever in the sinner's prayer. But given the critical importance of the subject matter—namely, salvation—we must seriously examine the concept of the sinner's prayer.

The sinner's prayer is an example of a wrong presupposition that plagues much of modern evangelism. It comes from the errant notion that a sinner's decision to receive Christ is the determining factor in salvation. The sinner's prayer is an offshoot of this concept of decisionism, despite the fact that it utterly removes the idea that it is actually God who draws people to Himself. In fact, because of this presupposition much of modern evangelism implies that if people ask to be saved then God is obligated to do so. This turns Jesus' description of the new birth coming from God on its head (John 3:3–8), and represents a serious distortion of the gospel. While Jesus said that no one can come to the Father unless the Father draws him (John 6:44), the sinner's prayer implies that people are ultimately the ones initiating and sealing their own salvation. Thus, the sinner's prayer actually is an obstacle to true evangelism.

The reality is that nowhere in the Bible does anything remotely resembling the sinner's prayer appear. Nowhere does anyone invite Jesus into his heart, or say something along the lines of "I now allow you to take over my life." Yet if someone were to ask the average evangelical what it takes to become a Christian, he or she may very well reply with something akin to the sinner's prayer. I have even counseled people who have been living a life of sin, with not even a pretense at godliness and not a shadow of affection for the Lord, who claim to be believers. Why? Because they remember praying the sinner's prayer as youths.

Remarkably, the sinner's prayer is popular, despite the fact there is no biblical justification for it. The Scriptures demonstrate that it is shortsighted and biblically naive for anyone to base his standing with God primarily upon on a single prayer.

DISCLAIMERS

Generalizations are dangerous. Not every point of criticism here will apply equally to everyone's use of the sinner's prayer. Faithful evangelists who are committed to the Lordship of Christ in salvation, the biblical gospel, and the purity of the church may have used the sinner's prayer method for years. I honor the fervent evangelists that faithfully spread the gospel. Nevertheless, all evangelism methods should be subject to biblical scrutiny.

Also, my general criticism is not intended as a critique of the legitimacy of anyone's personal salvation experience. I know many godly Christians who trace their salvation back to pastors or family members asking them to make a decision for Christ. At times, the sinner's prayer may coincide with the moment that a sinner is saved. However, we must still ask if it is a helpful and biblical model.

I recognize that many people have never considered an alternative to the sinner's prayer. It is so commonly used and so widely accepted as an evangelistic technique that few people would think it problematic. The goal of this chapter is not to make accusations, but rather to consider the sinner's prayer biblically and encourage a way of evangelism that is true to the Word of God.

Examples of the Sinner's Prayer

There are many variations of the sinner's prayer. A quick Internet search provides dozens of examples, including the following: "Lord Jesus, I believe you are the Son of God. Thank you for dying on the cross for my sins. Please forgive my sins and give me the gift of eternal life. I ask you in to my life and heart to be my Lord and Savior. I want to serve you always."[1]

Here is another: "Dear Lord Jesus, I know that I am a sinner and need Your forgiveness. I believe that You died for my sins. I want to turn from my sins. I now invite You to come into my heart and life. I want to trust and follow You as Lord and Savior. In Jesus' name. Amen."[2]

What these prayers share is a verbal acknowledgment of one's own sin, Christ's deity, the need for God's forgiveness, and a desire to turn from sin. All of that is good. And at the end, there is an invitation or request for Jesus to come into the sinner's heart and life. This notion of asking Jesus into one's heart is a fundamental part of most American evangelical rhetoric. You may also hear similar decisionistic language such as "I accepted Christ as my Savior" or "I rededicated my life to the Lord" or "I walked down during the altar call and got saved."

Although the motives behind this kind of prayer are generally good, the sinner's prayer can, unfortunately, do a great deal of spiritual damage because it does not square with the biblical examples, vocabulary, or theology. Before we analyze the deficiencies of the sinner's prayer, though, let us consider the source of the popularity of the sinner's prayer.

The Prayer's Popularity

I recently received an e-mail from a non-Christian friend who has been exposed to Christianity for many years. He was under the impression that praying a certain prayer would help "make it official." He wrote: "I want to 'officially' become a Christian. I guess 'born again' is the term I hear everyone use, and so

I was just wondering how to do that. Is it as simple as saying a certain prayer, or are there classes I need to complete, or do I need to be baptized first?"

Thankfully, this sincere e-mail began a discipleship relationship where I met with my friend to clarify the gospel and Jesus' terms of discipleship. I did not want to affirm his thinking that something needed to be done to make it official. He submitted his life to Christ and I baptized him three months after his initial e-mail.

How has the sinner's prayer method of evangelism become so popular that even nonbelievers know it? First, it is doable. It is a concrete, specific, observable act that often is emotionally satisfying for both the evangelist and the hearer. As finite human beings with a limited capacity for knowledge, we yearn for certainty and closure. By reducing salvation to an act such as the sinner's prayer, we simplify matters to the point where a person can "check the box" of Christianity and move on with his life with little to no understanding of what life in Christ really means. If someone asks, "What must I do to be saved?" the sinner's prayer provides a convenient and easy answer.

Second, the sinner's prayer is reproducible. It is difficult and time consuming to teach someone what it means to follow Christ, the truth about the gospel, baptism, and all that Christ commanded (Matt. 28:19–20). It is so much easier to encourage someone who wants to become a Christian to say a simple prayer. In this sense, the sinner's prayer is a shortcut in evangelism. Knowing and teaching the full gospel—such as Christ's deity and lordship, man's utter inability to please God on his own, the nature of true repentance, the substitutionary work of the Cross, and the resurrection—is essential to effective evangelism. But instead, the sinner's prayer offers an abbreviated lesson. It is the TV dinner of modern American evangelicalism.

Third, the sinner's prayer is measurable. In an age of church growth madness, numbers are supposedly critical for understanding success. The sinner's prayer provides an easy way to trumpet evangelistic success. In many cases the health and growth of converts is significantly less important than the "number of decisions made." However, when counting decisions becomes a measure of a ministry's effectiveness, there is the latent idea that the evangelist's skill or the church's presentation is what brings people to Christ.

THE SINNER'S PRAYER DIMINISHES
THE IMPACT OF THE GOSPEL

While the sinner's prayer is often used by well-meaning evangelists, the reality is that it diminishes the gospel that it is supposed to serve. Almost every significant tenet of the prayer in some way minimizes the power of the gospel. A reasonably complete presentation of the gospel can often be organized under four headings: (1) The character of God, (2) the sin of mankind, (3) Jesus Christ the savior, and (4) people's response. The sinner's prayer distorts the truth in each of these essential gospel categories.

The Character of God

First, the sinner's prayer misrepresents God, reversing the roles of God and mankind. It casts God as the passive Savior-in-waiting, and describes Him as an exclusively merciful God who is pining, waiting for another soul to accept Him. This is not an accurate depiction of the God of the Bible. Yes, He is merciful, and yes, He rejoices over sinners who are found (Luke 15:6, 9, 20). But He is also enthroned in power (Ps. 103:19) and exalted in splendid majesty (Isa. 45:5–7; 46:9–10). He rules the world, and yet the typical sinner's prayer reduces Him to a sideline capacity, where He is watching and waiting for the sinner to respond.

Moreover, the presentation of God in the prayer is exclusively that of His mercy, and it disregards God as the Creator and Judge. Thus, when people pray the sinner's prayer, they see only half of God. Consequently, they do not truly see Him at all. If you see His forgiveness but do not know of His furious wrath, or if you see His mercy yet miss His majesty, then you have an incomplete picture.

Further, the very idea of God being in heaven, waiting for people to respond, leads to precisely the type of boasting that the Scriptures reject. The net effect is that the sinner sits in judgment on God, and even if he does say the prayer, it is still an elevation of a human over God. Imagine inviting God to do anything, as if He needed our permission before He could act. This simply is not the biblical depiction of deity.

Decisionism drives God from the throne of His sovereignty by pretending that salvation is dependent solely on the choice of mankind. This prominent focus on mankind's choice and action is dangerous, because it can easily lead people away from dependence on God. This dependence is necessary not only in salvation but also in the Christian walk. Proverbs 1:7 says that fear of God is the beginning of wisdom, and yet right at the beginning of a person's spiritual walk, the sinner's prayer elevates the person above the fear of God. This is perhaps why Jesus never drove anyone to a decision in His evangelism.

The Sin of Mankind

Second, a right relationship with God begins with an accurate assessment of our need and our sinful state. In Ephesians 2:1–2, Paul powerfully communicates mankind's sinfulness, teaching that humans are spiritually dead and devoted to Satan. A rote prayer seems almost flippant compared with the gravity of mankind's problem.

When a person truly realizes the depth of his rebellion, the result is a deep sense of unworthiness and desperation. He must be driven to a place of spiritual bankruptcy when he understands his sin (Matt. 5:3). Like the publican who beat his breast and was unwilling to lift his face to heaven, we must similarly cry out to God for salvation (Luke 18:13).

Conviction of sin is good for the soul. In fact, it is a key ministry of the Holy Spirit (John 16:8). We are warned against mere worldly sorrow and exhorted to true biblical repentance so that our conviction will not end in death but in eternal life (2 Cor. 7:8–11). Because conviction of sin is so important, it is harmful to relieve the sinner's burden prematurely. Just like a broken leg does not need anesthesia but instead needs a cast, so too is the soul harmed if conviction is neglected in place of a hastily applied bandage. People should feel the crisis of being lost to the extent that they are driven to strive after salvation (Luke 13:24).

Praying a sinner's prayer short-circuits God's work within the burdened heart. The burdened heart that is grieved over sin does not need a formulaic "repeat after me" prayer. Instead it must cry out in unworthiness to Christ, clinging only to the cross. Yes, salvation is urgent. But its urgency should not cause us to be sloppy or to fabricate destructive methods.

Jesus Christ the Savior

Third, the sinner's prayer robs glory from Jesus Christ by focusing on the human choice in salvation. If people walk away from an evangelistic encounter believing that their choice is why they are now saved, the power and authority of Jesus Christ are not magnified.

This poses a watershed question: who ultimately makes the decision for someone to be saved? Ultimately, does the choice lie with people who are dead in their sin, or does it lie with God, the One eager to redeem mankind? Who is the primary worker in salvation?

The language of the sinner's prayer focuses on people and seemingly empowers them with the ability to save themselves. The death and resurrection of Christ becomes minimized when it is presented as insufficient to actually save anyone. Salvation is granted solely by the grace of God, and obviously it is mankind's duty to respond to that grace (Eph. 2:8–10). However, in most sinners' prayer encounters, the emphasis is placed almost exclusively on the person's response, rather than on the irresistible grace of God. This imbalance misses an opportunity to revel in Jesus Christ the Savior.

At the end of the day, no simple prayer has saved a sinner; only God saves. The question is not whether we will accept Christ, but whether Christ will receive us. Jesus Christ is not a nervous high-school teenager, waiting by the prayer phone for anyone to just call and accept Him. He is the Savior, the Redeemer, and the Author and Finisher of our faith (Heb. 12:2).

Consider the many passive terms associated with salvation in the Bible: people are rescued (Col. 1:13), their debt is canceled (Col. 2:14), and they are released from sins (Rev. 1:5). He saved us, Paul writes, and we are "justified freely by His grace" (Rom. 3:24; Titus 3:5). It is clear that mankind is responsible for how it responds to the gospel message, and it is also clear that there is a theological tension as well as mystery with this issue. But the sinner's prayer avoids the issue and the tension altogether, by teaching a new believer a minimized view of God's sovereignty. When Nicodemus asked how one is born again, Jesus did not give him a prayer to pray. Rather, He affirmed that salvation is a work of the Spirit of God who does what he wills when he wills: "The wind blows where it wishes, and you hear the sound of it, but cannot tell where it comes from and where it goes. So is everyone who is born of the Spirit"

(John 3:8). Salvation is never apart from the hearing of the gospel (Rom. 10:17; 1 Peter 1:23), but only by the sovereign choice of God.

If God is the ultimate worker of salvation, why does the sinner's prayer place such emphasis on a person's choice? If we are comforted by the God who is rich in mercy and who gives salvation (Eph. 2:6), then we can certainly entrust evangelism to Him as well. If God begins a work within the heart, He will complete it (Philem. 6).

People's Response

Wherever the gospel goes, a call to respond goes with it. People are morally culpable for the revelation of God in them (Rom. 1:18–23) and are responsible in a greater way when they hear the gospel and the command by God to believe. The Bible is not silent as to what that response should be. The gospel calls sinners to repent and believe.

Repentance is an essential part of salvation. Jesus repeatedly commanded His hearers to "repent" (Matt. 4:17; Luke 13:3). All men and women everywhere must repent (Acts 17:30). Repentance is the forsaking of sin and self, and the devotion of one's all to serving and seeking after Christ. Most commonly, the sinner's prayer does not convey a sense of real repentance. Second Corinthians 7:8–13 contains over a dozen descriptors of genuine repentance that lead to salvation and warns against false repentance, which is simply worldly sorrow. The faithful evangelist must understand the difference and carefully guide the hearer to understand the significance and depth of true repentance. To miss repentance is to miss the gospel (Acts 2:38).

Generally, the prayer contains some comment along the lines of "Lord Jesus, I believe in you." It is true that part of salvation is believing the gospel, but those whom we evangelize must believe differently from the shuddering demons who will never enjoy God in heaven (James 2:19). The demons believe orthodox facts about Christ but have no personal allegiance to Christ. Some evangelists take a sinner's agreement about the facts of Jesus' life and act as if that is evidence of saving faith. But in reality it may be little more than shallow demon-like faith, and shallow faith—like shallow repentance—is damning. Biblical belief demands trust (2 Cor. 1:9), reliance (Prov. 3:5–6), and submission to God as the creator. Real belief is the desire to live a life dependent on His power and dedicated to His righteousness (Rom. 10:9–11).

Again, the problem is not that the sinner's prayer calls the sinner to express belief in God. The problem is that the way the prayer is structured gives false assurance to a person based on a nebulous faith to begin with. Of course people should believe in God and the gospel, but a simple confession of a generic belief should not induce a sense of assurance.

THE SINNER'S PRAYER DAMAGES
THE PROGRESS OF NEW BELIEVERS

Not only does the sinner's prayer fail regarding these components of the gospel, but it actually can hinder the progress in the heart. This is because the sinner's prayer assumes the relationship with Christ is complete when it may not be, stopping short of the sinner's submission to Christ's lordship and commitment to wholehearted discipleship to Christ.

The first way that the sinner's prayer damages the progress of saints is that it does not feature the lordship of Christ in salvation. What is most often lost in the moment of the sinner's prayer to receive Christ is the even greater need for that sinner to follow Christ as Lord.

Do people who are introduced to the gospel by the sinner's prayer realize that when they embrace Christianity, they are promising to "deny [themselves], and take up [their] cross" (Luke 9:23)? Caution is called for here; there are many warnings in Scripture about people who "profess to know God, but in works they deny Him" (Titus 1:16; cf. Isa. 29:13). Without an encouragement to count the cost of discipleship, the sinner's prayer has the unintended consequence of creating people who begin a task without even understanding what is required to complete it (Luke 14:28).

In Matthew 7:21, Jesus tells His disciples, "Not everyone who says to Me, 'Lord, Lord,' shall enter the kingdom of heaven, but he who does the will of My Father in heaven." This passage clearly illustrates the truth that "many" people will claim to know Christ, but of that large group, only a "few" will actually know the Savior and enter the kingdom of heaven. Indeed, Scripture is full of examples of people who had a false conversion, whether it is the people described in 1 John 2:19, or Demas in 2 Timothy 4:10, or even Judas Iscariot, perhaps the most famous false convert of all. Without challenging people to count the cost of discipleship, the sinner's prayer has the result of adding people like

Demas to the church. They want to follow Christ, and they want to believe, but nobody told them about the sacrifice that it would entail.

In this way the sinner's prayer damages the progress of new believers by failing to feature the necessity of obedience. The demands of discipleship are an essential aspect of true salvation, and yet the sinner's prayer glosses over them completely. Too often the sinner's prayer is a means to make a convert to Jesus, while the Lord is seeking to make disciples (John 8:31; 13:35).

A right understanding of salvation, including its gravity and magnitude, will make a person careful in how he evangelizes. Those who followed Jesus certainly understood that "whoever does not bear his cross and come after Me cannot be My disciple" (Luke 14:27).

Jesus expected His followers to count the cost of their discipleship (Matt. 10:37–39). Modern evangelistic techniques often are so hasty that the only thing counted is the number of decisions. Jesus' preaching included sober warnings and honest challenges for those who came to Him seeking salvation. He repeatedly called people to the difficult path of following Him (Matt. 7:13–14). Becoming a Christian was and is synonymous with becoming Jesus' obedient disciple (Matt. 28:19). The sinner's prayer almost never features this reality. The hard truth of discipleship is jettisoned so that the point of decision is reached as easily and painlessly as possible.

Jesus emphasized that the gate of salvation is hard to find (Luke 13:24), although it is the broad path that has an easy opening (Matt. 7:13). However, for many purveyors of the sinner's prayer the gate of salvation is not hard to find—much less hard to enter. The sinner's prayer makes people think that salvation is as easy as repeating a formula. This simply does not honor the gravity of the decision.

In light of the many threats that the sinner's prayer poses, I strongly suggest that it is unhelpful for evangelists, counselors, and preachers to offer a prayer that the noncommitted can repeat in order to "get saved." We are commanded to make disciples and teach people to obey all the commands of Christ, not shorten the Great Commission to "go into the world and get as many people as you can to repeat a prayer to become a Christian." We are obligated to teach unbelievers about their sinfulness, the grace of God, the power and wrath of God, as well as the Cross and resurrection.

The Sinner's Prayer Dulls the Purity of the Church

Numerous Christians today decry the current state of evangelical churches. In some countries, the church has growing numbers and decreasing influence. There are churches teeming with people, yet many of them utterly fail to live differently from the world.

In an age when evangelicalism disappoints more than it delivers, we should be taking a close look at the entrance gate. The result of generations weaned by the sinner's prayer is masses of unconverted people sitting in the pews, compromising the purity of the church. With so many non-Christians thinking that they are Christians, it is easy to understand why the modern American church is so ineffective: it is full of millions of "false starts," people who lack the Holy Spirit and thus fail Christianity's basics. Bringing unconverted people into the church results in a "carnal" Christianity where "backsliding" and pointless "rededications" to Christ are no help.

Jesus warned about nonbelievers in the church when He told the parable of the wheat and the tares (Matt. 13:24–30). The parable declares that tares will spring up among the wheat, and He warns us to be watchful for these false professions. Many of the problems in the church are due to the presence of those who have prayed the sinner's prayer and yet remain unconverted. They hinder the testimony of the church that is supposed to be a shining light (Phil. 2:15). The result is that the church becomes filled with people who give lip service to Christianity, yet fall short of true conversion. Imagine a person who comes to church, hears the pastor preaching, and then hears the pastor ask for people to make a commitment to Jesus. That person responds, and is led in the sinner's prayer. At this point, his life is not changed, and while the person may believe everything he has heard, he has not been challenged to repent, or to count the cost of discipleship and acknowledge Jesus as Lord. But because he has not been truly regenerated, and because he does not understand true discipleship, his life actually harms the testimony of the church. Real discipleship is traded for a quick, easy, and external decision.

THE SINNER'S PRAYER GIVES FALSE ASSURANCE

Many sinner's prayer advocates quickly offer assurance of salvation to the one praying. I remember hearing an evangelical leader lead thousands of people in the sinner's prayer at a stadium, after a crusade. When he was done, he told them, "You are now Christians, born again, and don't let anyone ever question that." These people had not heard a word about discipleship, repentance, or submitting their lives to the Lord. Instead, they were led to believe that they were saved simply because they said the prayer. Imagine the horror of living a carnal life that dishonors Christ, believing the entire time that one is saved, only to come face-to-face with the Savior and hear those terrifying words, "Depart from Me, you who practice lawlessness" (Matt. 7:23).

It is tragic to see the carnage of false conversion in Christianity, and much of this unnecessary deception comes as a result of the sinner's prayer. It would be far more loving to help a person rightly understand what it means to be a Christian than to give a person false confidence in a nonexistent conversion. Providing people with a true understanding of Christianity causes them to count the cost of what it truly means to take up one's cross, believe the gospel, and follow Christ. This understanding might result in fewer immediate professions of faith but will be instrumental in genuine conversions. This introspection is what Paul commanded in 2 Corinthians 13:5, "Examine yourselves as to whether you are in the faith. Test yourselves. Do you not know yourselves, that Jesus Christ is in you?—unless indeed you are disqualified." It is absolutely true that any person who is truly regenerated is sealed forever and kept by the power of God (Eph. 1:14; 1 Peter 1:5). But we are commanded in 2 Corinthians 13:5 to examine ourselves to see if we are in the faith. The point is not that Christians can lose their salvation, but that there are many false professors (Titus 1:16; 1 John 2:19) and that people's hearts, which are "deceitful above all things" (Jer. 17:9), can sometimes fool them into believing they are Christians when their lives show otherwise. To combat this, Paul asks his readers to test themselves. This test is not seen in a momentary prayer, but rather is expressed through a lifelong commitment of continual self-examination. Our Christianity is not grounded in a decision we made years ago; it is grounded in our abiding in God now and forever (John 15:1–5).

Since false profession was such a concern in the New Testament, Christians cannot be so ready to dispense assurance with no real knowledge of the sinner's true state. Instead, a faithful evangelist will imitate Christ's evangelism and challenge people to count the cost (Luke 14:28).

The burdened sinner does not need a dated and signed piece of paper for assurance; he needs the promises of Scripture. Allow the Holy Spirit to provide assurance based on obedience (1 John 3:18–19), instead of a repeated prayer or a response to a gospel invitation.

An Alternative: The Great Commission

Some may ask, "What approach should I take if I don't use the sinner's prayer?" I recommend the method of worldwide evangelism taught by Jesus: call sinners to repentance for forgiveness (Luke 24:47), make disciples, teach them, and baptize them (Matt. 28:19–20; Mark 16:15–18; Acts 1:6–9). Making disciples includes helping people understand the magnitude of following Jesus (Luke 14:25–33). Teaching is the labor of patient instruction. Baptism represents a public declaration of understanding and belief in the gospel with a commitment to follow Christ devotedly.

In fact, I have heard many people defend the sinner's prayer by saying, "whomever Jesus called, he called publicly," as if Jesus himself had used the sinner's prayer! It is true that most of the people Jesus called, he did call publicly. And it is also true that Christians are called to make a public profession of Jesus as the Christ. But the scriptural version of this public profession is baptism, not a repeated prayer. By elevating the prayer to this level, the result is actually a minimization of baptism.

Considering the fact that nothing like the sinner's prayer is found in the Scriptures, and considering the dangers of the prayer, it simply does not seem reasonable to continue to use it as if it marked the entrance to the Christian life. Instead of succumbing to the weaknesses of the sinner's prayer system, an evangelistic encounter that is moving to the point of response should follow the Great Commission and teach the gospel so that responses can truly be from the heart. Challenge hearers to count the cost, and, in fact, even encourage them to pray. Just do not have them repeat a prayer after you, as if it were your words that mattered rather than their hearts.

If a person says he wants to become a Christian, react with joy. Encourage a believer to attend church, read the Bible, pray, and to make changes in his life. Encourage him to hold fast to Jesus and His word, and agree to help the person get started in his Christian life. But the idea of leading the person in a prayer and then giving a false assurance is certainly counterproductive to Great Commission evangelism.

Our evangelism would be much more robust, our fruit much more evident, and the church much healthier if we focused on Jesus' hard call to make disciples instead of our modern, harmful substitute. Follow the biblical model and we will see the Spirit's fruit: a powerful gospel, growing believers, and a pure church.

Section 3

Evangelism in Practice

11

Jesus as Lord: Essential Components of the Gospel Message[1]

John MacArthur

Behind all of the theological questions about evangelism is this issue: for a person to have saving faith, what exactly needs to be conveyed so that he understands the message? This chapter deals with the nuts and bolts of a gospel message: who God is, why people are alienated from Him, what Christ has done to mediate the two, and how people must respond.

When sharing the gospel with nonbelievers, what are the main elements that we should make sure we communicate? Here is where this book gets practical. The real question we are asking is: "How should I evangelize my friends, family, and neighbors?" For parents, an even more important question is "How should I present the gospel to my children?"

Recent segments within Christianity have tended to take a minimalist approach to this question. Unfortunately, the legitimate desire to express the heart of the gospel clearly has given way to a less wholesome endeavor. It is a campaign to distill the essentials of the message to the barest possible terms. The glorious gospel of Christ—that which Paul called "the power of God to salvation to everyone who believes" (Rom. 1:16)—includes all the truth about Christ. But American evangelicalism tends to regard the gospel as a "plan of salvation." We have reduced the message to a list of facts stated in the fewest possible words—and getting fewer all the time. You have probably seen these prepackaged "plans of salvation": "Six Steps to Peace with God"; "Five Things God Wants You to Know"; "Four Spiritual Laws"; "Three Truths You Can't Live Without"; "Two Ways to Live"; or "One Way to Heaven."[2]

Another trend, equally dangerous, is to reduce evangelism to a memorized conversation. Often, evangelism training consists of having Christians memorize a series of questions, anticipating that each question will fall into one of a few categories that has a preplanned response.

But the gospel is not a message that can be capsulated, abridged, and shrink-wrapped, then offered as a generic remedy for every kind of sinner. Ignorant sinners need to be instructed about who God is and why He has the right to demand their obedience. Self-righteous sinners need to have their sin exposed by the demands of God's law. Careless sinners need to be confronted with the reality of God's impending judgment. Fearful sinners need to hear that God in His mercy has provided a way of deliverance. All sinners must understand how utterly holy God is. They must comprehend the basic truths of Christ's sacrificial death and the triumph of His resurrection. They need to be confronted with God's demand that they turn from their sin to embrace Christ as Lord and Savior.

Furthermore, in all the instances where Jesus and the apostles evangelized—whether they were ministering to individuals or crowds—there are no two incidents where they presented the message in precisely the same terminology. They knew that salvation is a sovereign work of God. Their role was to preach truth; the Holy Spirit would apply it individually to the hearts of His elect.

The form of the message will vary in each case. But the content must always drive home the reality of God's holiness and the sinner's helpless condition. Then it points sinners to Christ as a sovereign but merciful Lord who has purchased full atonement for all who will turn to Him in faith.

Christians today are often cautioned not to say too much to the lost. Certain spiritual issues are labeled taboo when speaking to the unconverted: God's law, Christ's lordship, turning from sin, surrender, obedience, judgment, and hell. Such things are not to be mentioned, lest we "add something to the offer of God's free gift." There are some who take this reductionist evangelism to its furthest extreme. Wrongly applying the Reformed doctrine of *sola fide* ("faith alone"), they make faith the only permissible topic when speaking to non-Christians about their duty before God. Then they render faith utterly meaningless by stripping it of everything but its notional aspects. This, some believe, preserves the purity of the gospel.

What this actually has done is undercut the power of the message of salvation. It has also populated the church with "converts" whose faith is counterfeit and whose hope hangs on a bogus promise. Numbly saying they "accept Christ as Savior," they brazenly reject His rightful claim as Lord. Paying Him glib lip service, they utterly scorn Him with their hearts (Mark 7:6). Casually affirming Him with their mouths, they deliberately deny Him with their deeds (Titus 1:16). Addressing Him superficially as "Lord, Lord," they stubbornly decline to do His bidding (Luke 6:46). Such people fit the tragic description of the "many" in Matthew 7:22–23 who will one day be stunned to hear Him say, "'I never knew you; depart from Me, you who practice lawlessness!'"

What We Say in Evangelism

If there is no simple description for an evangelistic conversation, then what should the evangelist say when proclaiming the gospel? There are many helpful books that give guidelines on how to witness.[3] In this chapter, I want to focus on some crucial issues relating to the content of the message we are called to share with unbelievers. Specifically, if we want to articulate the gospel as precisely as possible, what are the points we need to make clear? What follows is a list of truths about the gospel that the evangelist should strive to include in every gospel conversation. They are not listed or given in a chronological order; this is not to suggest "start with 1, then 2," but rather are just listed to be helpful. The following is what the evangelist wants to convey in any gospel conversation.

Teach Them About God's Holiness
"The fear of the LORD is the beginning of wisdom" (Ps. 111:10; see also Job 28:28; Prov. 1:7; 9:10; 15:33; Mic. 6:9). Much of contemporary evangelism aims to arouse anything but fear of God in the mind of sinners. For example, "God loves you and has a wonderful plan for your life," is the opening line of the

typical evangelistic appeal today. This kind of evangelism is far from the image of a God who must be feared.

The remedy for such thinking is the biblical truth of God's holiness. God is utterly holy, and His law therefore demands perfect holiness: "For I am the LORD your God. You shall therefore consecrate yourselves, and you shall be holy; for I am holy....You shall therefore be holy, for I am holy" (Lev. 11:44–45). "You cannot serve the LORD, for He is a holy God. He is a jealous God; He will not forgive your transgressions nor your sins" (Josh. 24:19). "No one is holy like the LORD, / For there is none besides You, / Nor is there any rock like our God" (1 Sam. 2:2). "Who is able to stand before this holy Lord God?" (1 Sam. 6:20).

Even the gospel requires this holiness: "Be holy, for I am holy" (1 Peter 1:16). "Without [holiness] no one will see the Lord" (Heb. 12:14).

Because He is holy, God hates sin: "I, the LORD your God, am a jealous God, visiting the iniquity of the fathers upon the children to the third and fourth generations of those who hate Me" (Ex. 20:5).

Sinners cannot stand before Him: "The ungodly shall not stand in the judgment, / Nor sinners in the congregation of the righteous" (Ps. 1:5).

Show Them Their Sin

Gospel means "good news." What makes it truly good news is not just that heaven is free, but that sin has been conquered by God's Son. Sadly, it has become stylish to present the gospel as something other than a remedy for sin. "Salvation" is offered as an escape from punishment, God's plan for a wonderful life, a means of fulfillment, an answer to life's problems, and a promise of free forgiveness. All those things are true of course, but they are by-products of redemption, not the main issue of the gospel itself. When sin is left unaddressed, such promises of divine blessings cheapen the message.

In Scripture, evangelism often begins with a call to repentance and obedience.[4] Jesus Himself preached, "Repent, and believe in the gospel" (Mark 1:15). Paul wrote, "If you confess with your mouth the Lord Jesus and believe in your heart that God has raised Him from the dead, you will be saved" (Rom. 10:9). At Pentecost, Peter preached, "Repent, and let every one of you be baptized in the name of Jesus Christ for the remission of sins; and you shall receive the gift of the Holy Spirit" (Acts 2:38). John wrote, "He who does not believe the Son shall not see life, but the wrath of God abides on him" (John 3:36). The writer to the Hebrews said that Christ "became the author of eternal salvation to all who obey him" (Heb. 5:9). James wrote: "Therefore submit to God. Resist the devil and he will flee from you. Draw near to God and He will draw near to you. Cleanse your hands, you sinners; and purify your hearts, you double-minded" (James 4:7–8).

Jesus and the apostles did not hesitate to use the law in their evangelism.[5] They knew that law reveals our sin (Rom. 3:20) and is a tutor to lead us to Christ (Gal. 3:24). It is the means God uses to make sinners see their own helplessness. Clearly, Paul saw a key place for the law in evangelistic contexts. Yet many today believe the law, with its inflexible demand for holiness and obedience, is contrary to and incompatible with the gospel.

Why should we make such distinctions where Scripture does not? If Scripture cautioned against preaching repentance, obedience, righteousness, or judgment to unbelievers, that would be one thing. But Scripture contains no such warnings. The opposite is true. For example, when Jesus was asked by a man how he might obtain eternal life, He responded by preaching law and lordship (Matt. 19:16–22). If we want to follow a biblical model, we cannot ignore sin, righteousness, and judgment because they are the very matters about which the Holy Spirit convicts the unsaved (John 16:8). Can we omit them from the message and still call it the gospel?

Apostolic evangelism inevitably culminated in a call for repentance (Acts 2:38; 3:19; 17:30; 26:20). Can we tell sinners they do not have to turn from their sin, and then call that evangelism? Paul ministered to unbelievers when he "declared...that they should repent, turn to God, and do works befitting repentance" (Acts 26:20). Can we reduce the message to simply "accept Christ" and still believe we are evangelistically ministering?

One wonders what sort of salvation is available to those who do not even recognize their sin. Did Jesus not say, "Those who are well have no need of a physician, but those who are sick. I did not come to call the righteous, but sinners" (Mark 2:17)? To offer salvation to someone who does not even understand the gravity of sin is to fulfill Jeremiah 6:14: "They have healed the hurt of My people slightly, / Saying, 'Peace, peace!' / When there is no peace."

Sin Is What Makes True Peace Impossible for Unbelievers

"But the wicked are like the troubled sea, / When it cannot rest, / Whose waters cast up mire and dirt"(Isa. 57:20). This trouble comes from the fact that sin brings consequences (the thief is constantly in fear of being caught), but also comes from living a life separated from God (Eph. 4:18).

All Have Sinned

Paul explains in Romans that "there is none righteous, no, not one; / There is none who understands; / There is none who seeks after God" (Rom. 3:10–11). Nobody is able to claim he is going to heaven because he is a good person.

Sin Makes the Sinner Worthy of Death

"And sin, when it is full-grown, brings forth death" (James 1:15). "For the wages of sin is death" (Rom. 6:23).

Sinners Can Do Nothing to Earn Salvation

"But we are all like an unclean thing, / And all our righteousnesses are like filthy rags; / We all fade as a leaf, / And our iniquities, like the wind, / Have taken us away" (Isa. 64:6). "By the deeds of the law no flesh will be justified in His sight" (Rom. 3:20). "A man is not justified by the works of the law...by the works of the law no flesh shall be justified" (Gal. 2:16).

Sinners Are Therefore in a Helpless State

"It is appointed for men to die once, but after this the judgment" (Heb. 9:27). "There is nothing covered that will not be revealed, nor hidden that will not be known" (Luke 12:2). "God will judge the secrets of men by Jesus Christ" (Rom. 2:16). "The cowardly, unbelieving, abominable, murderers, sexually immoral, sorcerers, idolaters, and all liars shall have their part in the lake which burns with fire and brimstone, which is the second death" (Rev. 21:8).

Instruct Them About Christ and What He Has Done

The gospel is good news about who Christ is and what He has done for guilty sinners. While the call to repent from a life of sin is in every part of the gospel presentation, repentance alone is not the gospel message. The heart of the gospel message is how God bridged the gap between sinful humans and His own holiness. This is wonderfully seen in the person and work of Christ.

He Is Eternally God

"In the beginning was the Word, and the Word was with God, and the Word was God. He was in the beginning with God. All things were made through Him, and without Him nothing was made that that was made.... And the Word became flesh and dwelt among us, and we beheld His glory, the glory as of the only begotten of the Father, full of grace and truth" (John 1:1–3, 14). "In Him dwells all the fullness of the Godhead bodily" (Col. 2:9). In order to understand what God has done, the sinner needs to understand who Christ is.

He Is Lord of All

"He is Lord of lords and King of kings; and those who are with Him are called, chosen, and faithful" (Rev. 17:14). "And being found in appearance as a man, He humbled Himself and became obedient to the point of death, even the death of the cross. Therefore God also has highly exalted Him and given Him the name which is above every name" (Phil. 2:8–9). "He is Lord of all" (Acts 10:36).

He Became Man

"Who, being in the form of God, did not consider it robbery to be equal with God, but made Himself of no reputation, taking the form of a bondservant, and coming in the likeness of men" (Phil. 2:6–7).

He Is Utterly Pure and Sinless

"[He] was in all points tempted as we are, yet without sin" (Heb. 4:15). He "committed no sin, / Nor was deceit found in His mouth." (1 Peter 2:22). "He was manifested to take away our sins, and in Him there is no sin" (1 John 3:5).

The Sinless One Became a Sacrifice for Our Sin

"He made Him who knew no sin to be sin for us, that we might become the righteousness of God in Him" (2 Cor. 5:21). He "gave Himself for us, that He might redeem us from every lawless deed and purify for Himself His own special people, zealous for good works" (Titus 2:14).

He Shed His Own Blood As an Atonement for Sin

"In Him we have redemption through His blood, the forgiveness of sins, according to the riches of His grace which He made to abound toward us in all wisdom and prudence, having made known to us the mystery of His will, according to His good pleasure which He purposed in Himself" (Eph. 1:7–9). "[He] loved us and washed us from our sins in His own blood" (Rev. 1:5).

He Died on the Cross to Provide a Way of Salvation for Sinners

"[He] Himself bore our sins in His own body on the tree, that we, having died to sins, might live for righteousness—by whose stripes you were healed" (1 Peter 2:24). "And by Him to reconcile all things to Himself, by Him, whether things on earth or things in heaven, having made peace through the blood of His cross." (Col. 1:20).

He Rose Triumphantly from the Dead

Christ "declared to be the Son of God with power according to the Spirit of holiness, by the resurrection from the dead" (Rom. 1:4). "[He] was delivered up because of our offenses, and was raised because of our justification" (Rom. 4:25). "For I delivered to you first of all that which I also received: that Christ died for our sins according to the Scriptures, and that He was buried, and that He rose again the third day according to the Scriptures" (1 Cor. 15:3–4).

He Makes a Way for Reconciliation with God

Sinners are separated from God because of their sin. They have no access to Him through prayer (Isa. 1:15), and they are alienated from the fellowship experienced by those who know their heavenly Father (Eph. 2:12). But Christ's death and resurrection make it possible for people to be reconciled to God (1 Peter 3:18).

Tell Them What God Demands of Them

Repentant faith is the requirement. It is not merely a "decision" to trust Christ for eternal life, but a wholesale forsaking of everything else we trust, and a turning to Jesus Christ as Lord and Savior. At the center of evangelism is the call for a person to stop being a slave of sin, and become a slave of God.[6]

Repent

"Repent, and turn from all your transgressions" (Ezek. 18:30). "'For I have no pleasure in the death of one who dies,' says the Lord God" (Ezek. 18:32).

"[God] now commands all men everywhere to repent" (Acts 17:30). "Repent, turn to God, and do works befitting repentance" (Acts 26:20).

Follow Jesus

"If anyone desires to come after Me, let him deny himself, and take up his cross daily, and follow Me" (Luke 9:23). "No one, having put his hand to the plow, and looking back, is fit for the kingdom of God" (Luke 9:62). "If anyone serves Me, let him follow Me; and where I am, there My servant will be also. If anyone serves Me, him My Father will honor" (John 12:26).

Trust Him as Lord and Savior

"Believe on the Lord Jesus Christ, and you will be saved" (Acts 16:31). "If you confess with your mouth the Lord Jesus and believe in your heart that God has raised Him from the dead, you will be saved" (Rom. 10:9).

Advise Them to Count the Cost Thoughtfully

Salvation is absolutely free. So is joining the army. You do not have to buy your way in. Everything you will need is provided. But there is a sense in which following Christ—like joining the army—will cost you dearly. It can cost freedom, family, friends, autonomy, and possibly even your life. The job of the evangelist—like that of the army recruiter—is to tell potential inductees the full story. That is exactly why Jesus' message was often so full of hard demands:

> If anyone comes to Me and does not hate his father and mother, wife and children, brothers and sisters, yes, and his own life also, he cannot be My disciple. And whoever does not bear his cross and come after Me cannot be My disciple. For which of you, intending to build a tower, does not sit down first and count the cost, whether he has enough to finish it—lest, after he has laid the foundation, and is not able to finish, all who see it begin to mock him, saying, "This man began to build and was not able to finish?" Or what king, going to make war against another king, does not sit down first and consider whether he is able with ten thousand to meet him who comes against him with twenty thousand? Or else, while the other is still a great way off, he sends a delegation and asks conditions of peace. So likewise, whoever of you does not forsake all that he has cannot be My disciple. (Luke 14:26–33)

The free or costly, death or life enigma is expressed in the clearest possible terms by John 12:24–25: "Most assuredly, I say to you, unless a grain of wheat falls into the ground and dies, it remains alone; but if it dies, it produces much grain. He who loves his life will lose it, and he who hates his life in this world will keep it for eternal life."

The Cross is central to the gospel precisely because of its graphic message, including the awfulness of sin, the profundity of God's wrath against sin, and the efficacy of Jesus' work in crucifying the old man (Rom. 6:6). A. W. Tozer wrote, "The cross is the most revolutionary thing ever to appear among men."[7]

The cross of Roman times knew no compromise; it never made concessions. It won all of its arguments by killing its opponent and silencing him for good. It spared not Christ, but slew Him the same as the rest. He was alive when they hung Him on that cross and completely dead when they took Him down six hours later. That was the cross the first time it appeared in Christian history.

The cross always has its way. It wins by defeating its opponent and imposing its will upon him. It always dominates. It never compromises, never dickers nor confers, never surrenders a point for the sake of peace. It cares not for peace; it cares only to end its opposition as fast as possible.

With perfect knowledge of all this, Christ said, "If any man will come after me, let him deny himself, and take up his cross daily, and follow me" (Luke 9:23 KJV). So the cross not only brings Christ's life to an end, it ends also the first life, the old life, of every one of His true followers. It destroys the old pattern, the adamic pattern, in the believer's life, and brings it to an end. Then the God who raised Christ from the dead raises the believer and a new life begins. This, and nothing less, is true Christianity.

Urge Them to Trust Christ

"Knowing, therefore, the terror of the Lord, we persuade men" (2 Cor. 5:11). Paul sternly explains:

> God was in Christ reconciling the world to Himself, not imputing their trespasses to them, and has committed to us the word of reconciliation.

Now then, we are ambassadors for Christ, as though God were pleading through us: we implore you on Christ's behalf, be reconciled to God. (2 Cor. 5:19–20)

"Let the wicked forsake his way, / And the unrighteous man his thoughts; / Let him return to the LORD, / And He will have mercy on him; / And to our God, / For He will abundantly pardon." (Isa. 55:7). "If you confess with your mouth the Lord Jesus and believe in your heart that God has raised Him from the dead, you will be saved. For with the heart one believes unto righteousness, and with the mouth confession is made unto salvation" (Rom. 10:9–10).

THE CALL TO BAPTISM

Nowhere in either the Old or New Testaments do we find an invitation for sinners to believe now, but obey later. The call to trust and obey is a single summons. The word *obey* is sometimes even used to describe the conversion experience: "He became the author of eternal salvation to all who obey Him" (Heb. 5:9).

Does anyone really suppose it is possible to believe, to really fathom everything that Jesus did in suffering and dying for sin? Could anyone accept the offer of forgiveness from His hand—and then turn away, not exalt Him with one's own life, and even grow to despise, reject, and disbelieve Him exactly like those who put Him to death? That kind of theology is grotesque.

The truth is, our surrender to Christ is never purer than at the moment we are born again. In that sacred moment we are wholly under the sovereign control of the Holy Spirit, united to Christ, and recipients of a new heart. Then, more than ever, obedience is nonnegotiable, nor would any genuine convert desire it to be so (Rom. 6:17).

The first command for every Christian is baptism. Baptism is not a condition of salvation but an initial step of obedience for the Christian. Conversion is complete before baptism occurs; baptism is only an external sign that testifies to what has already occurred in the sinner's heart. Baptism is an ordinance, and it is precisely the kind of "work" Paul states cannot be meritorious (compare with circumcision, Rom. 4:10–11).[8]

Nevertheless, one can hardly read the New Testament without noticing the heavy stress the early church placed on baptism. They simply assumed that every genuine believer would embark on a life of obedience and discipleship. That was nonnegotiable. Therefore they viewed baptism as the turning point. Only those who were baptized were considered Christians. That is why the Ethiopian eunuch was so eager to be baptized (Acts 8:36–39).

Unfortunately, the church today takes baptism much more casually. It is not unusual to meet people who have been professing Christians for years but have never been baptized. That was unheard of in the New Testament church. Because our evangelical culture downplays the importance of obedience to Christ, we have lost the focus on this initial Christian act.

Charles Spurgeon wrote, "If the professed convert distinctly and deliberately declares that he knows the Lord's will, but does not mean to attend to it, you are not to pamper his presumptions, but it is your duty to assure him that he is not saved."[9] This principle, of course, does not prohibit new believers' classes, catechism, or even a brief time between conversion and baptism. But it does mean that when a person professes faith in Christ, the new convert should learn about baptism, and desire to profess his or her faith publicly.

Jesus as Lord

The first creed of the early church was "Jesus is Lord" (cf. Rom. 10:9–10; 1 Cor. 12:3). The lordship of Christ permeated apostolic preaching, and it permeates the New Testament. In the very first apostolic sermon, Peter's message at Pentecost, this was the pinnacle:

> This Jesus God has raised up, of which we are all witnesses. Therefore being exalted to the right hand of God, and having received from the Father the promise of the Holy Spirit, He poured out this which you now see and hear. For David did not ascend into the heavens, but he says himself:
> "The LORD said to my Lord,
> 'Sit at My right hand,
> Till I make Your enemies Your footstool.'"

Therefore let all the house of Israel know assuredly that God has made this Jesus, whom you crucified, both Lord and Christ. (Acts 2:32–36)

The context leaves no doubt about Peter's meaning. This was a message about Christ's absolute authority as the blessed and only Sovereign, the King of kings and Lord of lords (1 Tim. 6:15–16).

Throughout the book of Acts Jesus' absolute lordship is a recurring theme. When Peter opened the gospel ministry to Gentiles at the house of Cornelius, he again declared, "He is Lord of all" (Acts 10:36). The truth of His lordship was the key to apostolic preaching. Christ's lordship is the gospel according to the apostles.

T. Alan Chrisope, in his wonderful book *Jesus Is Lord*, writes, "There is no element of apostolic preaching more prominent than the resurrection, exaltation and lordship of Jesus."[10] He adds:

> The confession "Jesus is Lord" is the single most predominant Christian confession in the New Testament. Not only does it occur in several passages which emphasize its singular character as *the* Christian confession (e.g., Philippians 2:9–11; Romans 10:9; 1 Corinthians 12:3; 8:5–6; cf. Ephesians 4:5), but it also occurs numerous times in a variant form in the phrase "our Lord," a designation of Jesus which was so widely used that it became the distinctive and universally recognized Christian confession, known and acknowledged by all believers.[11]

In fact, he writes, "All the basic facts of the gospel story are implicit in the single brief confession, 'Jesus is Lord.'"[12]

The apostle Paul said, "We do not preach ourselves, but Christ Jesus the Lord, and ourselves your bondservants for Jesus' sake" (2 Cor. 4:5). Jesus as Lord is the evangelistic message we bring to a world that is lost without it.

12

Starting the Conversation: A Practical Approach to Real-Life Evangelism

Jim Stitzinger III

Perhaps the most difficult part of evangelism is directing conversations to the point where the gospel can be explained. This chapter provides practical advice on how to initiate relationships with those whom the Lord has placed around us, and then how to direct those relationships toward evangelistic opportunities.

Many believers stereotype evangelism as an activity done at a designated time and place, by people with the "gift" of evangelism. They wrongly think of evangelism as being quarantined to a "cold-calling" strategy, contacting people we have never seen before and most likely will never see again.

While spontaneous evangelistic conversations should be a part of every believer's life, the majority of gospel presentations take place within the framework of existing relationships. If we are to fulfill the commission of Christ (Matt. 28:19–20), we must always be ready to explain the gospel to those around us.

For this reason, a believer's life should be characterized by evangelism. Simply put, bringing the gospel to unbelievers should be a consistent part of our lives. If it is not, we are neglecting the very reason God has left us on earth.

While it is true that there are specific people with the gift of evangelism, all believers should be active in sharing the gospel with the world around them (Acts 21:8; Eph. 4:11). Even Timothy, while gifted as a pastor, was exhorted to "do the work of an evangelist" (2 Tim. 4:5). The bottom line is that Scripture knows nothing of a believer who does not consistently, passionately, and boldly proclaim Christ.

As Paul stated clearly in 2 Corinthians 5:20, we are ambassadors for Christ. In the Roman world, an ambassador was sent by a more powerful country to forge and repair good relationships with a smaller, alienated country. If the ambassador was resisted or mistreated, swift punishment was likely to follow.[1] This is what Paul means when he describes Christians as ambassadors. We have been sent by God to repair relationships with an alienated world. If our message is rejected, God is our defender and will bring judgment to those who scorned Him. As His ambassadors our aim is to faithfully bring the message with which we have been entrusted. This is not a burdensome task, but rather is a joy, and there is no mistaking the privilege we share in proclaiming the person and work of Christ.

Because love for God always manifests itself in obedience to Christ, evangelism is one of the quickest ways to check the pulse of our love. We must never neglect the unbelievers whom God has sovereignly chosen to place in our lives. Without a proper understanding of both the "why" and "how" of evangelism, we tend to grow indifferent and begin speaking of unbelievers as if they were an enemy to be resisted rather than individuals to be pursued with the loving confrontation of the gospel. But when we understand that sinners are separated from God, are slaves of sin, and have no hope in this world, then we have compassion for them. When we realize that we have been left on earth to reach them with the good news of restoration to God, then we should be eager to bring the message to them.

What we want is a lifestyle of evangelism; not a sporadic focus, but a consistent walk that brings people to an increasing knowledge of Christ. By aligning our thoughts on the subject with Scripture, we begin to change our patterns of living. Charles Spurgeon once said, "Every Christian here is either a missionary or an impostor!"[2] He continued:

The saving of souls, if a man has once gained love to perishing sinners, and love to his blessed Master, will be an all-absorbing passion to him. It will so carry him away, that he will almost forget himself in the saving of others. He will be like the stout, brave fireman, who careth not for the scorch or for the heat, so that he may rescue the poor creature on whom true humanity hath set his heart.[3]

A focused evangelist will take time to cultivate a relationship with unbelievers, asking questions and being aware of issues that usher in the gospel conversation.

THE PRIORITIES

Living evangelistically does not come naturally, even for the mature Christian. After all, the gospel is a foolish message (1 Cor. 1:25), and that adds difficulty to the task. Nobody delights in bringing a foolish message to people who by nature start from the position of hating God. Thus there can be a certain logical uneasiness when it comes to evangelism. But this uneasiness can be overcome when a person organizes his life around some basic priorities.

The Priority of Personal Holiness

Effective personal evangelism begins with living a transformed life. Paul wrote that every believer must "not be conformed to this world, but be transformed by the renewing of [the] mind" (Rom. 12:2).

How we think determines how we speak and act (Prov. 23:7; Luke 6:45). Sinful words and actions come from sinful thinking; righteous words and actions result from righteous thinking. Even though a believer's mind has gone from being enslaved to sin to being submissive to Christ, we still must continue to renew our minds by frequently meditating on God's Word. The Holy Spirit works through the Word implanted in our conscience (Ps. 119:9–11) to help set our minds "on things above" (Col. 3:2) and help us to focus on things that are true, noble, just, pure, lovely, and of good report (Phil. 4:8).

The outcome of our prayers and meditation is our Christian influence on an unbelieving world. Our lifestyle must authenticate the message. Because we are believers, our lives should "adorn the doctrine of God our Savior in all things" (Titus 2:10).

Peter shows the connection between our lives and our evangelism when he calls believers to:

> sanctify the Lord God in your hearts, and always be ready to give a defense to everyone who asks you a reason for the hope that is in you, with meekness and fear; having a good conscience, that when they defame you as evildoers, those who revile your good conduct in Christ may be ashamed. (1 Peter 3:15–16)

These verses speak to the purity that should characterize the life of every believer. Purity of life grows from a sound conscience continually trained under the authority of Scripture. As believers, we must guard the challenge to be effectual doers of the Word and not merely hearers who delude themselves (James 1:22–26). It is not enough to clinically know the facts of the gospel; we must strive for Christlike humility.

Hypocrisy in a believer's life destroys evangelism like mold destroys bread. Eloquence and persuasive speech cannot overcome the blatant nature of unrepentant sin. We must remember that long before unbelievers hear what we say, they will observe how we live. Just as unbelievers are identified by their "fruit" (Gal. 5:19–21), so too believers are identified by their "fruit" (Gal. 5:22–23).

The example we set may be the only view of Christian living that many will know. Sin is still a part of our lives and at times the unbelievers we are witnessing to will be affected by our sin. Yet even in those moments of failure, we have the opportunity to demonstrate humility in seeking forgiveness and reconciliation both from God and those we offend.

A believer who lives as salt and light in a dark and decaying world (Matt. 5:13–16) will not detract from the gospel message, but will put Christ on display as the world sees Him working through us. Christ said in Luke 6:45 (NASB) that "the good man out of the good treasure of his heart brings forth what is good; and the evil man out of the evil treasure brings forth what is evil; for his mouth speaks from that which fills his heart." The consistent example of a changed life is compelling proof of salvation.

The Priority of Relentless Prayer

The work of evangelism is advanced through prayer. Paul told the Thessalonians to "pray without ceasing" (1 Thess. 5:17), and one component of that life of prayer is interceding for those who have yet to embrace Christ as Lord and Savior.

Evangelistic prayer pleads with God to be glorified through drawing specific unbelievers to Himself. We see this in Paul's life as he wrote in Romans 10:1 (NASB): "Brethren, my heart's desire and my prayer to God for them is for their salvation" (see also 1 Tim. 2:1–4). This is consistent with how Paul requested that the Colossians be "praying also for us, that God would open to us a door for the word, to speak the mystery of Christ" (Col. 4:3).

Evangelistic prayer petitions God to provide opportunities to present the gospel. It asks God for courage and boldness so that He would be honored. Paul asked the church at Ephesus to pray for him "that utterance may be given to me, that I may open my mouth boldly to make known the mystery of the gospel, for which I am an ambassador in chains; that in it I may speak boldly, as I ought to speak" (Eph. 6:19–20).

Pray specifically, pray earnestly, pray relentlessly for those in your sovereignly chosen mission field. I have noticed in my own life that the more I pray for evangelistic opportunities, the more occasions I have to share the gospel. I am not sure if my praying merely opens my eyes to opportunities I would have otherwise let pass by, or if this increase is a direct answer to my prayer. I suspect a little of both. Either way, evangelistic prayer is a priority in building a life that brings the gospel to others.

The Priority of Gospel Memory

An evangelist can only share what he knows. Obviously, if people do not know the gospel, they cannot explain it. Thus, evangelism begins with the facts and verses that we have committed to memory. By taking the time to memorize and regularly review the gospel message, we not only aid our own sanctification, but will continually grow in being clear and understandable in evangelism. Because salvation is entirely a work of God, we must study the Bible to be workers who need not be ashamed (2 Tim. 2:15).

This is far more important than even our own testimony. While the reality of Christ's work in our lives is important to account for, it lacks the authority that is only found in the actual words of Scripture (Heb. 4:12). The use of your testimony is powerful when you detail the work of Christ in your life, but remember that we must put Christ on display—not highlight past wickedness or accomplishments.

The following is a simple gospel outline to commit to memory. While it is not exhaustive, it does cover the basics of what one must know to be saved.

Who God is. The Bible explains that God created us and sustains us. Therefore He is the absolute authority in our lives. He is perfect, loving and requires us to obey Him perfectly.

1. God created and owns everything, including you (Gen. 1:1; Ps. 24:1).
2. God is perfectly holy (Matt. 5:48).
3. God requires your perfect obedience to His law (James 2:10).

Who we are. Instead of seeking God, everyone lives in disobedient rebellion against God. The Bible calls that disobedience "sin." Good works never erase the guilt of sin. The penalty for sin is more than the physical death everyone will experience; it is eternal separation from God in hell. Man deserves this judgment for refusing to obey God.

1. You have broken God's law (Rom. 3:10, 23).
2. You will pay the eternal penalty for your sin (Rom. 6:23).
3. You cannot save yourself by your good works (Titus 3:5).

Who Jesus is. God's great love and mercy can extend a pardon to every sinner. God sent His Son, Jesus Christ, to die on the cross to pay the penalty of sin for all who believe. In His death, Jesus endured our punishment, satisfying the wrath of God. In His resurrection, Jesus proved He is God declaring victory over sin and death.

1. Christ came to earth as both God and sinless man (Col. 2:9).
2. Christ demonstrated His love by dying on the cross to pay sin's penalty (Rom. 5:8; 2 Cor. 5:21).
3. Christ rose from the grave and is alive today (1 Cor. 15:4).

Our response. God commands you to confess and repent of your sin. You must believe in Jesus Christ as Lord and Savior. You must submit your entire life to Jesus Christ obeying Him as your Lord and Savior. Only by believing in Christ may you be forgiven.

1. You must repent of all that dishonors God. (Isa. 55:7; Luke 9:23).
2. You must believe in Christ as Lord and Savior. (Rom. 10:9).

The Conversation

With the gospel committed to memory, the next step is starting conversations with unbelievers. As I mentioned earlier, many people view evangelism as occurring predominantly in the context of complete strangers. The reality, however, is that most of our evangelism will actually be in the context of those whom we already know. A practical way to understand this is to make three lists:

1. *All of the unbelievers you regularly interact with, but with whom you have never had any gospel conversation.* Understandably, this list might be rather large, so limit it to just those you communicate with on a regular basis such as neighbors, family, coworkers, friends from social gatherings, and so on. Think of people you see regularly (the mailman, the dry cleaner, or others with whom you often have interaction).
2. *All of the unbelievers with whom you have had some level of gospel conversation.* With these people, you have discussed portions of the gospel, perhaps advancing their understanding of various components. On this list might be the people whom you have invited to a Bible study, comforted during difficult times, prayed with when given the opportunity, answered some questions they had about the gospel, and so forth.
3. *All of the unbelievers with whom you have had extensive gospel conversation.* Those listed here have heard the full gospel presentation perhaps multiple times. They have had questions answered, and you have pleaded with them to repent and believe in Christ.

Many believers who have worked through this exercise find it easy to populate list one, somewhat more difficult to fill in list two, and very difficult to itemize list three. It reveals a sad reality that while we talk about evangelism, we often satisfy ourselves with vague comments and suggestions rather than strategic and passionate proclamation.

Our goal is to keep track and advance each person's understanding of the gospel and at the same time carefully work to build their knowledge of Christ's saving message.

By viewing those we know in this simple grid, we focus more intently on the actual work of evangelism. Rather than being haphazard, we become deliberate. Rather than a distant thought, it is the first line of concern in every point of contact. All of this helps to gear our thinking toward greater persistence and precision in the gospel ministry to those we know and love.

The Strategy

Whether we are witnessing to someone we have known for only a few minutes or a lifelong friend, it all starts with launching a conversation.

For many believers, the most difficult part of evangelism is initiating a conversation about the gospel. Much like riding a bike, once you get started, the rest is easy—it is just that the "getting started" part can leave you with some scrapes and bruises. We find it easy to talk to our friends about almost any other subject, but we often have trouble directing the conversation to spiritual issues. How do we bridge the gap between the ordinary matters of life and the eternally valuable truth of Scripture?

There are many "launching questions" that are suggested by different subjects. Work, sports, politics, news, and mundane daily activities all can be the base for a gospel conversation. Think about what comments to make that might stimulate friends to think about spiritual issues. This is an acquired skill, not a gift relegated to only a few Christians. The only requirement is that we love people and have a desire to glorify God by being obedient to evangelize the world.

Think of the following steps as training wheels for launching a gospel-oriented conversation.

Step One: Start with a Common Conversation

Getting to know someone is the beginning of a relationship. Showing interest in the person's life gives that person a reason to talk to you and listen to you. Our goal is to talk on a level more personal than the weather—perhaps about the person's family, work, education, music, hobbies, or pets. As you find out what interests the unbeliever, you will know and understand him and be able to relate to his feelings and ideas.

Begin by learning the names of the people with whom God has surrounded you. Introductions are a natural starting point for any conversation. By knowing and using someone's name, we communicate authenticity and genuine interest. It is realistic that a person can learn his neighbor's names, or the names of people he or she sees regularly. It never ceases to amaze me how many Christians want to be more evangelistic, but do not even know who their neighbors are.

There are all kinds of excuses for this. I used to live in an apartment complex, and after a long drive home I really wanted to just go inside and see my family. I could use that as an excuse to not talk to my neighbors, many of whom I ended up seeing several times a week. But discipline in viewing the world as a mission field should drive us to take the basic step of getting to know the people we hope to reach.

Once you have met those around you, listen carefully to what they say. You will gain valuable insight to their thinking processes and feelings. A good listener will pick up on issues or events that trouble unbelievers. A good listener will notice themes that are important to unbelievers and will communicate genuine concern and love for them.

Good listening skills involve more than just your ears. Body language is important too. Maintain good eye contact, be patient, and resist distractions. The goal is to communicate true interest by giving your full attention.

Part of listening is to stop talking and ask questions.[4] Ask people where they work, and if they like it. Find out where they went to school, what they do on the weekends, and other basic information that helps you get to know them. Some Christians feel that these kinds of questions are unspiritual or cunning, but the truth is that getting to know someone is an important part of evangelism. It makes no sense to say that you love your neighbors if you do not even know who they are.

As you develop a relationship with those whom the Lord has placed in your life, the kind of questions you ask should lead to more in-depth conversations. Seek to draw out thoughts while providing opportunity to share personal feelings and ideas. For example, here are some open-ended questions you may ask:

1. "How did you make that decision?"
2. "What motivated you to choose this job?"
3. "Why is that so important to you?"
4. "What would you have done in that situation?"
5. "Can you give me an example of that?"

Do not affirm and accept all that the unbeliever says, but enter every conversation with your mind set on understanding him, looking for the best opportunity to present whatever portion of the gospel the Lord allows. Most people love to talk about themselves, so listen. Do not be in a hurry to answer your own questions or to give your opinion. Take the time to develop a trusting relationship.

Step Two: Pose a Probing Statement or Question

Throughout the conversations you have, look for the right bridge to the gospel. For some people this bridge is natural, but many Christians find difficulty here. A helpful tool for me has been to ask a question or make a statement that gets the conversation directly to what the person believes about sin and salvation. Sometimes a conversation will move directly to the gospel, but most often it will not—unless we steer it that way. The Bible gives us several examples of this kind of evangelism.

In John 4, Jesus was talking with a woman whom he met at a well about the subject at hand: water. Jesus said, "Whoever drinks of the water that I shall give him will never thirst" (v. 14). This moved them from the secular topic of water to the spiritual topic of living water.

Simon Peter stood by the lake, drying nets and talking to Christ about fishing. Jesus used a challenge only fishermen would understand: "Follow Me, and I will make you fishers of men" (Matt. 4:19). Jesus moved the conversation from the secular topic of fishing to a spiritual dimension of fishing for believers.

Here are a few examples that may work for you:

1. "With your health weakening, are you thinking about where you will spend eternity?"
2. "Why is it wrong to steal or kill? Where does that moral law come from?"
3. "Who determines whether something is right or wrong?"

4. "What do you think God requires of us to get into heaven?"
5. "Why do you think it is that rich people seldom seem happy?"
6. "Where do you get your information about [God, Christ, eternity]?"
7. "How does someone of your religion get to heaven?"

The more you talk to a person, the more opportunities you have to make the jump from the normal conversations to the spiritual. When you know what the person is going through in life, you are better able to bridge the conversation to the gospel. If he is frustrated about something at work, ask why. If he is delighted about things in life, share the joy, but ask why that particular thing brings such happiness. Be deliberate to make a connection from the person's life to the gospel.

Step Three: Ask Permission, and Ask a Direct Question

Having inquired about work, family, and church, and maybe even having shared your personal testimony, you can move your conversation to deeper spiritual things by asking direct questions. Before asking those questions, it is helpful to ask the person's permission. This deters a response such as "I do not talk about my deeper beliefs."

At this point, ask a direct question, such as "If you were to die today, where would you spend eternity?" "What are God's requirements to enter heaven?"

You will probably get a wide range of responses to those questions. Unbelievers often respond by saying:

1. "I think God will accept me because I am a pretty good person."
2. "Man is basically good and can work his way into heaven."
3. "God loves too much to condemn anyone to hell."
4. "I think Christ was just a good man, nothing more than that."

These responses are "works-based" and may provide a useful springboard to sharing God's Word. You might respond by saying:

1. "The Bible says God's standard for entering heaven is much different. May I show you what God requires?"
2. "You have put some thought into your answer, but it is different from what the Bible says. May I show you what the Bible says about that issue?"

3. "I heard what you said about God being too loving to send someone to hell, but the Bible says you missed a very important fact. May I share with you what He said about Himself?"

4. "I am sure you try to be a good person, but the Bible says you are missing something. May I share with you what it is?"

You might ask, "Why do you think God lets people into His heaven?" or "What is your best hope for going to heaven?" If the person still has no answer, you might say, "These are important questions to be able to answer. Could I share with you what the Bible says about the subject?"

At this point, proceed with the gospel, being sure to contrast what the Bible says with the person's previous thinking on the particular points of the message. Of course, not everyone will be interested, and you may be met with some rather firm resistance.

Our job is to clearly present the gospel message. With this responsibility, our effectiveness is gauged by the clarity of the message given, not simply by the response of the unbeliever. God is sovereign over salvation, and there are those who will reject the gospel message.

When an unbeliever begins to mock the message, we should refocus our efforts on other people. Christ said to His disciples in Matthew 10:14, "Whoever will not receive you nor hear your words, when you depart from that house or city, shake off the dust from your feet." The point is that when the unbeliever has made a fully informed decision to reject the gospel and has become hostile, we focus on others whom the Lord may be preparing to receive the gospel.

If and when you are rejected, remember: do not engage in fruitless arguing with an unbeliever. We must not destroy evangelism by needless argument. Remember that God's sovereignty never changes. He may use our example of humility and love to confront a hard heart. The gospel, not the personality of the messenger, must be the rock of offense. We must leave the results to God. Our responsibility is simply to be faithful to proclaim the gospel message clearly.

Also, do not take an unbeliever's rejection personally. Remember, unbelievers cannot respond positively to the gospel on their own. When unbelievers reject the gospel, they are rejecting Christ, not us. We must be faithful to present the message accurately and lovingly, then leave the results to God.

Recognizing that the conversion is a work of God should keep us from becoming discouraged.

Finally, continue to pray for the unbeliever's repentance. Let the person know that you are available to answer any questions about spiritual issues. Assure him that you will continue to keep him in prayer. Pray for him and use the testimony of your changed life to evangelize the unbeliever. You do not know how God may be using you in the drawing process.

As J. I. Packer wrote: "We glorify God by evangelizing, not only because evangelizing is an act of obedience, but also because in evangelism we tell the world what great things God has done for the salvation of sinners. God is glorified when His mighty works of grace are made known."[5]

The aim of this chapter is not to present a series of sample conversations for a Christians to memorize, but rather to encourage you to develop relationships faithfully and intentionally with people so that you can effectively bring the gospel to them. Strive to keep your life focused on holy living and evangelistic prayer. Be on the lookout for opportunities to bring the gospel to those who need it. If you are disciplined in scattering seed, the Lord will be faithful to bring the harvest.

13

The Call of Repentance: Delivering the Message to the Conscience

Tom Patton

There can be no conversion without repentance, yet this is perhaps the single most neglected aspect of contemporary evangelism. After decades of easy-believism, the heart of the church has seemingly flat lined into cardiac arrest. Instead of allowing Scripture to penetrate the unrepentant heart, the current cultural trend is to excuse away sin and recognize human success as the secret to abundant living. True brokenness seems like a relic of a bygone era. Deep mourning for sin, tears of sorrow, and agony over the crushing weight of iniquity are all virtually nonexistent expressions today. Nevertheless, it remains the purpose of the evangelist to call people to repent from all that dishonors God.

A recent poll reveals that most Americans do not believe they are in need of repentance because they do not recognize any sin from which they must repent.[1] Since the very concept of salvation implies deliverance from the imminent peril resulting from sin, it logically follows that today's tendency to redefine sin removes the need for repentance from society's conscience. The moral construct of our culture is such that even the slightest hint of ethical failure is quickly interpreted through the grid of relativism and excused away as irrelevant. Few dare to expose the central wound of the human soul as the sin of unbelief.

In order to be saved, people do not merely need to believe the basic facts of the gospel. They do not, as some evangelists might claim, simply need to trust God for a better life. Instead, people need to repent from their sin. This includes specific sins in their life—such as lying, greed, and self-righteousness—but also they need to repent of unbelief in the God of the gospel.

It may surprise you to realize that most gospel presentations in the Bible begin with a call to repentance. As Richard Roberts wrote, "The first word of the gospel is not 'love.' It is not even 'grace.' The first word of the gospel is 'repent.'"[2]

The first New Testament preacher was, of course, John the Baptist. The first recorded words of John's ministry were "Repent, for the kingdom of heaven is at hand!"(Matt. 3:2). Similarly, Jesus began His ministry with those exact words (Matt. 4:17). In fact, Mark describes Jesus' initial preaching as appeals to "repent, and believe in the gospel" (Mark 1:15).

Likewise, when the twelve apostles were sent out, they too began their ministry with the same call: "They went out and preached that people should repent" (Mark 6:12). This is not only true corporately, but individually as well. Peter's first sermon was a command for people to repent and be baptized (Acts 2:38). This is true too of John (Acts 3:19), Paul (Acts 26:18), and Timothy (2 Tim. 2:25). At the heart of evangelism has always been the command to repent from sin.

Sadly, too many evangelicals no longer view themselves as proclaimers of repentance from unbelief, but rather as self-styled connoisseurs in the art of inspiration and contextualization. Today's concern is more about achieving dreams than about acknowledging depravity. Not only is it common for our psychologically savvy society to endorse superficial cures, it is the church-at-large who has condescended to gloss over divine directives in exchange for an attempt to simply clean up people's lives rather than ardently seek radical transformation.

The core message delivered to the multitudes today proclaims a gospel of positivity rather than a gospel of rescue. The cry of God upon the human heart has slowly been redirected into a kind of holy pep talk rather than a demand for total transformation. True repentance has slowly been replaced by a user-friendly counterfeit.

GOD, PEOPLE, AND REPENTANCE

The root cause of people's disdain of the doctrine of repentance is their fallen nature (Matt. 13:14; John 8:43). Because of Adam's disobedience, the whole world now participates in the guilt of original sin and by extension has inherited an innate propensity to sin (Rom. 5:14). The divine call of God to fallen humanity is a call to radical, inward, spiritual transformation. From their birth, everyone is confronted with the divine command to know and become like God. Because of the Fall, people are unable to do this, and thus the call upon the human heart is a call for repentance.

All sin is a violation of the moral law of God. Thus, when people sin they are living proof of the human heart's refusal to conform to the image of God. People refuse to be perfect as God is perfect (Matt. 5:48), or to love others as they love themselves. By loving sin and resisting God, they demonstrate that their unbelieving hearts are far from him.

In the face of this global rebellion, God is not silent. Rather, He is constantly declaring His own excellencies through every imaginable avenue that His creation can sustain (Ps. 19:1). The very nature of God can be understood in how He has determined to call out to His creation, so that they might acknowledge Him as God and turn from the sin of their unbelief. God brings glory to Himself by allowing all persons the opportunity to recognize their Creator's inherent claim upon them and thereby enables them to turn away from their sin in repentance and faith.

God continually calls out for people to repent by revealing Himself through common grace (Matt. 5:45; Acts 14:17). This grace is seen through the internal awareness of moral law and the conscience-infused sense of right and wrong (Rom. 2:12). It is creation's design creation's design to point all people back to their Creator by way of general revelation (Ps. 19; Rom. 1:20), and through the specific revelation of the Word of Truth, which saves those who believe (Ps. 119).

Because of the depth of mankind's sinful rebellion against God, the self-revelation of God had to be inescapable. People are called upon at every level of their being to repent from their deep-seated refusal to acknowledge and worship the God who created humans, with the hope of sharing the unfathomable blessing of communion with God through belief. God continues, in His mercy, to call those created in His image to turn away from the delusion of their own autonomy, and to embrace the incontrovertible evidence of His divine sovereignty over them.

The Character of God and Repentance

In concert with this calling of God comes yet another vital truth to consider: the character of God in salvation. The key proclamation of the Bible is that the Creator of the universe has condescended to His creation by revealing to them the truth concerning His transcendent existence, His holy perfections, and His righteous judgments with a view toward calling to Himself a people for His own possession (Titus 2:14). God extends His gracious invitation to mankind by literally showering His creation with evidence of His ownership over them through every conceivable means imaginable so that they might know and worship Him as God, rather than continue in their condition of unbelief.

All who do not conform to the supreme holiness of God are placed, as it were, in the courtroom of heaven, standing before the awful fury of impending judgment, awaiting the inescapable response to their unrighteous rebellion while experiencing the degrading horrors of divine abandonment. The essence of human lawlessness is an act of personal defiance against the character of God. Walter J. Chantry summarizes this well: "Evangelists must use the moral law to reveal the glory of the God offended. Then the sinner will be ready to weep, not only because his personal safety is endangered, but also, and primarily, because he has been guilty of treason to the King of kings."[3]

Stephen Charnock, in *The Existence and Attribute of God*, states it this way:

> We deny his sovereignty when we violate his laws; we disgrace his holiness when we cast our filth before his face; we disparage his wisdom when we set up another rule as the guide of our actions than that law he hath fixed; we slight his sufficiency when we prefer a satisfaction in sin before a happiness in him alone; and his goodness, when we judge it not strong enough to attract us to him.[4]

Suppressing the truth about God's divine attributes results in His supernatural turning over of humanity to the fullest expression of their unbelief in judgment because they reject being conformed to God (Rom. 1:18–32). Therefore, the supernatural summons of God for humanity to know Him is also a call to be like Him (Rom. 8:29; 2 Peter 1:4; 1 John 3:2).

The Conviction of Unbelief in Repentance

Because the self-revelation of God and the call to conform to His likeness is at the heart of true biblical repentance, it follows that the foremost sin of which mankind must repent is the denial of God.

Jesus Christ is the full expression of God in human form. Thus it is through belief in Jesus Christ for the forgiveness of sins that man is made at peace with God. That is why at its core the call of repentance is a call to turn from the sin of unbelief in Jesus Christ, who is the substance of the gospel (John 16:8–9).

James Montgomery Boice makes the following remark concerning the essence of unbelief expressed in John 16:9:

> The sin of which the Holy Spirit convicts men is the sin of unbelief. "In regard to sin because they do not believe in me," Jesus says. Notice that it is not conviction of the sin of gambling, though that may come in time. It is not the sin of adultery, or drunkenness, or pride, or stealing primarily, but the sin of refusing to believe on Jesus. Why is this? It is not because the other sins are not sin or that they need not be repented of and renounced, for they must be. It is just that belief in Christ, the one thing God requires for salvation, is that which is hardest for the natural man even to acknowledge, let alone attain.[5]

Therefore, to completely embrace the will of God the human heart must repent from its unbelief in Jesus Christ. To be conformed to God's character, a person must trust Him for both the forgiveness of sins and eternal life. This is not merely a change of mind concerning the existence of the person of Christ. Rather, this is a wholehearted release of the once-suppressed truth concerning God and a fully engaged apprehension of the hideousness of one's own sin as measured against the holy perfections of Christ. As J. Goetzmann has stated, "Repentance is now no longer obedience to a law but to a person."[6] This is the principal role of the Spirit of God in conviction and repentance unto life. It is the change from loving sin and hating God to loving Jesus and hating sin. Pastor John MacArthur comments:

> Primarily the Holy Spirit doesn't convict unbelievers of all the sins they've ever committed. Rather He concentrates on convicting them of the sin of rejecting Jesus Christ, which is consistent with the Spirit's ministry of revealing Christ … man's problem is the sin of not believing in Christ not the sins he has committed.[7]

Martyn Lloyd-Jones wrote this about this chief work of the Spirit at Pentecost:

> The Holy Spirit makes you come to the terrible realization, "I must be spiritually dead! I must be lifeless. I must have a heart of stone! There is something wrong with me. I'm in trouble. What can I do?" Those people in Jerusalem now realized that their rejection of Jesus was based on ignorance and deadness, and that as a result they were terribly guilty before God.[8]

Zechariah 12:10 proclaims repentance this way, "Then they will look on Me whom they pierced. Yes, they will mourn for Him as one mourns for his only son, and grieve for Him as one grieves for a firstborn." Christ states in John 8:24, "Therefore I said to you that you will die in your sins; for if you do not believe that I am He, you will die in your sins."

The issue is not whether one "believes" in Christ—even the demons "believe" and shudder (James 2:19)—rather, the issue is whether the sinner believes in Christ as He revealed Himself. Repentance unto salvation is a call to turn from unbelief in Christ (Matt. 11:20–27; John 3:18; Acts 2:36–38; 3:17–19; 5:30–33; 11:17–18; 17:30–31; 20:21) followed by laying aside every aspect of life associated with unbelief (2 Cor. 12:21; Eph. 4:17–20).

THE BIBLICAL TERMINOLOGY FOR REPENTANCE

In the Old Testament, the word most often translated *repent* (שׁוּב šub) literally means "to turn." It has the idea of turning from sin to God (Joel 2:12).[9] It implies a leaving behind of all one's entanglements so as to return to righteousness. In the Old Testament, there are "two requisites of repentance: to turn from evil and to turn to the good, namely a turning to God (Hos. 14:2; Ezek. 14:6; Isa. 30:15; 44:22; 55:7; 57:17; 59:20)."[10] The Old Testament presents the call to repentance as being a complete change of heart that creates sorrow for the sin committed against God and a complete turning to the Lord.

The words used in the New Testament for *repentance* (μετάνοια metanoia from the verb μετανοέω metanoeō) are similar, as they also have the idea of "changing one's mind."[11] What the Greek adds is a connotation of a change in respect to a previously held position.[12] The essential New Testament idea of repentance is expressed by a full change that affects the feelings, will, and thoughts of the person who repents.[13]

According to *The Dictionary of New Testament Theology*, the concept of repentance in the New Testament is not "predominantly intellectual," but "rather the decision by the whole man to turn round is stressed" (Mark 1:4; Luke 3:8; 24:47; Acts 5:31; 11:18; 26:20; Rom. 2:4; 2 Cor. 7:9; 2 Titus 2:25; Heb. 6:6; 12:17; 2 Peter 3:9).[14] So when the New Testament speaks of repentance, it is talking about the most radical change imaginable in a person's life. The prevailing root of the evil from which the sinner must turn is his underlying condition of unbelief. Only when a sinner recognizes that under his self-righteousness and independence is the sin of disbelief will he be rescued from the minutiae of evil that plagues him on a daily basis.

All of this has profound implications on evangelism. A person proclaiming the gospel to nonbelievers has to realize that the evangelist is not asking someone to simply change her mind about Christ. Rather, the evangelist is telling the person to fundamentally change her life, to flee her previous way of living, and to start over.

THE INTELLECTUAL, EMOTIONAL, AND VOLITIONAL ASPECTS OF REPENTANCE

Repentance is first realized intellectually. This happens when the mind learns about sin, and sees the evils of sin in a person's own life. Before sin can be repented of, there must be both an intellectual comprehension of God's demand for repentance and a clear understanding of the weight of sinful rebellion. Though the witness of conscience upon the human heart is one of the chief instruments created by God for the assignment of guilt to a person, the conscience must still be made aware of the violation before conviction can appear.

Even the conviction of sin may not necessarily lead to a change of heart. Before his conversion, Paul said he would not have known that sin was sin, if it were not for the law of God (Rom. 7:7). He understood that he sinned against a person's law. Sin is personal. Thus, merely an intellectual recognition of sin did not lead him to repentance. Rather, Paul was converted because he recognized that unbelief was sin against a person, Jesus Christ. God used this realization as the means to open his eyes (Acts 26:13–19).

Second, repentance is seen in the emotions. When the intellect understands that sin exists in a person's life, that understanding will produce sorrow over that sin. Biblical change does not come as a result of avoiding the sorrow, but rather through the embracing of sorrow that sees sin for what it really is.

Because the intensity of emotion in any act of repentance depends on a number of factors the depth of emotion will differ from person to person. As Thomas Watson so aptly put it, "Some patients have their sores let out with a needle, others with a lance."[15] There will always be some degree of sorrow in repentance. However, though its presence is to be expected, sorrow is never the sole barometer for repentance, because repentance is not the mere presence of tears. Some individuals are born with such a natural softness and tenderness of heart that weeping is a normal occurrence, and does not indicate true penitent sorrow.

In 2 Corinthians 7:10 the apostle Paul reveals that there is an ungodly kind of sorrow that "produces death." The sorrow that the apostle is speaking of concerns the sadness of heart that regrets or rather feels sorry for what it has done. It is a sorrow in that it has regret for something that was lost and feels a grief for missing the opportunity to indulge in the sin that the world had freely offered. Worldly sorrow is pain that is ultimately born out of longing for more of the world. It is resentment for being found out; it is a hatred for not getting away with sin.

There is an additional observation about sorrow in 2 Corinthians 7:10. One type of sorrow is produced as a result of God's work in the heart and the other sorrow is not. The Corinthian people were "made" sorrowful, and theirs was the grief that produces repentance. However, the sorrow of the world that Paul contrasts is not from God, in the same way that the "lust of the flesh, the lust of the eyes, and the pride of life" are not from the Father but are from the world (1 John 2:16).

Both true biblical repentance and the repentant sorrow that flows from it proceed directly from the heart of God and cannot be produced on human terms. It is the Spirit of God Himself who produces godly sorrow, not human effort. Repentance is of God (Acts 5:31; 11:18).

Repentance is more than a change of mind, and more than a change of heart, because true biblical repentance requires a change of behavior and therefore requires a volitional response. Repentance demands radical conversion, a transformation of nature, a definitive turning from unbelief and evil, and a resolute turning to God in total obedience. This is more than a change of mind but a determination to surrender to Christ. It is the "fruits worthy of repentance" (Matt. 3:8).

Simply put, for a person to truly repent, she needs to see sorrow in her life, grieve over it, and then do something in response to it.

THE KEY EVIDENCES OF REPENTANCE

Second Corinthians 7 provides an encyclopedia of seven qualities of true biblical repentance. There Paul writes, "See what earnestness this godly grief has produced in you, but also what eagerness to clear yourselves, what indignation, what fear, what longing, what zeal, what punishment!" (v. 11 ESV). Each one of these features is extremely helpful, vivid, and contains measurable truths that can apply both to the lives of unbelievers coming to faith, as well as believers who are living by faith. Paul provides in this text a clear contrast between two different kinds of sorrows that culminate in two different eternal destinies.

Earnestness

When Paul describes repentance as having earnestness to it, he means that it is a repentance that is both diligent and speedy. Paul had seen a marked difference in the Corinthians' lives, especially in contrast to the way they had once been marked by a certain kind of carelessness. Now their lives were demonstrating an attitude of seriousness and gravity about their sin. They were conscious of how God viewed their sin, and thus they were now earnest in that they were beginning to see life from the divine perspective. They were serious and eager to follow Paul's command and to obey his words knowing that they were from the Lord. The Corinthians had come to have a divine perspective about sin.

Eagerness

After they repented, the Corinthians were eager to clear themselves of all unrighteousness. They wanted to prove themselves trustworthy to rid themselves of the guilt. Paul had no doubt accused them in his earlier letter and now they wanted to prove themselves as no longer holding to their once sinful ways. The sense given by this term is that there was no indifference whatsoever in their turning toward God.

Indignation

Here, Paul speaks of repentance as being so severe emotionally that it can cause physical pain. When the Corinthians repented, they had a righteous indignation for how they had lived previously. They now opposed their own prior actions and they hated the shame that their sin had brought upon the church and upon Paul. They were angry with themselves for allowing themselves to entertain the rebellious thoughts and actions of which they were guilty. They despised the way they had been seduced away from righteousness.

Fear

When the heart responds to the greatness of God in light of its desperate need for forgiveness, there is a godly fear that is present. This fear is seen in the soul that knows "there is forgiveness with You, / That You may be feared" (Ps. 130:4). This is the sign of a truly awakened conscience in that it sees its sin first and foremost as a sin against God (Ps. 51:4).

Longing

Repentance brings with it a deep desire and yearning toward the one they had wronged—in this case, Paul. This is the natural aching of the soul to be restored to the privileges and the relationships within the body of Christ that they once enjoyed.

Zeal

When a person turns from sin, he is not turning to a blank set of desires. Rather, he is turning to holiness. Real repentance is not lukewarm or ambivalent about holiness. Rather, it yields a zeal for the things of God (in this case, to be reunited with Paul).

Punishment

People inherently want to avoid punishment for their sins. But when repentance is real, godly, and genuine, there is a new desire to make right what was wrong. An obvious example of this is Zacchaeus, who went immediately to make reparation and restoration because of the authenticity of his salvation (Luke 19:8). Real repentance reaches beyond the superficial and the casual to make every effort to reveal the present grace of the moment.

Paul states all of this in order to show how radical true repentance is. It is earnest, eager, and indignant. It includes fear, longing, zeal, and it embraces punishment. It is not superficial, and it is certainly not captured in a fleeting decision. Obedience to such a call stands in direct contrast to the previous condition of unbelief, and can aptly be described as turning away from sin to Christ. Of course an evangelist calls people to embrace the gospel. But the starting block of that embrace is repentance, and this is what evangelists should be explaining to people.

THE PRACTICAL APPLICATION OF REPENTANCE

The evangelist must understand the practical applications concerning the use of the doctrine of repentance. First, it is necessary to confront unbelievers with the foolishness of their refusal to accept their sinfulness while facing a holy and just God. Unbelievers must recognize that they know of God already, but in unrighteousness they have denied Him. They must come to realize, by God's grace, He has created all things and seen fit to place in each of His human creations the knowledge that He has done so. They must know that because people were born in sin, they must learn that they suppress the truth about God within themselves, denying both the fact that God created them, as well as every other thing that surrounds them. They must learn that this active state of denial deceives them into thinking that every thought they have can be thought without reference to the very truth they deny. They must see that they are thinking thoughts that do not claim God while all the time borrowing from internal and external information that cannot help revealing God. Sin is both denying God and disobeying His law (Rom. 1:28–32; Eph. 2:1–3). They must come to realize that even one single act against the moral law of God is a breaking of it all and an affront to His holy character, thus betraying their underlying condition of unbelief. Thus, because of this unbelief, even a single act of sin is enough to condemn them as much as if they broke every single law of God (James 2:10).

After sin is realized it is essential to reveal the indictment of God against sin and sinners. No presentation of the gospel is complete unless the wrath of God against sin is clearly explained as being a guaranteed coming judgment for those who disobey. Unbelievers must come to see that God has judged sin and must be satisfied (Rom. 2:5–8). They must recognize that their good deeds are not acceptable currency before God (Eph. 2:8). Unbelievers must see God as holy and good and unapproachable by sinful humans (1 Peter 1:15–16). They must understand the wrath of God, revealed through the moral pollution of their own souls and the world around them (Rom. 1–3). They must see that God is a God of holiness who judges sin (John 3:18), and this judgment separates people forever from God (Luke 16:26).

Lastly, there must be a presentation of the identity of God in Jesus Christ as the Savior of mankind from sin. People must see that God has revealed a Savior who is Lord (Rom. 3:21–26). They must see the sinlessness of Christ, the moral perfection of Christ, the demonstration of His deity (John 1:1–5, 14–18; 8:58) and either the offer of His salvation (Matt. 11:28) or certain judgment. It is here that the need for repentance must be revealed within the framework of judgment and that it is a turning from sin and a turning to God in Christ (Luke 9:23–26). There must be no rationale, no philosophical musing, no common ground concerning salvation other than the one God has spoken concerning the "Man" Christ Jesus who proved His power over death by resurrection.

The declaration of the repentance should not be hidden in order to attract someone toward Christianity. The gospel of repentance is radical, and it must be presented as God designed it: in such a way so that lives are radically influenced.

Section 4

Evangelism in the Church

14

Acorns to Oaks: Farming the Field of Your Child's Heart

Kurt Gebhards

Christian evangelism begins in the home. During a child's formative years, it is essential that Christian parents communicate the gospel in a loving and compassionate fashion. As parents, our responsibility is to plant the seed of truth in our children's minds, to think often of their spiritual condition, and pray that God will bless our evangelism. Parents are to make every effort to protect childlike belief, while trusting God to ultimately grow the acorn of their children's faith into a strong oak.

One evening when my family was at a park and my kids were running around, I struck up a conversation with a mom who was pushing her young son on a swing. When I asked about her family, she said that she had a teenage son who wanted very little to do with her. "He just goes into his room and only comes out when he's listening to his iPod," she said with disappointment. "He never wants to talk. He never wants to do anything with me anymore. I don't know what happened …." Her voice trailed off. I could tell she was deeply affected by her son's disinterest, and was sad that she had "lost" her son without knowing why.

We exchanged some more small talk, and then she pointed to the four-year-old she was pushing in the swing. "Joshua's going into preschool this fall. I can't wait. It'll be such a relief." Her words shocked me, in both their honesty and their blindness. All parents have moments of frustration, but few express that to a complete stranger. I was powerfully struck by this mom's seeming inability to connect her vocalized apathy toward her preschooler to the indifference of her teenager.

Christian parenting needs to be substantially different from this kind of selfish and shortsighted disinterest. However, many Christian parents are fearful that they too will "lose" their kids when they get older—that they will lose them to the world. But such loss and hardship is not inevitable. It should encourage you to know that Christian parents are not helpless when it comes to protecting against such sin and rebellion.

Consider two basic facts about parents and kids. First, it is natural for parents to love their children. Second, it is natural for children to love their parents. God naturally places in parents and children a heart of love for each other. Still, many parents feel inadequate and fearful. Parents, take heart: the fields of parenting evangelism are white for the harvest (John 4:35).

It is common for people to be intimidated by evangelism. Talking to co-workers about the gospel can seem out of place. Neighbors come and go, and there never seems to be the right time to have a spiritual conversation with them. And many people are just terrified by the thought of evangelizing strangers. I do not want to excuse these excuses, because Christians should be passionate about the gospel to the extent that it overcomes those barriers; however, there is another mission field closer to home. Every Christian parent has an open and God-given invitation to evangelize their children.

When children come into the world, they are separated from God by their sinful nature, but they also do not know anything about the world. While morally they are already corrupt, intellectually they are a blank slate. Christian parents have the ability to pour into their lives, and teach them the truth about the world, God, and the gospel. This, if you think about it, can be more overwhelming than a three-minute conversation with a neighbor.

Occasionally, the apostle Paul also felt overwhelmed by the ministry God had entrusted to him. Yet Paul overcame his inadequacies because he had a confidence that came from God. He wrote, "Not that we are sufficient of ourselves to think of anything as being from ourselves, but our sufficiency is from God, who also made us sufficient as ministers of the new covenant" (2 Cor. 3:5–6). Paul's source of adequacy for his gospel ministry to pagan Corinthians is the same source of our adequacy for the gospel ministry to our children. Reliance on God gave confidence to Paul, and it should give confidence to us as well.

The Definition of Christian Parenting

Christian parenting really should be defined as parenting-evangelism, because a Christian parent's primary responsibility is to disciple and evangelize the child. The Great Commission should be lived out in the home first, for "if anyone does not provide for his own, and especially for those of his household, he has denied the faith and is worse than an unbeliever" (1 Tim. 5:8). This principle of providing for one's household does not just apply to physical needs; it also applies to spiritual needs.

Christians innately have a desire to see their children walk with Christ. Accordingly, parents must remember the responsibility of discipleship. God grants us the privilege of caring for our children by teaching them what a gospel-centered life looks like. Parents should see their children as their primary evangelistic field.

The process of parenting is just that: a process. Parents have their children's entire childhood to teach them to recognize their own sin, the gospel, and how to live a Christian life. It is not a one-time opportunity, and is not a single conversation. It is very much like how Paul portrayed evangelism in 1 Corinthians 3:6. There he described how the Corinthians came to know Christ: "I planted, Apollos watered, but God gave the increase." The analogy of planting is appropriate because, like evangelism, it is a process that takes time, effort, and that is ultimately dependent upon the Lord.

The planting is not supernatural, but the growing of the seed is. Just as the farmer cannot physically make his crops grow, he can be faithful to plant, water, and care for the seed. The God who makes a tiny seed grow into a large, fruit-bearing tree should receive all the glory. In evangelism, Christians are privileged to plant, water, and tend the plants of Christian growth. But it is God alone who has the miraculous prerogative to create growth, and He alone deserves the glory for performing the wonderful work of salvation.

So how does Paul's point relate to parenting? In this: the goal of parenting is not the salvation of your children. That is outside your capacity and control. The goal of parenting is faithfully teaching your children what the gospel is, and how it should affect their lives. The parent plants the seed and provides the water. God gives the growth. This simple verse also provides parents with a threefold strategy for evangelism: prepare the soil of your child's heart, plant seeds of truth, and pray and protect the crop from enemies.

PREPARE THE SOIL OF YOUR CHILD'S HEART

I will never forget one sunny Friday morning when a few close friends and I went to breakfast with Dr. Sinclair Ferguson. One of us asked Dr. Ferguson for counsel about parenting, and his response was profound. He said, in his deep Scottish brogue, "As Christian parents, you must make sure you wrap more than one cord of love around your child's heart." He went on to explain that he knew of many parents who catechized their children very well and yet had not formed a strong relationship with them. He spoke of the essential value of crafting with our children a biblical and well-rounded relationship of love.

As parents we must provide soil for our children to grow. One factor that greatly influences the productivity of any plant is the soil in which it is planted. For example, the hydrangea plant features a beautiful bloom, and I have seen hydrangeas in many colors. Did you know that the color of the hydrangea bloom is dependent upon the acidity of its soil? Soil also is a determinative factor in the yield of a fruit-bearing plant. In Matthew 13, Jesus teaches that although the seed of the gospel is pure, not all soils are equally receptive and fruitful. Accordingly, as Christian parents, our goal is to prepare the soil of our child's heart. We want to make the best possible environment for our child to be receptive to the gospel.

The soil of your child's heart is the relational environment of your home. Just as the hydrangea bloom is influenced by the soil in which it is planted, so our children are shaped by the relationships in the home. While poison in the soil would kill a plant, hypocrisy in the home could adversely affect your child's heart. Conversely, when a home is marked by integrity and love, children see the authenticity of the gospel. At the heart of a godly relationship is

love—true biblical love. This kind of love is to fill the home, and it can be cultivated through discipline, encouragement, humility, and enjoyment.

Discipline

One practical way to demonstrate love to children is through discipline.
While it may seem counterintuitive to demonstrate love to a child through
discipline, the fact is that discipline is a form of protection for children. By
teaching them right and wrong from a young age, you prepare them to recognize their own sin.

A house without discipline produces a child who does not recognize that
certain things are simply wrong in this world. Lying, disobedience, and selfishness are basic wrongs that children must not only learn to recognize, but to
associate with punishment. When they see that the standard is truth, delight-
ful obedience, and selflessness, then they are prepared to recognize their own
inability to behave.

The goal of discipline is not merely correction. A parent could train his
children like he would trains his dogs—a parent can get children to come, stay,
and be quiet. But this is of course not the point. The aim of discipline is to
prepare the child to realize that when he or she sins, the child receives punishment. This basic association establishes in a child's mind the concepts of right
and wrong, sin, and pain associated with sin. These rudimentary concepts are
critical elements of preparing the soil of a child's heart. Beyond that, discipline
prepares children to realize that the standard is beyond their reach. Not only
do children need to obey completely the first time they are told anything, they
also need to do so with joy. As children learn this, their hearts are prepared to
understand how far short they fall of God's commands.

Of course, godly discipline is balanced with mercy. James writes, "For judgment is without mercy to the one who has shown no mercy. Mercy triumphs
over judgment" (James 2:13). James's point is clear: in God's dealings with His
beloved children, His mercy overrules judgment. By balancing discipline with
mercy, we also prepare our child's heart to understand that while they fall short
of God's standard, God also is prepared to offer mercy.

Parents who are reluctant to show mercy to their children are in danger of
creating a home environment that is not only harsh to the child, but antagonistic to the gospel. J. C. Ryle explained it this way: "It is a dangerous thing

to make your children afraid of you. Fear puts an end to openness of manner; fear leads to concealments; fear sows the seed of much hypocrisy, and leads to many a lie."[1]

As Paul tenderly cared for his spiritual children, so parents must be tender with their children (1 Thess. 2:7).

To be sure, godly discipline is an integral aspect of faithful parenting (Prov. 23:13–14; Heb. 12:4–11). Discipline, however, must be practiced in a compassionate, merciful environment. For more insight on parental discipline, I strongly recommend *Shepherding a Child's Heart* by Tedd Tripp.[2]

Encouragement

Just as a flower does not open under gloomy skies, so a child's heart will not bloom under harsh conditions. Our children need warmth, care, and encouragement to gain the courage to open up. You want the soil of your child's heart to be richly fertilized by frequent, Christ-magnifying encouragement, which shows love in a powerful way. Paul highlights the significance of paternal encouragement in his own ministry when he writes, "You know how we exhorted, and comforted, and charged every one of you, as a father does his own children" (1 Thess. 2:11).

Consider Colossians 3:12–13 (NASB): "So, as those who have been chosen of God, holy and beloved, put on a heart of compassion, kindness, humility, gentleness and patience; bearing with one another, and forgiving each other." Here, Paul gives hands and feet to the notion of encouragement. It is this type of encouragement that should fill Christian homes like a pleasant aroma, because generosity and love are powerful motivators. Build on the positive. Children respond powerfully to affirmation, so love them by encouraging them.

Ryle correctly pointed out that "children must be wooed with kindness, if their attention is ever to be won. ... Just so you must set before your children their duty—command, threaten, punish, reason—but if affection be wanting in your treatment, your labor will be in vain."[3] So, as Ryle suggests, it is important to encourage your children with enthusiasm and joy.

Humility

Pride is an inhibitor of gospel growth in your child's heart and an assured path to destruction. Pride is the opposite of the safe path to salvation (Prov.

16:18), because God resists the proud person (1 Peter 5:5) but draws near to the humble (Ps. 138:6). Knowing this, perhaps the single way you can prepare the soil of your children's heart is by demonstrating humility.

Jesus provided that example to us. In Matthew 11:29 He said, "Take My yoke upon you and learn from Me, for I am gentle and lowly in heart, and you will find rest for your souls." Notably, this is the only time in the Gospels that Jesus defines Himself with adjectives. The gentle and humble Teacher commands us to learn from Him expressly because He is humble. We should follow His example and teach our children with humility, desiring that they will "receive with meekness the implanted word, which is able to save [their] souls" (James 1:21).

Humility can only be cultivated with deliberate steps. Here are four examples of actions that can demonstrate humility as a means of preparing your child's heart to understand the gospel:

1. Find a more mature Christian to disciple you. If you want to show your children how much they need wisdom, show them how much you need wisdom by humbling your heart and pursuing a mentor to teach you.
2. Admit when you are wrong and seek forgiveness when you sin against your family, including your children.
3. Meditate on contrition, humility, brokenness, spiritual hunger, and dependence. C. J. Mahaney's book *Humility* is a great resource for further study.[4]
4. Demonstrate dependence on God's holy Word. Isaiah 66:2 (NASB) teaches an important truth: "To this one I will look, / To him who is humble and contrite of spirit, and who trembles at My word." Your children should see you reading the Bible, and they should hear you talking about it to others.

When a parent models these behaviors to her children, she is in fact demonstrating humility. The parent is teaching her children that there is a limit to human wisdom, and that godly wisdom comes when sought after with a humble heart. This prepares your children to realize that God's wisdom is higher than their own limited understanding.

Enjoyment

Christ enjoyed the presence of children (Matt. 18:1–6; 19:13–15). Can you imagine Him blessing them through pursed lips and a veiled frown? No. He loved the presence of children.

Parenting should be fun. If you delight in being a parent, you are preparing the soil of your child's heart by demonstrating the joy that God gives those who are obedient to Him.

What does it mean to enjoy parenting? It means to have fun with your children. Get on the floor with them when they are young. Join them in their areas of interest as they mature. Joyfully join them in their world, enthusiastically relishing their activities and games.

Preparing the soil is crucial to future fruitfulness. Parent-evangelists should be fertilizing the soil of their child's heart with discipline, encouragement, humility, and enjoyment. All of this arduous preparation is designed to create the best possible environment for the seed of truth.

Plant Gospel Seeds

The most important aspect of farming is the seed that you choose to plant. If you sow peach pits, you will never reap a harvest of plums, no matter what else you do. Successful farmers take great care with their seed. We should protect the seed of the gospel much more. There are two main ways to plant seeds of the gospel in a child's heart: speak with words of biblical integrity, and live a life of gospel credibility.

Words of Biblical Integrity

Galatians 6:8 (NASB) teaches a clear and powerful principle: "For the one who sows to his own flesh will from the flesh reap corruption, but the one who sows to the Spirit will from the Spirit reap eternal life."

This passage highlights that all Christians carry two seed bags, and we must ensure that we are casting seed from the Spirit, not of the flesh. The last thing that our children need is for us to sow seeds to the flesh in their lives. So much in our children's lives, including their own wayward hearts and the world, sows seeds to their flesh. As parents, we are called by God to protect the grove of their lives and to plant and cultivate godly trees. When we act in a consistently fleshly manner, what hope do they have of reaping a harvest of godliness? Where are they going to get seeds of the Spirit unless we spread those seeds liberally in their lives? Charles Spurgeon said: "You are teaching children, mind what you teach them. … Take care what you are after! … It is a child's soul you are tempering with. … If it be evil to mislead grey-age, it must be far more so to turn aside the feet of the young into the road of error, in which they may for ever walk."[5]

When we take the opportunity to explain the gospel to our children, we are sowing seeds. This includes everything from the long, patient, and thorough conversations, as well as the brief daily comments. Every reference to the gospel is seed that is sown. This seed is then corroborated by actions.

It is important to look for occasions to explain the gospel to our children. These conversations can be habitual—such as a devotional every night, or a family time once a week—or they can be spontaneous, as the parents teach through the normal course of life.

A parent should not feel like she has to include all elements of the gospel in one conversation, because she is parenting for life. If the parent has a long-term view, she can go deep on specific elements (such as the Cross, resurrection, repentance, sin, the nature of God, the humanity of Christ, etc.) as the need arises. A parent has the child's entire life, so drill deep and over time you will cover the breadth.

With this approach, there is no need to water-down or minimize the message to your children. Obviously, we should use age-appropriate terminology. But when Scripture talks about teaching children spiritual truth, the emphasis is on thoroughness: "And these words which I command you today shall be in your heart. You shall teach them diligently to your children, and shall talk of them when you sit in your house, when you walk by the way, when you lie down, and when you rise up" (Deut. 6:6–7).

Oversimplification is a greater danger than giving too much detail. Do not soften the parts that are unpleasant, such as Christ's death, atonement, or the effects of sin in a person's life. But take the time to carefully explain how these elements relate to the gospel, while constantly reminding your children of the centrality of the lordship of Jesus over the world.

When a parent makes important decisions in life, he should explain to his children how the gospel influenced that decision. Use the differences between your family and others to explain the gospel. Explain why you do not buy certain things, do certain things, or want certain things, and constantly point back to the gospel as the motivation. When you see disturbing news on TV, or are confronted with suffering, take those opportunities to explain sin and forgiveness. Essentially, parents are constantly on the lookout for the right occasions to teach their children about the gospel. All these conversations are forms of scattering the seed.

Lives of Credibility

Once we spread God's seeds, we must water them with prayer and the words and works of God. We must cultivate the soil with biblical care, love, and friendship. But since the seed is the most critical thing, we need to know what it is, and how to tell good seed from bad seed. In other words, we need to become experts in the gospel.

If we desire to teach our children faithfully, we must first master the curriculum. Because we cannot teach well what we do not know well, we need to be experts in the gospel. Since Christians and non-Christians alike need the gospel, our children should hear gospel themes regularly. Study the gospel, and trust in its power (Rom. 1:16).

Speaking words of biblical integrity is only half of the gospel equation. That is why 1 Timothy 4:16 commands "Take heed to yourself and to the doctrine. Continue in them, for in doing this you will save both yourself and those who hear you."

Paul extends an amazing promise: if our lips preach the gospel with theological accuracy, and our lives are filled with integrity, others will be drawn to Christ. Gospel words plus consistently godly lives is the most potent combination in evangelism. If our children can understand the truth of the gospel because of our clear, accurate, and loving explanation, and can see the power of the gospel because of our earnest, prayerful, and Spirit-enabled desire to imitate Christ, we have faithfully discharged our duty to sow the seed of the gospel into our children's lives.

Remember, our responsibility is to do all we can to prepare the field of our children's hearts. Proverbs 21:31 says, "The horse is prepared for the day of battle, / But deliverance is of the LORD." In the days of their battles, Israel was responsible to depend fully on God and to do all they could to be ready for battle. It is likewise our responsibility as parents to do all we can to become gospel experts—not only for the benefit of ourselves and the people we evangelize but also for our children. We need to live lives of gospel credibility, especially with the young people who see us all the time.

Pray and Protect as God Causes the Growth

In agriculture, after the soil is prepared and the seed is planted, there is a lot of waiting. The season of waiting for God to cause growth, however, is not a time of inactivity, but of great effort. Remember, there is always work to do in the field of a child's heart. While you continue to build a relationship of love and emphasize the gospel with every opportunity, there are also a few more acts that a faithful and rightly motivated farmer needs to perform. A farmer waits for the growth by watching for weeds, watering, and caring for the fields. A parent, after planting, waits by praying for, protecting, and nourishing the seeds that have been planted.

Pray

Prayer is our most important responsibility and yet is often neglected. Just as Samuel considered it a sin not to pray for Israel, not praying for and with our children is an abdication of our responsibility as parents (1 Sam. 12:23). In praying, we bring our children into God's presence and leave them there for God to perform His work. Our reliance must be solely on the One who can bring about the miracle of spiritual rebirth. Pray that God would change your children's hearts and draw them to Him.

You can do this by praying with your child daily. Encourage your child to pray on his own. Give your child ideas about what to pray for, and help him express needs, failures, and sins to God. Pray with your spouse for the spiritual needs of your child. Share with your children how you pray for them, and how you see the Lord answering those prayers in their lives.

Protect

While we trust in the Lord, we also want to protect our children from weeds that can grow up and choke out the new growth. In the parable of the soils, Jesus taught that the seed that falls among weeds grows up very quickly, but the weeds of worldliness and riches grow up and choke it out (Matt. 13:22). As diligent farmers, we must beware of weeds that will take nutrients from the soil, overshadow the seed with its leaves, and kill the sapling as it develops.

To determine threats to your child's faith, ask yourself these questions: (1) what does my child want to do more than anything? (2) in what circumstances does my child respond sinfully? (3) does he or she become angry when something is taken away or an activity is interrupted? Especially in these areas, parents should be careful of childish excess and indulgence.

When we talk about defending against the weeds of idolatry, we need to have a strong relationship with our children. We must be comfortable engaging them on a heart level, so that when idols encroach, we can intervene with truth, empathy, and love. This protection is essential.

As any parent knows, we will not be able to protect our children forever. At the end of the day, trusting in God's power is essential to sanity in parenting. We must trust God for His great work of salvation.

Nourish

One of the most common questions that I received as a children's pastor is How should parents respond to their child's profession of faith? I answer this by using the acrostic GROW. Christian parents desire for their children to become Christians but need to be wary of false professions. So adopt the GROW model for responding to your child's profession of faith:

1. **G**uard your child against false assurance.
2. **R**efresh your child's interest with encouragement.
3. **O**bserve your child's fruitfulness.
4. **W**ait for mature fruit from mature trees.

Guard

Protect your children against false assurance by teaching them the nature of true salvation. John MacArthur writes:

> Certainly we cannot assume that every profession of faith reflects a genuine work of God in the heart, and this is particularly true of children. Children often respond positively to gospel invitations for a host

of reasons. Many of these reasons are unrelated to any awareness of sin and are apart from any real understanding of spiritual truth. If we prod children to "faith" by external pressure, their "conversion" will prove to be spurious.[6]

Salvation is not attained by reciting a prayer (or by any other human act). Salvation is the work of God in the heart of man and results in a lifelong journey of fruitful commitment to Christ. Many sectors of American evangelicalism accept a mere profession of faith without any reservations. However, Jesus taught, "Not everyone who says to Me, 'Lord, Lord,' shall enter the kingdom of heaven" (Matt. 7:21). Wise parents, therefore, will not assume that a child's simply having asked Jesus into his heart means that he is born again.

Recognize that children are likely to follow their parents' lead and mimic their parents' faith without understanding the gospel. Because they naturally want to please their parents, some children are naturally inclined to make a decision for Christ. Consequently, it is spiritually reckless to give them assurance of salvation based on a prayer. Our evangelical heritage has done great harm by asking children to "receive Jesus into your heart." It is common for youth workers to lead young children in the sinner's prayer. As parents, we need to understand evangelism to the extent that we can watch over the sapling of faith. It is far better to think of salvation as a life commitment rather than a momentary decision.

Again, MacArthur writes: "Teach children the gospel—all of it—but understand that you may be planting the seeds for a harvest that may not be mature for many years. If you mow a field as soon as it sprouts you will never be able to reap a full harvest."[7]

Refresh

Encouraging your children is a way to refresh their interest in the gospel. Be careful not to discourage their interest in the things of Christ. Do not drive a wedge between a profession of faith and subsequent actions by saying things like "If you were a Christian, then you wouldn't say things like that" or "If you were truly born again, you would have a different attitude." Also, it often is not productive to say "You are not a Christian" to a young child who is still developing. Do not discourage her interest in Christianity. When the child says that she wants to accept Jesus into her heart, think more about what God is beginning to do in the child's heart, and less about the biblical accuracy of the child's wording. Correct your children's theology and inform them about biblical salvation, but build on the positive. So if you want to grow your child's faith, guard against false profession and refresh interest with encouragement.

Observe

Examine your children's fruitfulness. Our greatest desire is for children to glorify God by bearing much spiritual fruit (John 15:8). If your child professes to be a Christian, 2 Corinthians 13:5 applies to that child: "Examine yourselves as to whether you are in the faith. Test yourselves." Also, our Savior's warning applies to all professing Christians: "By their fruits you will know them." (Matt. 7:20). Refuse to give your children a formula for salvation. If you give them a works-focused formula or recipe such as "repent and believe," even if the formula is biblical, your children can emphasize jumping through hoops without working through the central heart issues. Constantly point to the fruit of salvation (love for God's Word, joyful sacrifice for others, passion for Christ, etc.) so that they can assess their progress.

Waiting

There is one more consideration in stimulating your child's profession of faith, and that is waiting. Christian parents should not expect mature fruit from young saplings but should expect to wait for maturity of the tree to produce the highest-quality fruit. Do not judge a young sapling by mature-tree standards. Yes, inspect the fruit of your child's profession. Yes, keep your eye on spiritual evidence. But do not expect a young, healthy tree to produce adult fruit.

Faithful farmers wait for God to work the miracle of growth. "Let us not grow weary while doing good, for in due season we shall reap if we do not lose heart." (Gal. 6:9). Dennis Gundersen adds:

> The fact is a child is very much an unfinished product. Childhood, viewed biblically, is a stage in which parents are patiently cultivating the persons their children are to become. Childhood is a time of preparation and not a time of completion, of immaturity and not of

maturity, of seed-planting and not of fruit-bearing. To view things otherwise is shallow thinking about children and about evangelism.[8]

God is the actor in salvation. He is the One who saves us. He made us alive while we were dead, and it is because of His work that believers are found in Christ (1 Cor. 1:30). We need to work while we wait for God to do His work. As parents, once again we find ourselves in a position of humble trust, waiting on God to work His miraculous power of salvation.

THE COMING HARVEST

In the great work of parenting, God equips his parent-evangelists to prepare the soil and sow the seed. Then He enables them to pray for and protect the sapling. Because of this labor, God often chooses to grow the seed and perform His miraculous deed of regeneration. Ryle admonishes parents by saying:

> Precious, no doubt, are these little ones in your eyes; but if you love them, think often of their souls. No interest should weigh with you so much as their eternal interests. No part of them should be so dear to you as that part which will never die. The world, with all its glory, shall pass away; the hills shall melt; the heavens shall be wrapped together as a scroll; the sun shall cease to shine. But the spirit which dwells in those little creatures, whom you love so well, shall outlive them all, and whether in happiness or misery (to speak as a man) will depend on you.[9]

Ryle speaks the truth. The great endeavor for Christian parents is to sow the gospel into the souls of our children. So, Christian parents, prepare the soil, plant pure gospel seed, pray to God in trust, and protect against the weeds of this world. Perhaps, then, it may be said of our children, "So they will be called oaks of righteousness, / The planting of the LORD, that He may be glorified" (Isa. 61:3 NASB). It is our desire to look out onto the fields of our families and see large trees that are robustly fruitful for the Lord Jesus Christ.

The Youth Pastor as Evangelist: The Church's Most Fruitful Evangelism

Austin Duncan

Youth ministry is often relegated to the sidelines of ministry. Youth pastors are stereotyped as "fun and games" entertainers who love students, but mostly serve as pied pipers to keep church kids out of trouble. The caricatures of a worldly, hedonistic, fluff-filled, event-driven youth group is all too often warranted by youth ministries that do not operate with a biblical philosophy of ministry. In fact, these pseudo-ministries actually harm the cause of evangelism. Rightly understood, the youth pastor is first and foremost an evangelist.

There was a young man who came from an irreligious family; he was a popular public high school junior, a soccer player, and a pothead. He was dating a Mormon girl and wasting his life. He had never heard the gospel. His soccer coach was a volunteer youth worker at a church. The coach shared the true gospel with the young man, and invited him to attend the church's youth ministry where he heard the message of Christ preached for the first time. God opened this young man's heart to believe the gospel and his life was radically changed. He left the Mormon girl, stopped partying, and became a devoted follower of Jesus. But the change did not stop there. This student's transformed life was so alluring and his gospel witness so compelling that within a few years his parents and sister had also turned to Jesus.

There was another young man whose mother attended church, but the streets had been welcoming to her son. His rebellion against his mother's faith was obvious. He disrupted the youth group with his constant and obvious disdain for anything related to the church. He started hanging around gang members in one of the most dangerous neighborhoods in Los Angeles. But this young man's life began to fall apart. His gang friends turned on him; he was completely alone. One of the leaders in the youth group saw that the young man had begun to taste the bitter sorrow of sin and reminded him that his life would only continue to bring him pain and dissatisfaction, and eventually the wrath of God would come down upon him, unless he repented. This young son was broken by his sin and cried out to Jesus to forgive him. He reconciled with his mom, became a productive member of the church, and today is an evangelist who aspires to participate in overseas missions.

When youth ministry is run with biblical and ecclesiastical convictions, it becomes one of the most compelling evangelistic focuses of the church. Obviously, today's teenagers are growing up in a society that is simply not Christian. They find themselves in a bastion of hedonism and relativism, and the Christian church stands out as a beacon of hope. For this reason, an effective youth minister must be an evangelist at heart. Instead of building a youth group that is a watered-down version of the main service couched in the current popular youth language and culture, a youth pastor needs to have a biblical philosophy of ministry.

A youth minister may be a competent creator of programs; he may be an expert at running camps; he may have great leadership over a staff of volunteers, but if he is not being faithful in evangelism he is not fulfilling his ministry (2 Tim. 4:5). He must realize that one of the ways he is most useful to his church is by being an evangelist.

Even a cursory survey of modern youth ministry would suggest that rather than evangelism and discipleship, most ministries to teens are characterized by hype and defection. The hype surrounds their endless activities, and defection characterizes their results. Not only are we not winning youth to Christ, we are losing the ones we have. The failed retention rate of churchgoing teens is alarming and widely recognized. What is seldom recognized is that those who leave the church do so because they were never really part of the church. The apostle John writes, "They went out from us, but they were not of us; for if they had been of us, they would have continued with us" (1 John 2:19).

In other words, the fact that the majority of youth group students are abandoning the church in college is evidence of the fact that the majority of students in youth groups are not saved. This means that one of the main roles of a youth pastor is as an evangelist.

In spite of this urgent need, the stereotype of the typical evangelical youth pastor is that of a camp director and event coordinator. He is expected to give the students in the church something to do, and his success is measured by the number of people at social events. But true evangelism—actually, true ministry—is not about filling empty chairs. The focus of true evangelism should be on souls, not seats.

When I see youth group leaders get fired up with an almost missionary zeal in an appeal to get more people to sign up for a lock-in, my heart breaks. What is needed is that same zeal applied toward the gospel. Getting students to attend is not the goal; rather, the aim is to clearly and faithfully proclaim the message of the Cross.

Simply put, what makes a good youth ministry is what should make a good adult ministry: the accurate and persuasive presentation of the gospel. But event-driven ministries tend to purposefully shield their young people from the strong call, hard truths, and straightforward demands of Jesus. Youth ministry leaders seek to mask their services in popular culture in order to draw a crowd of unbelievers who will feel as comfortable in church as possible. Instead of maximizing these ideally formative years for spiritual instruction, they dumb down Scripture and ramp up the fun, games, lights, and prizes. Teens are left with the impression that following Christ is easy, holiness is optional, and church should always be fun and catered to one's preferences. No wonder too many kids who grow up with a fun-and-games youth ministry mentality shop for churches pastored by glorified game show hosts.

The result of this wrong approach to youth ministry is a generation of high school students who have no concept of the lordship of Christ, much less an understanding of discipleship. When those students go off to college they are ill equipped to withstand the assault that will take place on their faith. They were never integrated into the adult community of the church as a whole.

Attending youth functions is not the same thing as committing yourself to Jesus Christ. This is an obvious point, and one with which not even the most pragmatic youth pastor would disagree. The ministry that focuses on a simple and worldly message and fun games, and strives after attendance is actually the enemy of evangelism. True evangelism focuses on none of those, but rather is bent on gospel proclamation.

A compelling student ministry has not done its job if students can graduate from the ministry without ever having been confronted with the demands that Jesus Christ has on their lives. When the gospel is presented clearly, a call is given to respond. Many students have made false professions of faith because they were given a false gospel. They were told if they believe in Jesus they are going to heaven. They were led to believe that the half-truths they were exposed to at youth group were the real deal. But because they never turned from their sin, they never learned to treasure Jesus above everything else in the world. The result is the same in teenagers as it is in adults; eventually the desire to live for themselves is stronger than the assurance they gained from the sinner's prayer.

But when a full gospel is presented—one that includes the call to repentance, discipleship, sanctification, and the charge to love Jesus more than this world—students will be compelled to respond. Those who are not saved will leave like the masses in John 6. Those who do respond to the claims of Christ do not need to be coddled by youth pastors and isolated from the church body; they need to be baptized and accepted into membership in our churches. They need shepherding and discipleship. They need to be involved in the ministry, demonstrating their love for God by putting into practice the gifts God has given them (Eph. 4:12). All of this is made possible when the youth pastor is focused on evangelism.

Not everyone believes that it is possible to have a youth ministry that produces strong Christians, theologians, and passionate evangelists. The biggest skeptics of a deep and profound youth ministry are not the students, but often are the youth pastors themselves. By having a games-based ministry that panders to the lowest common denominator of a fleeting youth culture, high school students in the church are modeled capitulation rather than Christianity.

It is my privilege and joy to minister to students and it is my aim, by the grace of God, to encourage and point fellow laborers toward student ministry that is biblically motivated, theologically sound, and overwhelmingly evangelistic. If a high school student can be won to Christ, then his or her life can be a shining example of faithfulness. I desire to see teens who are Christians demonstrating that reality through lives devoted to Christ, His Word, and His church. This chapter will outline some practical principles for building a youth ministry that has an evangelistic focus, and that produces mature and godly teens.

BUILD ON SCRIPTURE

The question of how to best reach a young person with the gospel is actually an ancient one: "How can a young man cleanse his way? By taking heed according to Your word" (Ps. 119:9).

The answer sounds simple. If a young person wants to keep his way pure, he must meditate, read, and study the Bible. If a youth pastor wants to serve his students, if nothing else, he will teach them to love the Word of God. Easily, the most important element of a strong youth ministry will be its Bible teaching. I wish youth pastors would abandon video curriculum, stop wasting the church's money on graphic-rich youth lessons, and quit wracking their brains trying to figure out what topic might be discussed next. Instead, if they taught the students the sufficiency of the Word by modeling it in their own ministry, the effect would be profound.

The Scriptures themselves are the most important tool for the youth pastor. There is no other way for a person to come to Christ except through the preaching of the gospel, and there is no place where the gospel is presented more clearly than in the Scriptures. When a youth ministry is built on verse by verse teaching of the Bible, the students learn how to live and what to believe. As a God-ordained side effect, students also learn how to study and interpret the Bible for themselves as they watch Scripture rightly divided and properly explained.

The pastor's preaching should illustrate that the gospel is news, not advice. Jesus Christ, the son of God, died on the cross for sins as a substitute. He was raised to life on the third day, showing God's acceptance of His sacrifice, proving His life and His words were true, and to be right before God you must repent of your sins and trust in Christ alone for salvation. That's the gospel, and that must be preached consistently.

Teenagers in the youth group need this message. They do not need cultural relevancy, and they certainly do not need a youth leader who really "gets them." They need a minister who will explain to them that they will not get to heaven on the coattails of their parents' Christianity, that God's hates sin, and that the most important issue in the universe is not if they are going to make the soccer team, but if they are reconciled to God. Have they turned from sin to the Savior? Have they embraced, in faith, God's perfect sacrifice of His dear Son? Is Christ's life theirs?

Beyond the gospel, an effective youth pastor must teach deep theology. Students should learn more about justification, sanctification, election, and the trinity than they should about culture or the dangers of sex. The goal of youth ministry is not to produce "morality," abstinence pledges, or good grades. God has something better for young people, namely radical commitment to God's truth. For this reason, using the Bible to teach superficial moral lessons simply is not sufficient. The counter to the shallowness of the trend-chasing youth culture is not games and a cool youth group; it is the deep and unchanging theology of the Bible. If a youth pastor shies away from teaching theology, he is making a mockery of his calling and is betraying his opportunity. In the long term he is failing to prepare students to counter the worldly philosophies they will be taught in college.

If students graduate from high school and have been confronted with the deep truths in the full gospel, and if they have been consistently exposed to the theological teachings of the Bible, they will go to college understanding that the Scriptures have the answers for the ethical and moral dilemmas that they will be exposed to. By teaching theology and modeling the sufficiency of Scripture, the youth pastor is giving teens an alternative to the temptation of sin, and this alternative is inherently evangelistic. That kind of youth ministry equips the saints and becomes a light to nonbelievers.

BUILD INTO THE CHURCH

Ecclesiology is sadly absent from the theology of too many youth pastors. The church is so precious to Christ that He calls her His bride. He has ordained that the church be the primary means to advance His kingdom on earth. The dangers of parachurch organizations usurping the church's role are perhaps most clear in youth ministry. But for the youth pastor, the real danger is of building a youth ministry that essentially functions like a parachurch organization, except that it meets in your own church. It should not be possible for students to faithfully participate in a youth ministry but not participate in the church. One of the major goals of a youth program is to equip students to live lives committed to the church.

The youth must be involved with adults in serving missionaries, participating in neighborhood outreach, and visiting the elderly. Above all, they should be a part of the corporate body of the church in worship, fellowship, and service. One of the reasons that young people withdraw from the church is because they grow out of what it has to offer them. Eventually, they will tire of games and skits, and look for something more profound. A key to student ministry—for a lasting student ministry—is to get young people involved in the church because they are in love with the gospel. Then, if they leave the church, they abandon an integral part of their lives. Church no longer is a place that serves them, but a place where they belong.

Isolating our teenagers from the rest of the body of the church is bad for everyone involved. Just as the foot cannot say to the hand that it is not part of the body, so the youth cannot say that he or she is not part of the body of believers (1 Cor. 12:15). Serving the church is how Christians are called to use their God-given gifts, as this is where believers live out the New Testament command to love one another. Teenagers must be taught to have affection for the church, to care for its needs, and to devote themselves to its health and growth.

Unhindered opportunity is the hallmark of being young and unmarried. First Corinthians 7 is a paradigmatic chapter concerning youth ministry. While it is primarily known for its teaching regarding marriage and singleness, it is a fact that the youth in our student ministries are generally single. As singles, they garner two advantages over married people. They have unhindered opportunity (v. 32) and undistracted devotion to the Lord (v. 35). This is not to say that young people are not distracted, but because of their singleness, energy, and strength, their personal devotion to Christ can be greater than at other times in their lives. At this stage in life, there are few suitors to compete with Jesus Christ for their love. A genuine and maturing relationship with the Lord during the teen years can be well-set cement for a life of ministry and devotion.

Youth do not have spouses, mortgages, children, bills, or full-time jobs; thus, very little stands in the way of them being the most active arm of the body of Christ. Their concerns and interests are not as divided as they will be when they get married. Most of them go to school with thousands of opportunities to evangelize and minister in Christ's name. Athletics and extracurricular activities are invitations to "proclaim the praises of Him who called you out of darkness into His marvelous light" (1 Peter 2:9). We neglect a huge mission field if we are not helping our young people reach their campuses for Christ.

Youth ministers are often considered to be on the sidelines of real ministry. Their role is sadly seen as keeping the teenagers busy and distracted. This is tragic because it communicates that teenagers may be the church of tomorrow, but they are not part of the church now. An alternative is to encourage teens, if they are saved, to use their gifts for the benefit of the body of the church and the glory of God. This is youth ministry done with ecclesiastical conviction.

BUILD WITH QUALIFIED LEADERSHIP

"But if I am delayed," wrote Paul, " I write so that you may know how you ought to conduct yourself in the house of God, which is the church of the living God, the pillar and ground of the truth" (1 Tim. 3:15). This verse is a reminder to us that the Bible is not silent as it relates to who should minister in the church. The context of 1 Timothy 3 is leadership. Paul had just finished explaining precisely what kind of person he wanted leading those in the church.

In order to properly encourage our youth in evangelism, we must cultivate and model exemplary biblical leadership. The volunteers in our youth departments should be biblically qualified as servant-leaders. We need to be selective in who is allowed to work with young people, because not everyone who wants to help is biblically qualified to begin with. Youth ministry offers opportunities for students to spend time with mature spiritual leaders who can establish personal relationships with them. Adults who work with youth must be devoted to involvement in the lives of our students because we know that personal discipleship is most effective on a more personal, one-on-one basis. Our qualified volunteers need to serve as living models of what we desire in our students. It is better to have too few leaders than any leaders who are not biblically qualified.[1]

It is a matter of fact that young people are easy to influence. If a leader is weak theologically or compromises in holiness, those same shortcomings will soon be mirrored by the students under his leadership. Conversely, if a leader is passionate about the gospel and for the lost, this strength will be emulated. Evangelism is making disciples, which involves teaching them through imitation (Matt. 28:19–20). Youth workers are disciple makers and should model shepherding, not socialization.

One of the key areas of maturity that should be evident in any volunteer's life is evangelism. If the youth group evolves into a haven for introspective or shy leaders, then evangelism will be stifled. This is seen in two ways. First, youth ministry leaders need to know how to talk to students about the gospel. Leaders need to know the spiritual condition of their students, and must be able to cultivate relationships that allow for direct conversations about the personal reality of the gospel. Second, leaders need to be able to communicate with visitors, non-Christians, family and friends of the students in the youth group. They need to know how to seize opportunities to give the gospel in a clear and concise way to people they may never see again. They need to do this tactfully, or students will be embarrassed to invite their friends, but they need to do this clearly, or students will have no reason to invite their friends. Our leadership must be competent as biblical counselors and evangelists. Leaders need to show students that God's Word is sufficient for all the issues they will face in life.

It gives me joy to take part in the same ministry of Paul as I seek to influence teenagers to follow Jesus Christ. Paul urged the Corinthians to "imitate me, just as I also imitate Christ" (1 Cor. 11:1). The joy is found in watching students begin to imitate Christ. Not only do they become good followers of their leaders, but they themselves become influencers of students around them. Leadership is influence, and youth leaders must remember that their lives and words are being watched and followed. This is a significant responsibility before God.

BUILD BY EVANGELISM

The wise youth minister is an evangelist at heart and desires to see young men and women give their lives to Christ. The students in our churches present tremendous opportunity as a mission field. There are teenagers who attend from the neighborhood who have not been reared in a Christian home and who do not know Christ. There are also those reared in the church, who are unsaved and living on a faith that is not their own. Church kids need Jesus too. These realities motivate me to fulfill the Great Commission, specifically at a youth level. If we neglect to minister to students, we lose an opportunity to preach the gospel.

For an example of how viewing the youth pastor role as predominantly evangelistic is helpful, consider the issue of assurance. High school students struggle with assurance. If you cannot declare with certainty that God has saved you, then how can you open up the mysteries of God in evangelism with another? Oftentimes teens are insecure, and getting them to understand their assurance in salvation is vital. Teens who have grown up "Christian" and find themselves moving closer to an age of independence begin to question whether their faith is valid or just a product of their parents' influence. They ask, "Is my faith my own? Am I attending church to please my parents or my Lord?" These are good questions and wise shepherds will help young people navigate through this work of self-examination.

Growing up Christian comes with benefits and pitfalls. Familiarity must not breed contempt concerning spiritual things. The two extremes in youth ministry are the students who are confident that they are saved but who actually are not, and those who question their salvation but misunderstand grace. Helping students navigate 2 Corinthians 13:5 is practically a weekly task: "Examine yourselves as to whether you are in the faith."

If a youth pastor views himself as an evangelist, he has a daunting task ahead of him. His students scatter during the week to different high schools, and most will be surrounded by thousands of unbelievers. The only hope for the pastor to have a consistent gospel witness with the community is to train his students to be evangelists.

As Christians, we are ambassadors for Christ (2 Cor. 5:20). Students who are Christians are just as much ambassadors as older saints are. No matter what a person's age, all must be trained to make disciples. Students should ask themselves two vital questions. First, are they saved? Second, are they seizing their opportunities for evangelizing others?

Teens must be reminded of the truths found elsewhere in this book. They must be taught that we live for God's glory and nothing glorifies God as much as a sinner turning from the world and to Jesus. Youth must understand that they have the privilege of bringing the good news about Jesus to their friends, many of whom will have never heard it before.

If we tell our students these things, we can then prepare them to become evangelists. We can teach them how to evangelize, what to say, and give advice on when to say it. We can equip them by praying for them, encouraging them, and by preaching evangelistic messages. We can also remind the youth group as a whole that nothing cripples evangelism faster than hypocritical messengers, and use those discussions as opportunities for the students to evaluate their own faith and witness.

When we preach theologically, and our expectation is for our students to live evangelistically, then we are preparing them apologetically. The apostle Peter declares, "Sanctify the Lord God in your hearts, and always be ready to give a defense to everyone who asks you a reason for the hope that is in you" (1 Peter 3:15). As shepherds, we need to equip our young people to be able to defend the gospel, to clearly articulate why the good news is so good.

This is especially true for our high school students who are daily given the opportunity to give an answer for their hope. They live in an environment ripe for gospel ministry. In our high school ministry we held an afternoon seminar for several weeks that focused on evangelism. It was one of our best-attended events, and students stayed after church for hours asking questions. We realized through the students' enthusiasm just how hungry teens are to be equipped evangelistically. The salvation of the lost and the defense of their faith were pressing concerns for them.

We can also prepare our students for evangelism by praying for them faithfully, and teaching them to be passionate about prayer as well. An evangelistic youth pastor will pray regularly and specifically for his flock and for the students he desires to see turn to Christ. He will teach his students to turn to God in prayer to empower their evangelism and beseech the Lord to save their lost friends at school. By emphasizing personal prayer, we demonstrate that it is not limited to Sunday mornings or flagpoles. We teach them that it is a discipline and not an event (1 Thess. 5:17). When they cultivate the close relationship with God that can only be gained through prayer, not only do they grow in their own maturity and humility, they also become more evangelistic.

Prayer is the fuel and work of missions. Encourage students to pray for unbelievers they know and to be specific in prayer. Have them pray specifically for individuals, and for an opportunity to give the gospel to those individuals. Help them learn the tension in Scripture between our prayers and our actions, by encouraging them to pray for others, then go and bring the gospel to those very same people.

THE JOY OF YOUTH MINISTRY

Colossians 1:28–29 says this: "Him we preach, warning every man and teaching every man in all wisdom, that we may present every man perfect in Christ Jesus. To this end I also labor, striving according to His working which works in me mightily." This verse is perhaps my biggest encouragement as a youth pastor. It drives me to minister to students in such a way that spiritual progress will take place in their lives. I love seeing Christ's maturing, sanctifying work in teenagers whose lives are devoted to Christ. Our goal is the same for every person in church regardless of their age. There is great joy in seeing God's people grow in their likeness to our Lord.

I specifically love youth ministry because I love the thought of young people's potential. It gladdens my heart to minister to those who are the future members, ministers, deacons, and elders of our church. I look out at the young faces in our high school service on Sundays and see that before them are life's greatest blessings and challenges. Trials, temptations, battles, and joys await them. This is the outset of their walks with Christ. It is in these initial years they have the opportunity to learn spiritual disciplines they will benefit from for the rest of their lives.

As under-shepherds of the church of Jesus Christ, we have the responsibility to be good stewards of the spiritual gifts given to us, the people entrusted to our care, and the resources that the Lord has provided to do ministry. Our goals for youth ministry should not be seen in the number of attendees, the sophistication of the events, or the "cool" factor of the youth pastor. Our standard must be biblical, and it is seen through the salvation and sanctification of our people. It is then that a youth pastor fulfills his calling as an evangelist.

Compel Them to Come In: Witnessing to Those with Special Needs

Rick McLean

When encountering those with special needs, even the most seasoned evangelist may hesitate, become nervous, or avoid them out of insecurity. How should the gospel be preached to these special people? Often the response is pity—not for the spiritual condition, but for the physical one. Understanding that in a sin-filled world "normal" does not exist, but that every human being has the same essential need, provokes the evangelist to overcome the perceived barrier that exists in reaching out to those with special needs.

The history of the treatment of those with disabilities is not pretty. In different eras they have often been abandoned at birth, banished from society, used as court jesters, drowned and burned during the Inquisition, gassed in Nazi Germany, segregated, institutionalized, tortured in the name of behavior management, abused, raped, euthanized, and murdered.[1]

The Christian community must recognize its responsibility to reach out to those with disabilities, especially in light of such a shocking past. Those with disabilities need to hear the good news. They need to know that Jesus Christ offers as much hope for them as for any other person in society. Compassion and love are called for—not pity.

People with disabilities are viewed in a variety of ways, but rarely are they seen as "normal." Because of the differences, we often struggle when we see someone who has a disability and qualify them as "abnormal." The view that people with disabilities are abnormal has been the justification for many years of abuse.

However, we do not look to history for our example, but rather to Jesus. He had a deep compassion for those who were broken and lost. Quite often many churches fall short in fulfilling their duty to evangelize and disciple individuals with disabilities. But if we desire to have a church that honors Christ then we must model Christ's example.

A BIBLICAL PERSPECTIVE ON DISABILITIES

To minister effectively to the disabled community it is important to understand why some people are born with disabilities and why God allows others to develop disabilities as they get older. The starting point is an understanding that originally, before sin was in the world, there were no imperfections. Genesis 1:27 states, "So God created man in His own image; in the image of God He created him; male and female He created them." Then verse 31 states, "God saw everything that He had made, and indeed it was very good."

Humans were created in the likeness of God. He created us with the ability to rule, love, reason, relate, and, most important, to obey God. When God finished His creation there was no pain, violence, struggle, conflict, nor death. It was perfect. Because our world is fraught with so much pain and imperfection it is difficult to imagine the joy and goodness prevalent in that pre-fallen world.

The Bible makes it clear that the cause of pain and suffering in the world is sin. Yes, we were made in the image of God, but we became fallen creatures. Adam and Eve, the first two humans that God created, disobeyed Him. In Genesis 2:16–17 God made it clear to Adam and Eve that they could eat freely from any tree of the garden except for one tree, and this was the tree of the knowledge of good and evil. God told Adam that if he ate of that tree he would surely die. But Eve, deceived by Satan, disobeyed God and ate from the tree.

Adam followed her example, and decay and death came to rule creation. Adam and Eve could never have predicted the global impact of their sin.

After their disobedience, they hid from God; for the first time they had evil thoughts and were conscious of their own guilt. Because of their sin God judged the man, the woman, and even the earth, bringing increased pain in childbearing, sorrow, toil, distress, disease, and death that plagues all of creation. Sin was growing, and it's reign would never stop in this world.

Adam and Eve's sin affected all of creation. Paul states in Romans 8:20, "For the creation was subjected to futility, not willingly, but because of Him who subjected it in hope." Adam and Eve's disobedience caused the world to become abnormal. For the first time, brokenness and suffering were introduced into the world. This brokenness would affect the human, spiritual, physical, intellectual, emotional, psychological, and social realms. This corruption is still in effect today and affects all areas of our lives. Paul states in Romans 8:22, "For we know that the whole creation groans and labors with birth pangs together until now."

The rebellion of Adam and Eve caused the perfect world to become imperfect with all of its pain, chaos, struggle, conflict, and death. God created us in His own image for a purpose, yet we all suffer the debilitating effects of sin in this life.

Because of the Fall we are all born with some kind of disability. Some people's disabilities are easily seen, while others are not visible to the human eye. Nevertheless, because of the sinful world in which we live, we have to realize that there is no such thing as "normal" or "abnormal." All humans have been incapacitated with sin, and all of us will one day experience death. Thus, from God's perspective, all of humanity has been handicapped, with only one hope, the gospel of Jesus Christ.

DIFFICULTIES THAT THE DISABLED COMMUNITY FACES

Those who do not suffer from a disability sometimes forget how difficult everyday activities can be because daily struggles are often very minor. Most of us have no idea what kind of daily struggles face a person with disabilities (or their family and friends), and this ignorance can lead to a lack of compassion. The family of a person with disabilities will be tested and tried in ways that they never expected. For a family whose child has been diagnosed with a disability from birth or a young age, the initial news can be devastating. The family will now have to deal with medical professionals, doubts, shattered dreams, and a host of other problems.

The financial and emotional strains on the family can be overwhelming. Joni Eareckson Tada stated once:

> In the thirty years of being disabled I have spent over 43,800 hours in the hospital or in bed from pressure sores, tens of thousands of dollars in medically related expenses, and 262,000 hours going through daily care routines. These medical issues absorb time, energy, and money that could otherwise be invested in relationships.[2]

Meanwhile, those disabled later in life may or may not have family to lean on as they adjust to changing circumstances.

DIFFICULTIES FINDING RELATIONSHIPS

As with most people, friendships can be very important to those with disabilities, and, like the rest of the world, they desire to be accepted for who they are. Yet many of them find friendships difficult because so many people shy away from them. What causes us to be so uncomfortable? Why is it that we shy away from being friends with a person with disabilities? Often, people become timid if a person with disabilities has a different appearance—different facial features, a crooked body—or just acts differently. Discomfort also comes from fear, which is due to a lack of understanding of how to approach and relate to these individuals.

Much of our discomfort and fear rises from incorrect assumptions. When we see someone who has either physical or mental disabilities we often assume the person is deaf or mute. We don't realize that a person's cognitive ability is not connected to their outward appearance. I know a man in our church who has severe cerebral palsy. For the first year he attended, I assumed he was mentally incoherent and could not talk, but one Sunday he approached me to ask about the sermon. I was taken aback that he was mentally alert and could speak with clarity about what was preached that morning.

Another misconception is that people with disabilities are not able to understand the gospel. I have discovered that they know more than we realize. Many may not be able to clearly articulate their faith, but they understand far more than we give them credit.

Unfortunately, there are many churches today that believe God wants a person with disabilities healed. Some go further and even tell this person that if the disability is not healed it is because the person has weak faith. This type of teaching compounds the problems of relating to a person with disabilities.

These principles can be summarized into one major theme: we need to think and treat those with disabilities the same as we would like to be treated. The essence of the person is the same as all of God's children who have sinned and need God's salvation. A person with disabilities is still a whole person.

The Purpose of Ministry to People with Disabilities

If people with disabilities are still whole, why should we minister specially to them? And what does the Bible teach us about these people?

Christ's ministry demonstrated a love and care for those with disabilities. Christ set the example of one who loved and reached out to them. The vast majority of Jesus' miracles were received by someone who had mental or physical disabilities. Jesus healed the blind, deaf, paralyzed, and mentally ill. He reached out to the blind with kindness. He ministered to children struggling with illnesses. Jesus loved to go out of His way for the deaf and the paralyzed.

In Mark 10:46–52 Jesus came in contact with a blind man named Bartimaeus. Blindness was a common problem during the time of Christ. Many would come to cities hoping to find a cure. Numerous diseases in the first century contributed to blindness, and many were blind from birth.[3]

Bartimaeus made his living through begging. One day as Jesus was coming by, Bartimaeus began to scream with an anguished shout, "Jesus, Son of David, have mercy on me!" (Mark 10:47). This was a desperate man. He threw himself totally on Jesus' mercy. He must have known of His great power to heal.

Bartimaeus stepped out in faith and cried out to Jesus. Many in the crowd, including the disciples, rebuked this man for being so loud and demanding. They told him to "be quiet" (v. 48). The multitude showed very little compassion toward this blind man. They, in some way, demonstrate how we sometimes treat those who are different in actions and speech.

So how did Jesus respond to this man? Jesus stopped and "commanded him to be called" (v. 49). Jesus instructed the multitudes to be quiet and bring the blind man to Him. The crowd paused their criticism and told the man that Jesus was summoning him. Bartimaeus was so excited, he threw aside his cloak and came to Jesus (v. 50). This man had great faith and he truly believed that Jesus could heal him. What is even more important is that Jesus was using this as an opportunity to teach the multitudes the importance of compassion, love, and care for those with disabilities. The disciples saw Jesus' priority to minister to those with disabilities. Jesus not only healed his physical eyes but also opened his spiritual eyes (v. 52). Jesus' example makes it clear that we should reach out to those who have mental or physical disabilities.

We are commanded to reach out to those with disabilities. In Matthew 25:34–40, Jesus describes the fruit of a person who is saved. He is not talking of doing good works to be saved, but these are works that show that a person is living for Christ. Jesus describes these six groups of people who have needs: the hungry, thirsty, strangers, naked, sick, and imprisoned. This represents the hurting and needy in the church and would certainly include those with disabilities.

James 1:27a states, "Pure and undefiled religion before God and the Father is this: to visit orphans and widows in their trouble." Widows and orphans are people who can be lonely, exploited, or in deep distress. These two groups represent two paradigms of the needy and dispossessed in society.[4] The word here translated "visit" does not mean "visit" in the casual sense. It is not a command to stop by these people and greet them. Rather, the word literally means "to care for, to protect, or to help."[5] From James's perspective, it is fundamental for "pure and undefiled religion" to love and care for the downtrodden.

Jesus explained why that is the case in Mark 2:15–17. While eating a meal with sinners in Matthew's house, the scribes and the Pharisees became upset with Jesus for eating with sinners. Jesus answered his critics by saying, "Those who are well have no need of a physician, but those who are sick. I did not come to call the righteous, but sinners, to repentance" (v. 17b). In Luke 19:10 Jesus said, "For the Son of Man has come to seek and to save that which was lost." Christ came to earth to save those who are hurting and lost.

We should look for opportunities to reach out to someone who has a disability. Develop a friendship with him. Take the person out to lunch or provide transportation for him. Make an effort to get to know someone who has a disability so that you can find out what his needs may be. Do not be afraid to ask the person how you can be of service to him. Encourage others to do the same.

We must also bring the good news of salvation to those who have disabilities. When Jesus healed those with disabilities He was concerned about their souls, as well as their bodies. In Mark 5:25–34 Jesus healed a woman who had been bleeding for many years. Because of this disease she was treated as a person who was unclean. This woman was unwanted, despised, and a castoff from society. She had such strong faith in Jesus that this woman came up from behind Jesus in a crowd of people and touched His outer garment and was healed. Jesus was so amazed that He looked around to see who this woman was who grabbed His cloak. Then He told her, "Your faith has made you well" (v. 34).

There are more than 516 million people in the world who have disabilities.[6] These people need the proclamation of the gospel. But only in Christ can people with disabilities be loved, and treated with respect and worth. The gospel must be accessible to all, including a person who has a severe disability.

It is important that people with disabilities receive the correct gospel. Just because they have disabilities does not give them a free ticket to heaven. They are sinners, yet Christ came into the world to die on the cross for their sins. If they savingly believe the gospel, they can receive forgiveness for their sins, and the hope of eternal life in the future. The gospel is the only message that joins those who are paralyzed, deaf, blind, sighted, intellectually capable, and have mental disabilities.

Sadly, there are many who give false hope to the those with disabilities. They tell them that if they give their life to Christ they will be physically healed. However, physical healing is not the message they need to hear; the message they need is that they can be spiritually healed, with the hope of heaven after death where then they will get a new body (Phil. 3:20–21).

As you develop relationships, do not be afraid to evangelize. Have honest conversations about the gospel, and talk about the blessings of being a Christian and the demands of discipleship. Often you will find that a person who has lost hope in this world is more than ready to find hope in the next.

If we desire to minister effectively with those who have disabilities we must learn how to communicate with them. Communication can at times be a challenge and it requires patience and a willingness to learn. You must slow down. You might struggle understanding what someone is saying, or the person might struggle understanding you. It could be easy to just give up and not make the effort that is required. The first few months of serving in Grace Community Church's ministry for people with disabilities were a challenge for me. There I was, the new pastor, and yet I was very uncomfortable talking with many of our friends. I struggled to understand some of them. But what helped was learning to be patient, persistent, and not being afraid to ask questions.

For more than thirty years we have had an outreach program called Grace Club. The purpose of this program is to share the gospel with adults with developmental disabilities. We meet every Tuesday evening during the school year. The evening starts out with games in our gym for thirty minutes. Then we meet in another room where we have a time of worship and prayer, and give a short message that always includes the gospel. The last fifteen minutes we break up into small groups for a more intimate interaction. We also have a ministry for adults with physical disabilities called "Grace on Wheels" where we take Saturday field trips that give people with disabilities opportunities to go to parks, museums, fairs, beaches, and have theme parties. The purpose of all of this is to develop friendships and also to share the gospel. The gospel is shared without pity, but with hope. It is important for us to remember that no physical or mental condition is outside the transforming power of the gospel.

Those with disabilities are an indispensable part of the church. If we truly follow the example of Jesus, it will be impossible for us to ignore them. In 1 Corinthians 12:22–24, Paul details the importance of the weaker members to the body of the church. This passage speaks of the hurting, fragile, vulnerable, weak, and lonely in the church. Paul expects the church to reach out to these people and also to provide opportunities for them to serve in the church. They have gifts and we need to encourage them to know and apply them in the church. We do not want to let their disabilities stand in the way of their service to the church.

WAYS TO CULTIVATE AN EFFECTIVE MINISTRY
FOR PEOPLE WITH DISABILITIES

There are several things your church can do to cultivate an effective ministry for those with disabilities.

What Should the Church Do?

First, the pastoral staff needs to create a vision for the church. The pastor could preach a message challenging his flock to reach out to those with disabilities, or use some other way to encourage his congregation to be faithful in this area. Second, the church should inform those with disabilities that they are welcome at the church and to come alongside them to minister to them.

What Does This Look Like?

Provide handicap-accessible bathrooms. Identify a location for wheelchairs to have full access to the worship center. Seek church ministry feedback from friends who have disabilities. Develop a transportation ministry to carpool people with special needs to church (at Grace Community Church we pick up nearly thirty people each week by van and bus). Look for professionally trained people in your congregation who might be skilled in nursing, special education, or physical or occupational therapy. It can be helpful to seek their input and advice. Make it known to your church that you do not have to be educated or have experience to serve. You need people who love God and have a heart to serve the hurting.

Over the years Grace Community Church has developed Sunday school classes for people who have developmental disabilities. The classes are attended by those who have a difficult time understanding the teaching in our main worship service or in the traditional Sunday school classes. The teaching for these classes is simple, with many visual aids to emphasize the lessons. Classes like these provide for more individual attention while we strive to let God's word work in their hearts.

Reach Out to Friends and Families

A very important aspect of ministering to people with disabilities is reaching out to their families and friends who can be mentally and physically stressed and exhausted. Their church attendance can be affected. The church needs to get to know the family and friends and learn their needs. The church has an opportunity to be the hands and feet of Jesus for those struggling to provide care.

In Luke 14:15–24, Jesus tells the story of a man who invited many guests to a banquet. He invited friends and influential people. But these friends found excuses not to attend the banquet. They had fields to plow, oxen to test, or a new wife to spend time with. This so angered the master that he ordered the servant to "go out quickly into the streets and lanes of the city, and bring in here the poor and the maimed and the lame and the blind…compel them to come in, that my house may be filled" (vv. 21*b*, 23). Jesus brought in all whose hearts might be open to Him.

Evangelizing those with disabilities is an issue of opportunity and obedience. Christians have the opportunity to evangelize a large segment of our population that is chronically neglected. Today there is a focus on reaching artists, athletes, businessmen, and others deemed important in society. But many such people are like the influential people in Luke 14 who are simply not interested in the gospel. I wish that Christians today would more often follow the example of the servant in Luke 14 and find those who will listen, many of whom no one else is talking to, and compel them to come in.

17

Reaching Addicts: Evangelizing Those with Addictions

Bill Shannon

Addictions can make the evangelist's task seem impossible. How do you give hope to someone when the person cannot even think clearly and seems to not have control over their own actions? Although all sin leads to death, the consequences of addiction are often more immediate and destructive. At its core, addiction is a form of idolatry. Understanding how addiction works will help the evangelist give hope to the addict, and it is a hope that is only found in the gospel.

Few sins are more destructive than those that become addictions. While all sin leads to death, addictions in particular have the power to ruin lives and devastate families. Drug addictions can end careers; alcohol addictions can separate families, and addictions of any kind can quickly thrust a person's life out of control—and sometimes beyond the sympathy of family and friends. Yet despite the ferocious nature of addiction, nothing is stronger than the transforming power of the gospel. For this reason the gospel can offer salvation from the enslavement of these life-dominating sins.

These sins are so controlling that it can seem as if a demonic power has overtaken the addict. Even so, addictions are not that dissimilar from other sins; after all, every sin, at its most basic level, is a form of rebellion against God. Sin reveals the sinner's real desire: to be independent from God and from God's commands. In this way, addictions are not unlike the first sin of Adam and Eve in the garden of Eden.

What Addiction is, and What It Is Not

Whether the addiction is to drugs, food, sex, video games, alcohol, pornography, or any other life-controlling substance or situation, it is an outgrowth of sinful decisions. When desire produces action, and that action goes against God's laws, then that action is sinful—whether or not it is labeled as an addiction. This truth is often clouded by confusion that covers the contemporary understanding of what the word *addiction* means.

Addiction has become a popular word that is used to describe or excuse any repetitive behavior that seems compulsory. These maladies of the soul are better understood as enslaving tendencies or afflictions. It is essential to remember that all these tendencies and afflictions (at least initially) are manifested in accordance with a person's will. While there certainly may be biological components to many addictions, ultimately, actions that violate God's laws are sin. In other words, biological factors may contribute to an addiction, but they do not cause an addiction, and they cannot be used as scapegoats to avoid responsibility for the addictions. God's law is broken by acts of the will, not by chemical reactions in the body.

This is essential to understand because for many, there is an eagerness to label a person's sinful and destructive behavior as an *addiction*. This eagerness reflects the world's concept of addiction as providing an excuse, as if the concept of addiction removes culpability for the sin that the person commits. It is our opinion at Grace Community Church that this label becomes problematic because if a person's sin is considered merely an addiction, then the assumption is that therapy or even psychotropic drugs is required for a cure. This mistaken notion—that the label of *addiction* necessitates therapy or drugs for hope of freedom—fails to understand the sufficiency of Scripture, the power of the Holy Spirit and the fellowship of believers as the means of grace to free people from their sin.

Ed Welch, in his book *Addictions: A Banquet in the Grave*, defined *addiction* this way: "Addiction is bondage to the rule of a substance, activity, or state of mind, which then becomes the center of life, defending itself from the truth so that even bad consequences don't bring repentance, and leading to further estrangement from God."[1] Anything that takes center stage in a person's life, even good things, can be considered a form of enslavement or addiction.

This bondage can be powerful because often the indulgence of certain desires can bring about feelings of euphoria and joy. When a person relies on things such as drugs, alcohol, sex, food, or even exercise for those feelings, then the process of enslavement has begun. Some indulgences bring about a sense of peace and comfort, such as playing video games, eating, or watching TV. Some can bring about an experience of energy, such as caffeine, nicotine, sugar, or chocolate. Still other actions can cause a sense of satisfaction, such as sex, weight lifting, running, self-pleasure, or pornography. These effects form the basis of an addiction. People develop addictions because the behavior is a way to change how they feel. People want to feel pleasure, acceptance, and comfort, and when a particular activity offers such temporary satisfaction, they will return to that activity again and again. The Bible describes this kind of person as out of control, being mastered by the world and the things in the world (1 John 2:15–17).

Proverbs 23:29–35 gives a picture of how this addiction is seen with alcohol. Alcohol's appeal stems from its ability to create artificial happiness and a sense of being carefree. When these substances are indulged in repeatedly, cravings are created that seem irresistible. The fact that there are negative consequences every time drunkenness is experienced does not reform the drunkard. The person can experience hangovers or lose a job and reputation, but none of this is enough to cause the drunkard to turn away from sin. In this context, the drunkard is a vivid depiction of a person enslaved to sin. Despite the consequences of the drunkard's actions and a track record of failure, the person maintains hope that the particular vice will still somehow bring satisfaction.

SEEING ADDICTION AS IDOLATRY

Addicts fervently pursue their vice, so much so that it is as if they are worshipping the object of their addiction. They turn to it for pleasure and peace, and it is in this sense that addiction is a form of idolatry. In reality, the worship of an actual idol (as the Israelites were prone to do three thousand years ago) is not substantially different from the behavior of the modern addict. In both cases the idolater does not want to be ruled by God, and instead allows idols to take control of his life. The idolater is consumed by the quest for joy, and his desires are set upon indulging in behaviors that will satisfy cravings. The longer the idolater pursues his quest to gain meaning and joy from an idol, the more reluctant the person is to recognize that it is powerless to deliver. Habits are formed, bodies are abused, and lives are ruined as a result of this sinful and rebellious idolatry.

Idolatry is not limited to those who are addicted to drugs or alcohol or even to those who have been diagnosed as sex addicts. This idolatry is seen even in the desire to indulge in legal and seemingly "normal" behaviors, particularly when that desire becomes a source for contentment or pleasure. I personally have counseled people who are worshipping idols in the form of anger, love, weight lifting, sleep, nicotine, pain, TV, self-pleasure, exercise, gambling, Facebook, work, sports, sugar, relationships, talking, sex, video games, caffeine, shoplifting, lying, chocolate, risk, success, Internet surfing, and pornography. These sins are often called addictions because of how powerfully they can grip a person's life. But like idolatry, the sin has power only because the person is clinging to it, longing for happiness, contentment, or some feeling that comes from it.

This longing makes the goal of the addiction the driving force of worship. The desire for the feeling associated with the addiction becomes all-consuming, and it becomes elevated to the level of worship. Drugs and sex are the modern golden calves erected by addicts to find meaning, power, or pleasure apart from God. Addicts often believe that they have found happier lives, but the payoff is short and not sweet. They are blinded and are soon out of control. They become victims of their own lust and an example of modern-day idolatry.

THE POWER OF ADDICTION

In order to understand why addictions are so powerful, and also why the gospel can bring deliverance, it is helpful to understand the source of addictions. People are dependent by nature. God did not design humans to be self-sufficient, but rather He created us to live dependent on Him. Therefore, a person cannot be truly happy or fulfilled without living in obedience to God's Word.

Because God is the creator, He is the source of life, and therefore a happy life is lived dependent on Him (see Col. 1:16*b*–18). But when a person rejects the lordship of Christ, and rejects the claim that God has on his life, that person is forced to suppress the truth about God (Rom. 1:18; 3:10–12). A person cannot live a life dependent upon God while simultaneously suppressing the truth about Him. When a person refuses to live in obedience to God, that person will become dependent upon fulfilling his or her own desires, even if they are sinful and destructive ones. A fallen person will feel conflicted. On the one hand, the person was created to worship God, yet on the other hand, in giving into sinful desires the person is actively rejecting worshiping God. When this is the case, the non-Christian is caught up in self-worship and personal comfort. This futile search for pleasure apart from Christ is what controls the unregenerate man or woman.

I once evangelized a heroin addict who told me that the reason he still took heroin was because his life was consumed with the quest to replicate the feeling he had the first time he got high—seventeen years before I met him. This illusive pleasure became his idol, and he was consumed by the chase. This pursuit became enslavement, and this enslavement became addiction. Because this man did not think true joy could come from the God who created him, he had wasted seventeen years of his life pursuing a god of pleasure. The addict believes the lie that there is something in the world that satisfies more than God does. This is the same lie that Eve encountered in the garden of Eden, and it is a lie that makes the addict a self-worshipper, an idolater, and—ironically—unable to worship the only One who can bring actual joy and meaning to life. As the addiction elbows God out of the addict's life, the person becomes consumed by the sinful quest for satisfaction, and believes Satan's lie that God is not all-satisfying. This is the lie that perpetuates the thinking of the addicted.

God created people to worship Him, and when they refuse to worship God, they will turn their focus to something else. In this way, addicts are like every other kind of sinner; they have rejected God and are serving something else instead. For the addict though, this pursuit becomes focused on a powerful, consuming, and usually self-destructive behavior. This is worship gone awry, and instead of producing satisfaction it enslaves the addict.

ADDICTION AS SELF-DESTRUCTIVE SLAVERY

Addiction can make genuine repentance seem impossible. I have worked with individuals who would be in my office sobbing and broken over how far they are from God, how they have abused their families, and how they have disgraced the church. Yet often as soon as our appointment is done, they leave my office and before they have even left the church parking lot I can see them doing drugs again. The addict often underestimates the power of enslavement to sin. The addict thinks that the habit can be broken when in reality the habit has already broken the person.

One of the reasons that these sins are so destructive is that they cause addicts to focus on a desire for short-term gratification. The addict wants to feel good immediately. When a person is so focused on the short term and on the ethereal success provided by an emotion or brief experience, that person is willing to do things that in the long run will be destructive. A drug addict is not concerned about how his immediate actions will affect his job tomorrow. The addict is captivated by the moment. This is why the analogy of slavery is so apt. The vice has consumed the user, and the user seems to have forfeited his own will. The addict's actions give truth to the common expression "It is not him, but the drugs." When an addict is ruled by desire to the extent that the person will sacrifice family, employment, friends, and even ignore personal conscience, the power of the addict's sin is manifest.

Drugs, alcohol, sexual desires, and other similar life-dominating sins do not make for good masters. They exploit the sinner. They seize on these facts:

1. People were made to worship God, but rejecting God causes a person to replace Him with something else.
2. When a person replaces the worship of God with the pursuit of pleasure in something else, the replacement is unable to deliver.
3. Nevertheless, the more a person pursues pleasure from a specific vice,

the more dependent the person becomes upon that brief feeling of joy, satisfaction, contentment, or accomplishment.

4. This dependency is a form of both worship and slavery.

Second Peter 2:19 (ESV) provides a portrait of this enslavement: "for whatever overcomes a person, to that he is enslaved." As the person serves his addiction, his life becomes dominated by sin, and sin invariably brings with it destructive results. The wages of sin is death, and addictions not only pay their wage, but addictions blind the person to the form of payment. In the meantime, the addict's life is destroyed, friends are lost, and the person feels trapped in a cycle of hopelessness.

People who are battling these kinds of sins often live in a world of guilt and shame. Drugs, alcohol, or whatever their vice is can function as their escape, and this perpetuates the cycle. Rather than facing their problems biblically, they turn to a sinful outlet for peace. This action brings with it guilt, and to deal with that guilt they are thrust back into the same sin. As the cycle continues, life spins out of control; God is forgotten, and they are suddenly enslaved and feel hopeless. At the heart of the issue is a lack of trust in God. Addicts do not believe that God alone can bring them peace.

In some cases addicts are motivated by a fear of failure, and drugs numb the pain of past disappointments. In addition, patterns and habits are formed so that they cling to their habit even when the behavior does not bring any pleasure or relief, even when it actually brings pain and distress. They feel like they are in bondage because they believe they have no freedom to do anything else. Moreover, this bondage is compounded by the fact that addicts often do not even see themselves as having a problem. They can become so blinded by their desires that they cannot see their lives falling apart around them. Sometimes they are even in denial as to the extent of their enslavement to sin. They may ask for help, they may make professions of faith perhaps even with good and noble intentions, but as soon as their desires return, so does their slavery. This can give a sense of hopelessness not just to those enslaved, but also to those around them. It is as if nothing can free the addict from the bonds of sin and shame.

Hope Found Only in the Gospel

The ultimate source of addiction is not in the substance itself, but in the heart of the person. When a person makes the decision to use a drug or act habitually, that person demonstrates that the addiction flows from within not from without. This is why only the gospel can offer hope, as only the gospel can transform the heart, which then transforms desires. Without this change there can be no lasting freedom from sins' enslavement.

It is our opinion that if a person puts his trust in medical sources or therapy for freedom from addiction—or if he labels the behavior a disease—that person's hope is actually diminished. Diseases have sources that are physical (such as genetics or infection) and can be treated with physical treatments. If the cause is physical, the treatment can be physical. But with addiction, if the source is the heart's desire to rebel against God, then only spiritual means provide true and lasting hope.

Ultimately, simply conquering addiction is not the goal. It is possible for a person to go through a secular program, find accountability in a group structure, or have a change of fortune in life such that addiction can be controlled. But if that happens without the gospel, the person may be clean from drugs yet remain an enemy of God.

The evangelist who deals with a person enslaved to life-dominating sin has the important and difficult task of discovering the addict's internal situation. What is going on in the person's life? What is the addict thinking? What does the person not like about what God is doing? What are the problems or pressures that the addict is facing in daily life? What does the person want from God, from life, or from others? Asking these kinds of questions may help reveal what the person actually worships. It will also probably show that the person has an inaccurate view of self; the addict might expect better things and treatment than what the person currently receives. Because the person does not understand the sin—or God's holiness—the addict does not realize that he deserves hell. This inflated view of self drives a person to pursue satisfaction through idols that can dominate his life.

The truth is that Jesus came to be the Savior of sinners. Because the gospel alone can take a heart from loving sin and hating God, to loving God and hating sin, it can provide salvation for even the most desperate of people. When

Jesus said, "It is not those who are healthy who need a physician, but those who are sick" (Matt. 9:12 NAS), He was actually giving good news to those enslaved by life-dominating sins. Jesus did not come to earth to save normal people with good lives and a hopeful future. He came to earth to find the rejected, the sick, the suffering, and those with serious issues. He came to seek and save the lost, and perhaps nobody is more lost than an addict.

EVANGELISM AND ADDICTS

So how do you bring the gospel to a person who is enslaved in this way? First, understand that for a person to truly repent from sin and trust the gospel, enslavement to sin must be acknowledged. The addict must come to terms with the fact that his life is being spent in the pursuit of sinful pleasures. The person must see that the very sin that is being pursued is unable to provide lasting satisfaction. If the evangelist can show the nonbeliever how he is pursuing sinful desires, and how that pursuit is an offense to a holy God, then the person is more likely to express genuine repentance rather than merely guilt.

Evangelists are in the business of convincing the enslaved to see how destructive the pleasures of the world are, and how glorious the glory of God in the gospel is. For example, Paul describes those who spend their lives pursuing these dominating sins as those "whose end is destruction, whose god is their appetite, and whose glory is in their shame, who set their minds on earthly things" (Phil. 3:19 NASB). They have been trained to satisfy themselves without any thought to the consequences of their actions in general, or their eternity in particular. The here and now, the pleasures of this world, and the search for joy—these are what enslaves the addict.

But here is where evangelism to addicts is perhaps even easier than presenting the gospel to an ordinary sinner. Your average non-Christian may be under the illusion that the person's life is together, and therefore the non-Chrisitan may not be interested in hearing about the Savior from sin. The addict generally does not fall into this category. While there are many addicts who refuse to see how their lives have fallen apart, this is not always the case. Some addicts have hit bottom, and have lost all they have ever trusted in. Their jobs, families, and friends are all gone. When this happens, oftentimes people are able to recognize that their lives are falling apart, and feel helpless in the face of their sin.

If the Christian can point them to the consequences of continued obedience to sinful desires, addicts can be warned about the destruction that awaits. By showing the judgment that God will bring to those who reject His will and insist on living for sin, the evangelist can warn addicts of judgment.

John 3:36*b* (NASB) says, "He who does not obey the Son will not see life, but the wrath of God abides on him." To many people, this verse might seem impossibly extreme and excessively harsh. But to the addict, the concept of powerful judgment for sin can seem possible and even reasonable. When a person has firsthand knowledge of the destruction and evil that sin can bring into a life, the severe judgment of God on sin suddenly does not seem far-fetched. Often, the addict is prepared to realize that there are eternal consequences to sin, and especially to the particular sin that is enslaving the person. This recognition can prepare the person to receive the good news of the gospel.

Judgment for sin seems reasonable and the opportunity for salvation seems precious if the person realizes humanity's enslavement to sin. This is why a clear presentation of the gospel is essential. When a person realizes that there is no hope in this life, then the person will understand that the person's life is spiritually dead.

The situation of the addict must be examined in order to truly help the person overcome the various temptations that will present themselves. Therefore, ask questions to learn about the nature of the person's sin. What is going on in the person's life? What are the family dynamics, job issues, and church relationships that are perhaps weighing the addict down? Is there anything in the person's life that he or she is trying to avoid? Check to see what false beliefs the addict has about God. Does the person live differently around friends than around strangers? Does the addict believe in the omniscience of God? Does the addict care about God at all?

People generally believe that they are better off than they really are. By explaining to the person how addiction is a form of slavery to sin, the bridge can be built to explain the gospel. Highlight the fact that Jesus died to set addicts free, and He rose from the grave because He defeated death. If He has power over death, then He certainly has power over the sins that hold people captive. If the sinner feels hopeless and helpless, explain how the gospel is the only thing in the world that can give lasting hope to the truly helpless. Reiterate that

Jesus calls the sinful to Himself, and help the person understand that the gospel changes lives. Ask the person to forsake sin and embrace belief in the gospel, even if it means fleeing from sin and the person's former life. Challenge the addict to see the holistic claims the gospel makes on a sinner's life.

The call to conquer a life-dominating sin is not a prerequisite for belief in the gospel. The Scriptures do not tell those who are mastered by sin to fight sin on their own power. It is not as if a sin must be defeated, temptation ignored, and habits broken before the gospel can be believed. In fact, the opposite is true; belief in the gospel provides the power and motivation to fight sin. Self-control is a fruit of belief, not the other way around. People can be encouraged that they do not have to be perfect to be a Christian; rather people just have to hate the sin, and believe that Jesus died and rose again to free individuals from the power of it.

The evangelist must be careful not to downplay the gravity of sin while also not preaching a works-based salvation. This balance is achieved by prayer, and by dependence on scriptural phrases in evangelism. Stress that the gospel justifies the ungodly (Rom. 4:5) because Christ came to save even the worst of sinners (1 Tim. 1:15). At the same time, it is good to count the cost of coming to Christ (Luke 14:28) because it requires fleeing the idolatry of this world (1 Cor. 10:14). In some sense this is the tension inherent in all evangelism: the gospel is free, but it will cost you everything (Matt. 10:38; 11:30). The presence of life-dominating sins merely makes this tension more acute and obvious.

Sinners can find hope, and a relationship with God can be restored through the power of the gospel. One of the many reasons an individual is languishing under the weight of sin is because the person does not know God, and access to God has been cut off through the power of sin. But when Jesus came to earth, He came to suffer for the sins of the unrighteous so that He might bring them back to God (1 Peter 3:18). When a person is not saved, that individual is fighting sin alone, and is doomed to failure. But in Christ, the power of prayer and hope of sanctification can give newfound life to the fight against sin.

Remember, when the evangelist calls someone to faith in Christ, he is actually calling the person to a new life, with new hope, new power, and the reality of becoming a new creation.

Post-Conversion

The repentant addict needs to understand the dynamic of the idol relationship. The addict must realize that addiction was in reality a worship problem, and as a new believer the individual needs to be actively turning away from the former things the person used to cling to as idols. (Leviticus 19:4 and Deuteronomy 11:16 explain this as it relates to actual wooden idols.) The newly converted must repent at the level of the heart and the mind. The person must confess all transgressions. The person must take responsibility for daily renewal through prayer and Scripture. The individual must consciously take every thought and imagination captive (2 Cor. 10:5). Titus 2:12 (NASB) commands the believer to "deny ungodliness and worldly desires." When the addict feels the urge or imagines former sin, the person must turn to the Word of God for encouragement and hope in the battle against the flesh and the former self.

More than likely, the person will have to deal with idolatry in other areas of life beyond what might have been apparent at first. In other words, there will be a need for a total life restructuring. The addict must begin a process of life renewal through new thinking so that the previous life-dominating sin does not recur in the heart. First Corinthians 6:12 tells the believer not to be mastered by anything. Sin is to be recognized as a robber of joy, happiness, comfort, peace, and sanity. In the life of the new believer, sin is seen as an intruder—as a thief who has broken into a house that is no longer belongs to the person.

The new believer must understand that permanent change is a twofold process of letting go of the habits and of thinking about the former life and picking up new ways of thinking that now can give glory to God (Eph. 4:22–24). There is a time of training that must occur for the new believer as the person learns about godliness (1 Tim. 4:7b–8). At the point of the temptation, new believers need to remind themselves that they are now set apart for godly purposes, and are no longer mastered by sin.

There is a certain ritual that has been formulated in those enslaved, and this is where the danger of sin is most closely lurking. A new believer will be afraid of falling back into addiction if set behaviors, attitudes, and patterns remain the same. These habits can make avoiding sin seem impossible. Proverbs 7:8 revels that proximity brings temptation: "Passing along the street near her corner; / And he took the path to her house." If someone's job or routine takes them near the center of temptation, get a map and help the person find new ways of going from home to work or to run errands. You must explain to someone the kind of changes needed to avoid temptation.

The newly saved addict must be willing to undergo radical amputation and deal harshly with sin by implementing a new approach to the trials of life (Matt. 5:29–30). There needs to be a total life restructuring. Because of the previous lifestyle there are probably many people that the person stole from or hurt in significant ways, and restitution should be made, if at all possible. Meanwhile, the things that were initiators of sin need to be put away. Some friendships will be dangerous to maintain because of the temptation that may go with them. A drug user, alcoholic, sex addict, and gambler might need to give up friends or places that would remind the person of his involvement with the substance or activity. First Corinthians 15:33 reminds us that "bad company corrupts good morals." Other friendships might provide fertile soil for evangelism. All of this should be explained and approached with prayer and wisdom.

Any new convert should be involved in the local church ministry but those previously enslaved by life-dominating sins must be accountable to fellowship in the local church in a particular way (Gal. 6:1–2). The good news is that addictions do not just happen. They are the product of desires and affections that stimulate imaginations and lusts. Thus they can be fought with new desires and new affections. Because the nature of their old sin is idolatry, in Christ addicts have hope because now, for the first time, their worship is rightly placed on the God who created them.

Romans 6:16–19 presents a clear picture of how life-dominating lusts are changed in Christ. Because of the work of Jesus Christ in salvation, the indwelling power of the Holy Spirit, and the work of the God, those who were once slaves to sin are now to be slaves of Christ. Romans 6:22 says, "But now having been freed from sin and enslaved to God, you derive your benefit, resulting in sanctification, and the outcome, eternal life." The Scriptures give such wonderful encouragement because they present God as one who is there to help overcome the various lusts or desires that cause people to sin.

Colossians 3:5 describes believers as those dead to the sins of "immorality, impurity, passion, evil desire, and greed." This is a past-tense experience for the true believer. The Bible understands enslavement to sin but by the power of the Holy Spirit and the truth of the gospel, enslavements or addictions can be overcome. This is the hope that the evangelist has to bring to those enslaved. It is not a flippant call to change, but it is an earnest offer for the person enslaved to be reconciled to God, to avoid hell, and to escape the snare of sin. It will not be easy, but it is the path to eternal life and lasting change.

18

When the Nations Come to Us: A Mandate for Immigrant Outreach

Michael Mahoney

The past decade has brought a change to missions through shifting world immigration. As immigrants flood to nations with a strong Christian witness, there is the potential to train an army of native missionaries by reaching out to this group. No longer is missions limited to sending people to a foreign land, because in many places the nations are coming to us. This chapter will help pastors think through how to best seize this new opportunity for global evangelization.

"Young man, sit down, sit down! You're an enthusiast. When God pleases to convert the heathen, he will do it without consulting you or me."[1] These were the words that William Carey heard after he proposed that Christ's command to "go into all the world" was still binding on the church. But the hyper-Calvinism that was rampant in the Baptist churches of England during the eighteenth century was not the only obstacle that Carey faced before he could make it to India.

Before there were hundreds of missions organizations, before churches had outreach committees and thumbtacked wall maps in the hallways, and before churches would hear from missionaries on furlough from all over the planet,

Carey was trying to figure out how a very poor village boy could raise the necessary support to go halfway across the world as a missionary.

Carey's solution was a pamphlet, the *Enquiry*, that eventually convinced churches to partner with him in what had never been done in missions history: they worked together to help small churches raise a seemingly impossible amount of money to send a missionary around the world.[2]

But Carey and his partner, John Thomas, had no idea that another seemingly impossible task was still in front of them. While raising the money and determining where to go was one thing, it was quite another to actually be able to find the means of getting there. The East India Company did not allow any Europeans to set foot on Indian soil without special licenses, which would be impossible for adventurous Baptist missionaries to obtain.

They got the idea of going as stowaways on a ship captained by a friend of Thomas. The captain agreed, but moments before they were supposed to leave, he received a letter informing him of legal consequences of his plan. With tear-filled eyes, Carey watched as the prospect of being a missionary literally sailed into the distance.

Eventually, they found a Danish ship willing to take them on board. With the confidence of the captain's protection of the missionaries, Carey's dreams of finally reaching the lost and dying world with the gospel seemed to be finally coming true.

But the problems did not stop once Carey and his family stepped on board the *Krön Princessa*. Carey and Thomas found themselves embarking on a dangerous five-month voyage. They were hit by severe currents that took them across to the Brazilian coast; then they traveled back around Africa where a midnight storm almost capsized the entire vessel. It took eleven days to repair the battered ship in order to finally make it to the Indian port of Bengal.[3]

When all of the delays are added up, it took Carey nearly ten years to find partner churches and to raise the funds to go to India, two more years to find a way to get there, and then more than five months to actually do so.

Today a person can get from London to any country in the world in twenty-four hours. This is not to say that missionaries do not still face significant obstacles. Rather, what has revolutionized missions in the last century has not merely been the feasibility of world travel. What has changed the whole approach to global evangelism is that now, along with sending William Careys to the nations, the nations are coming to us.

This change radically affects our approach to missions. With urban hubs world-wide flooded with immigrants, the world's demographics are shifting. While immigration certainly existed before, what makes today's trend different is the frequency in which it occurs. People can come from around the world to work, and they can travel home several times a year. The reality is that if an immigrant is saved and becomes part of a strong biblical church, that person becomes a practical missionary. As they are discipled and trained, they do so with the possibility of returning home, and being able to share the gospel with his friends and family members.

The possibilities for world evangelism that are connected to this influx of immigration demand an urgent and passionate response to reach those who live in the cities where we minister. No longer is it possible for us to think of missions as only an overseas extension of our church. It is now imperative that the heart of the church beat strongly in order to reach those whom God has placed within the radius of our church and influence regardless of the ethnic background of the community.

However, because many new immigrants have minimal English skills, it is unreasonable to expect a non-English speaker to attend an English-language service.[4] Thus, in addition to equipping our people for evangelism, pastors should be on the lookout for opportunities to start outreaches and even churches that target non-English speakers. This is an approach that for many people might seem novel, or even unnecessary. But the reality is that the potential fruit from this kind of ministry is simply too great to neglect. The nations are coming to us, and if we respond evangelistically, we have the opportunity to create a generation of missionaries who speak the language and are fully funded, ready to go back to the their own countries with the gospel.

Since its inception, the church has wrestled with how to fulfill its task of global evangelism. As early as AD 115, Ignatius of Antioch records how the early church was strategizing to send missionaries throughout the world.[5] It is clear in his correspondence that the issue of global evangelization had gripped the attention of the early church. Ignatius's hometown, Antioch, is where the followers of Jesus Christ were first called "Christians" (Acts 11:26). It is fitting that in the second century the continual struggle to take the gospel to all nations was focused there.

The struggle that the church faced came from Jewish Christians who wanted to keep Jewish and Gentile believers separate from each other. Paul, who became embroiled in the struggle, wrote his epistle to the Galatians from Antioch, where this problem had a serious impact on the church.[5] When Peter first came to Antioch he gladly accepted the Gentiles, even going as far as to eat with them. But when legalists from Jerusalem arrived, Peter became intimidated and pulled back from his acceptance of the Gentile believers. The apostle Paul then confronted Peter "to his face" for this compromise (Gal. 2:11). No amount of intimidation should have moved Peter to withdraw his acceptance of the Gentile Christians. This poignant encounter foreshadowed the struggles that the church would continue to have as it grappled with the reality of the Great Commission.

Just as Paul, Peter, and Ignatius were challenged by how the church should embrace the task of reaching all nations with the gospel, we who follow after them find ourselves engaged in an equally gripping challenge of how we can effectively fulfill the Great Commission today.

In Peter's day, the issue was how Jews should reach Gentiles. In Carey's day, the issue was if those in the West should evangelize the East. In our day, a new twist is how Christians in the United States should evangelize those who come to us. The mission field has arrived at our door, and is in need of our serious attention.

In Los Angeles alone the statistics are staggering. According to the 2000 U.S. Census Bureau, 58 percent of Los Angeles speaks a language other than English. Ten percent of Los Angeles residents were born in Asia. In the zip code where Grace Community Church is, there are forty different languages listed as being the primary language spoken in the home. In the United States as a whole, those figures are lower but still noticeable; 18 percent of the population speaks a language other than English in the home. This new facet of missions is a reality and the church must understand its implications.

THE CHALLENGE IS CLEAR AND THE NEED IS GREAT

It used to be only a small number of Christians who felt called to leave everything and go to another country, learn another language, adopt another culture, and bring the gospel to a foreign people. But today, the call to evangelize the world has suddenly left the realm of the romantic, and is now tangible for nearly all American Christians.

One response to this increased opportunity is for churches to start particular ministries aimed at reaching people in a nonnative language. These groups should be conducted in the primary language of the target audience. They should be evangelistic, with the aim of bringing the gospel to people who do not speak English, calling them to faith, discipling them, and then using them to reach their own families and even their own countrymen.

Before developing the concept of immigrant outreach further, I want to give a disclaimer: I am not advocating that churches exclude people of other cultural backgrounds. The church should be made up of people from different cultures, languages, and nations (see Acts 2). God's heart is clearly for the nations to be united through the church (see Matt. 28:19–20; Rev. 21:24). The more diverse a church is, the more God receives glory, because the gospel is the cause of unity in Christ. In diversity the transcendent nature of the gospel is manifest.

While a church that targets a specific culture certainly shows a lack of understanding of the power of the gospel, a church that neglects opportunities to reach different language groups—especially when those groups are in its own backyard—shows a failure to realize the potential of this opportunity. There are practical implications related to language ability. Because faith comes by hearing the gospel, a person who does not speak the language of the messenger cannot believe the message. The influx of non-English speakers necessitates a concerted effort from churches to reach out to the different language groups that surround us. If we fail to do so, we are not fulfilling the Great Commission.

PREPARATION FOR THE MISSION

In order to run this kind of language-specific ministry well, a deliberate approach from the leadership of the church is essential. The church must have the right man to lead this ministry. He must be fluent in the language of the group he wants to reach, as well as able to communicate clearly with the church's other elders. If he is successful, and people are won to Christ, he will be viewed as their pastor.

A ministry directed toward specific language or ethnic groups will only be as strong as the spiritual leaders that oversee it. If you are considering one of these ministries, it is wise to take heed to the admonitions given by Paul to Titus and Timothy regarding well-qualified leaders within the church. One point that is particularly important for ethnic ministry is the admonition to find a leader who is well respected within the church. If the leader does not have credibility within the existing English-language church, it will doom the feasibility of any outreach.

Essentially, this chapter is an appeal for pastors to find qualified men in their congregation who are bilingual and use them for this kind of outreach. If there is a new believer who is bilingual, disciple him with the goal of having him be able to reach others in his own language. The leader of the immigrant ministry should not be alone in this task; it will be the responsibility of the rest of the church leadership to show solidarity in supporting the new work. Sometimes this may even involve teaching the English-speaking members the importance of the Great Commission to their local community. But before any outreach to another immigrant group can be successful, there are essential qualities that must be its foundation.

Churchwide Support

Prior to starting an immigrant ministry, the senior pastor and church leadership must be solidly behind it. It will be their responsibility to educate the rest of the church members on the needs of the community, and to provide continued encouragement and vision. This kind of outreach will never be effective without support from the church leadership. The senior pastor must be the catalyst that allows the people of God to fulfill the mission of God in reaching the community for Christ. If the pastor takes ownership of this new work, the people will understand its importance. A church that is passionate in its outreach will have a leadership that models that strong commitment to evangelism.

From the staff to the congregation, every part of a church must work at building relationships with the immigrant community. The church body must accept and embrace this new outreach. If the English-language church is not supportive of the work, division will certainly enter into the body. It would be devastating to a church to have new believers come to Christ but never be treated with respect or a sense of brotherhood from the rest of the congregation.

Alex Montoya, a professor for church planting at The Master's Seminary, compared this effort to an organ transplant: "As in any transplant, unless the body is willing to accept the organ, all is lost."[7] Responsibility for the immigrant ministry cannot be delegated to a select few. The entire congregation must be moved to become involved in evangelizing the mission field that is at their doorstep. All church members, regardless of their language ability, should be enthusiastic about this endeavor.

Prayer

In any endeavor to start an evangelistic outreach, one must remember that only God can bless the work. Prayer must always undergird the ministry, and the entire body must demonstrate the seriousness of such a work. An effective ministry to internationals does not happen by accident. People involved with the ministry must be united when asking God to bring the growth of such a work. C. H. Spurgeon gives us a pertinent reminder of the importance of prayer: "I know of no better thermometer to your spiritual temperature than this, the measure of the intensity of your prayer."[8] The prayer support for such an outreach must be emphasized and continually strengthened.

Theology

The English-speaking church and the immigrant congregation must share the same theology and even the same statement of faith. The pastor and leaders of the new ministry must be responsible for overseeing the translation of the church's doctrinal statement into the language of the group you are evangelizing. This is important because having the same doctrinal statement further confirms the unity of the English speaking and non-English speaking ministry. This reinforces the doctrinal standard of the church and avoids any surprises in the teaching ministry. It also sets in place the basis for teaching church discipline, women's place in ministry, and so on.

Method of the Mission

When the church recognizes the need for outreach to immigrant communities, has qualified leadership, and realizes the desire to respond to the need, the primary task of the leadership is to put together a workable plan. This plan needs to approach the method (consider Bible study, outreach events, translation of Sunday messages, or a parallel church service). Basic questions about philosophy should be addressed at this stage. There are a number of options to explore, and there is not just one solution. Below are a few of the key options the church leadership should consider as they tackle the challenge of setting up an immigrant ministry.

Separate Worship Services

The most obvious—and also most complex—approach to this kind of outreach is to have two separate services within the same church. This is probably the most common approach to reaching another language group, but it does have its drawbacks. Be aware that having separate worship services can produce the feeling that two churches are meeting in the same facility.[9]

If a church does decide to do two worship services in different languages, the more similarities that overlap between the ministries, the better. For example, the pastors and elders of both ministries should serve on the same elder board. The members of both groups should be members of the same church. The finances should be pooled. All this helps prevent the "two church" feeling.

There are some other potential pitfalls as well. If the new outreach is relegated to an inferior facility or a less than ideal time slot, do not expect it to work. Stories of failed attempts at immigrant outreaches abound because of this error. I heard of a church that tried to start a Thai ministry in their basement, with no air conditioning, at 1:00 in the afternoon. The final straw came when the church asked the Thai ministry to cancel for a week because it needed to use the basement to store supplies for a youth camp the following week. Obviously, if a church's approach to launching a language-outreach program gives the new work a sense of inferiority, it quickly becomes demeaning and the work becomes hopeless.

Bible Studies

An easier and less intensive approach is to have a foreign-language Bible study. Rather than initiating a full church service, starting a small meeting led by an elder or teacher who teaches the Bible evangelistically is a viable solution. At Grace Community Church we currently have nine different Bible studies for internationals taught in the various languages of the attendees. Many of these members also attend the Sunday morning service conducted in English. Though this may be more difficult for them, they have the comfort of being taught later in the week in their own language.

A Bible study is probably the most practical starting point for most immigrant ministries. Many ministries have neither enough people nor the leadership to handle a full-blown foreign-language worship service.

POTENTIAL PITFALLS

As in any church, there are dangers and hazards to be avoided. These same snares exist when establishing your immigrant ministry, Bible study, or church. Just because your church may be sound and have good leadership does not mean that these dangers go away. If anything, they become more noticeable and the consequences and aftermath more tragic.

Financial Questions

We know that our offering belongs to God, but when the offering plates have been collected where does the money go? Does it go to the whole church, or should it stay within the ministry that collected it? A potential source of conflict with this kind of ministry is the idea of financial dependence. If the goal of the offering is to supply the needs of both the English and non-English speaking congregations, then it is usually best to pool all of the money together. Money given by anyone in the church should go to the ministry of the entire church, which includes both language groups.

This is where having unity between the leadership of the immigrant ministry and the English language church is crucial. It helps to ensure that the needs of the non-English language ministry are clearly represented and that they are not relegated to a second-rate status. The budget of the new ministry should be submitted to the eldership and approved as other ministries within the church.

Offerings from the immigrant ministry can go toward this budget, but especially in its infancy, the English speaking congregation must supplement where there is need.

Music Style

Of course, music can be a source of contention in any church, but it is important to remember that just as English language ministries have preferences in types and forms of music, so do non-English language ministries. It is important that the English language ministry does not attempt to impose its preferences upon the immigrant ministry. If you have put qualified elders and leaders in place, give them the autonomy to make decisions based upon the likes and dislikes of their audience, and be slow to criticize.

It must always be remembered that the content is far more important than style. Styles will come and go. Even styles within the same ethnic community will vary, but content should always drive the music ministry so that it correctly undergirds the preaching of the Word of God. Communication of biblical truth that motivates people to worship God is what is most important. When a style becomes the focus that drives a ministry, it can easily undermine the commitment to the high standard of the proclamation of biblical truth.

Prejudice

People are inherently egocentric. In this age of political correctness, it is easy to assume that we are above bigotry, but often this is simply not the case. Unfortunately, even Christians find themselves succumbing to this sin. There is a great need to apply Paul's words found in Galatians 3:28: "There is neither Jew nor Greek, there is neither slave nor free, there is neither male nor female; for you are all one in Christ Jesus."

Illegal immigrants, for example, have been the recipients of a great deal of hatred. There is heated debate in many countries about how churches should respond to this issue. Be careful that your church is not divided over this issue. If you are starting an immigrant ministry, be prepared to have an answer to this problem. Recently, the pastoral staff of Grace Community Church addressed this issue in desiring to pastor a growing number of those who are struggling through their immigration status.[10] It is pertinent that your church's leadership answer those who, out of prejudice or politics, want to keep illegal immigrants out of the church, as well as those who have reasonable questions about how someone's citizenship status relates to the church's relationship with government authorities.

The pastor and leadership must not only show solidarity with the immigrant ministry and its leadership but also subtly begin reinforcing the biblical truth that we are all created in the image of God, and there should be no distinction between ethnicities. Understand that in some localities you and your leadership may become unpopular for associating with particular immigrant communities, but do not let this deter you from your God-ordained mission to preach the gospel to all men, slave or free, illegal or legal.

Unrealistic Expectations

Language-based ministry can be more difficult than many people realize. Many immigrants come from countries where their religion is tied up with their nationality. The idea of coming to a church that is not the religion of their home country is too radical for some people to even entertain. Success should be measured in terms of years, not months. It can take years to develop a reputation as a church that actually does care about immigrants. For this reason, patience is absolutely necessary. Create expectations that are both biblical and agreed upon by the leadership of the immigrant ministry. Do not focus on "numbers" but emphasize the quality of the ministry that is being provided.

The most important reminder that can be given is to follow the instruction found in Ephesians 5:1–2, "Therefore be imitators of God as dear children. And walk in love, as Christ also has loved us and given Himself for us, an offering and a sacrifice to God for a sweet-smelling aroma." With this being the goal of your leadership, every one of the pitfalls above can be avoided. It will take diligent effort, and it will not be without obstacles. But by the grace of God you can accomplish this vital task.

DEALING WITH SUCCESS

If you are starting a ministry to internationals in your church, and it begins to grow, you may soon realize that your existing church leadership will not have sufficient time (and often language skills) to handle bulletins, picnics, culture-specific events, and even some of the counseling. At this point you will be faced with adding to the leadership of the immigrant ministry. The question then becomes how best to do it?

The purpose of launching a ministry to internationals must always be at the forefront: it is for the growth of the body of Christ. Unless you desire for it to become an entirely different church, it is best not to have a separate group of elders and leaders. Instead, the immigrant ministry should be encouraged to develop the gifts of its members and allow them to begin functioning in some of those roles. If a particular member of the new ministry stands out as exceptionally gifted, focus on him, and train him up with the goal of adding him to the church's elder board.

If this outreach attracts bilingual people to the church, allow them to choose which service or ministry to attend. Do not feel threatened if some decide to attend the English language service. At the same time, by developing the gifts of your non-English speaking members, you allow them to fulfill their biblical command to serve the church, and by having more elders you will have increased accountability between the non-English language ministry and the English language ministry.

God's plan has always been to take the gospel to all nations. In the Old Testament, it is made clear that God's heart was to extend the worship of God to the world. Deuteronomy 32:43 states, "Rejoice, O Gentiles, with His people." Psalm 117:1 reveals his plan clearly: "Praise the LORD, all you Gentiles! / Laud Him, all you peoples!"

The New Testament continues this clear indication that the heart of God is to reach all nations with the good news of Jesus Christ (Gal. 3:28). Paul also highlights that in Christ we now know "the mystery of His will, according to His good pleasure which He purposed in Himself, that in the dispensation of the fullness of the times He might gather together in one all things in Christ" (Eph. 1:9–10). The significance of the Great Commission is woven throughout the fabric of Scripture. The church cannot waver in her unyielding pursuit of continuing the mandate of reaching the world for Christ.

In Acts 1:8, God gives us the power to fulfill His call to reach the world with the gospel: "But you shall receive power when the Holy Spirit has come upon you; and you shall be witnesses to Me in Jerusalem, and in all Judea and Samaria, and to the end of the earth." The divine program is clear, and we must realize that the end of the earth has come to us, and immigrants from other nations are at our doorstep.

In the desire to fulfill the Great Commission, we need a demonstration of the Spirit's presence in our lives that produces a passionate and ardent zeal to reach every immigrant community within the realm of our ministry. We need a fervent dedication and an earnest longing for God to reach our world for Christ. Nothing else will so transform a church, give it vision, and strengthen its resolve as a determined plan of action to reach the immigrant community that God has brought within the reach of your own church. Being an integral part of fulfilling the call of God to reach all nations not only extends God's glory to the farthest reaches of the globe but also to the nations that are right at our doorstep.

19

To the Least of These: Ministry to the Social Outcast

Mark Tatlock

There is a tendency in many churches to perceive evangelizing the lost as being in conflict with acts of compassion and mercy toward the poor. The fact that many churches with good theology eschew mercy ministry is the result of historical coincidences and not biblical motives. The Bible makes compassion to the poor an essential part of Christianity, and to neglect it is to sin gravely against the Lord. Compassion is modeled in Jesus, commanded by James, and evidenced in the truth of the gospel.

For some reason, many Christians view ministry to the needy and evangelism as competing expressions of love to the lost. American evangelicalism has allowed a stereotype to exist that churches that focus on ministry toward the poor must somehow be neglecting gospel preaching, and vice versa. But this could not be farther from the biblical model, where mercy ministry is inextricably linked to gospel preaching. If Christians have been recipients of God's extensive compassion and mercy, then they should be first to demonstrate compassion and mercy toward others. In so doing, they provide an example of the greater spiritual reality of God's heart and His willingness to extend mercy and compassion through the redemption that they themselves have already received.

For evangelism to be taken seriously in a community, it is essential that it be connected to the testimony of changed lives. If one has experienced the mercy of God, it is necessary in a discussion of evangelism to include a proper view of mercy ministries. When people in the church repent from worldliness and selfishness, they put on contentment with God and mercy toward others. This sanctification is a public proclamation of the veracity of the gospel. Unfortunately, in the contemporary evangelical American church a great debate has arisen as to the legitimacy of mercy ministries as a part of the church's witness.

A Historical Perspective on Mercy Ministry

In 1907 Walter Rauschenbusch, a professor of Christian history at Rochester Theological Seminary, authored the influential book *Christianity and the Social Crisis*.[1] As a proponent of the widely accepted postmillennial ethos of turn-of-the-century America, Rauschenbusch held that improving social conditions in the world was an essential part of the soon-to-be-realized kingdom of God on earth. While the country was experiencing all of the social challenges of increased immigration, industrialization, and urban growth, the mainline denominations were caught up in the spirit of the day, believing that science and technology promised the betterment of society through efficiency and progress. Meanwhile, the promise of a more civil society stood in sharp contrast to the realities of the staggering numbers of orphans, widows, prisoners, and the sick who were the labor force behind such progress.

Having ministered in the Hell's Kitchen neighborhood of Manhattan, Rauschenbusch knew well the plight of the poor. He had worked tirelessly to extend ministry on their behalf through his church. This commitment to care for the poor gave hope for the future in the hermeneutically inadequate propositions of postmillennialism. With World War I still over the horizon, mainline Protestants were eager to embrace the promise that God's kingdom could be realized, not in a future eternity, but fully and completely in the present. These denominations were becoming more and more focused on social issues, and Rauschenbusch's book became the bridge that successfully fused the concept of mercy ministry with the increasingly liberal theology of denominations that were focused on social change, rather than upon gospel preaching.[2] This theology came to be known as the Social Gospel and was the product of the growing acceptance of postmillennialism at that time. The Social Gospel applied the language of redemption to acts of kindness, and it gave them soteriological implications. In this movement, the gospel became more about fighting poverty as a means to usher in the kingdom than it was about individual's salvation through Christ.[3]

While many conservative Christians during this era worked tirelessly on behalf of the poor, the eventual association of mercy ministry with liberal mainline denominations began to cause mercy ministry to be questioned as having any legitimate part within the fundamentalist church. The Social Gospel became the antithesis of sound biblical evangelistic practices, promising that redemption should be understand not only in personal salvific terms, but in social and structural terms as well.[4] The language of the kingdom took on different meanings for different Protestants, and the hostility directed by conservatives toward liberals came eventually to prevent the conservative church from maintaining social outreach as part of its ecclesiological framework.

Matters in the secular world influenced this divide as well. When President Franklin D. Roosevelt implemented an era of increased government participation in civic life with the New Deal, the nation turned its collective attention to the plight of the poor. In time, meeting the needs of the poor became regarded as a governmental obligation, and this corresponded to an absence of social ministries in the church. With the government providing housing, food, job training, orphan care, health care, and so on, a waning sense of duty came to be pervasive with American conservative Christianity.

This absence of concern was exponentially enhanced by the relocation of most conservative churches out of urban centers. By the end of World War II, the creation of affordable automobiles and suburban housing effectively produced a conservative church that was geographically removed from the greatest expressions of poverty found within the urban centers of the country. Meanwhile, the churches that stayed in the urban context were characteristically liberal in their doctrinal views.[5]

The strange fact that churches in the urban centers tended to be liberal is itself the fascinating result of historic occurrences. In the 1800s, American immigration had been predominantly from Western Europe and was mostly Protestant. But by the beginning of the 1900s there was a massive influx of non-Western Europeans. Coupled with the effects of the post-Civil War emancipation of African Americans, cities were becoming culturally and religiously diverse. When conservative churches moved away from the urban centers, the liberal mainline churches remained, along with generations of ethnically diverse church leaders who, in turn, were trained by mainline seminaries.[6]

Because these urban churches tended to be poorer than their suburban counterparts, they had more opportunity and need to minister to the poor. The result was that the churches that were most active in social ministry were also those that tended to be liberal. From the conservative perspective, this reality reinforced an image of mercy ministry being affiliated solely with theological liberalism.[7] The term "Social Gospel" became a euphemism for liberalism and the resulting affiliation was often employed by conservatives throughout the late twentieth century as a justification for not being actively engaged in reaching out to the poor.[8]

This transition marks a change in church history. Before the 1900s, Calvinist and Wesleyan branches of conservative Protestantism emphasized social ministry within their ecclesiological priorities.[9] Both traditions manifested the same shared commitment to serving the poor as an expression of God's love and mercy. This history was quickly lost as postmillennialism and liberalism became synonymous with mercy ministry. Of course, there were many conservative churches that attempted to practice compassion and mercy toward the poor, but nonetheless this oversimplified summary of history accurately portrays the fact that, for the most part, conservative churches disengaged from ministering to the downtrodden.

This transition had a profound effect on evangelistic strategies in the evangelical church of the 1900s.[10] By the middle of the century, churches focused their outreach on door-to-door literature distribution, campus evangelism, home visits for church visitors, and street preaching. While each of these strategies faithfully proclaimed the gospel, they often lacked the corresponding demonstration of God's love for the lost that is displayed in mercy ministry.

THE EXAMPLE OF JESUS

The net effect of this history is that in many contemporary churches God's compassion has become separated from the Great Commission. This is a radical change from the example of Jesus, who perfectly combined both of these elements. He was sent to seek and save those who were lost, and He did so differently than the predominant culture by traveling around the land of Israel. Had he established himself in Capernaum or Nazareth, His students would have been in a classroom or a synagogue, sitting at His feet. Instead, He chose to live simply and walk among the poor and needy. On the dusty paths and highways he ministered to those who were both physically and spiritually impoverished.

It was in this manner that he could illustrate what healing, forgiveness, and mercy looked like. In fact, Matthew explains that Jesus' compassion for the poor was what motivated him to send his disciples throughout the land preaching:

> Then Jesus went about all the cities and villages, teaching in their synagogues, preaching the gospel of the kingdom, and healing every sickness and every disease among the people. But when He saw the multitudes, He was moved with compassion for them, because they were weary and scattered, like sheep having no shepherd. Then He said to His disciples, "The harvest truly is plentiful, but the laborers are few. Therefore pray the Lord of the harvest to send out laborers into His harvest." (Matt. 9:35–38)

This is how Matthew 9 ends, but in 10:1, Jesus answered His own prayer by sending His disciples into the world to "heal all kinds of sickness and all kinds of disease." Notice that what motivated Him to send His disciples was His compassion for the poor. This compassion for their impoverished condition elicited a greater compassion for their spiritual condition, inspiring our Lord to pray for the Father to raise up many evangelists to go into the fields to reap the great harvest of spiritual fruit.

This engagement with the poor, helpless, and sick wonderfully afforded Jesus the chance to be a living parable of the greater kingdom promises of salvation. Obviously, there were elements of Jesus' ministry and His sending of the disciples that were miraculous and were linked to the miracle of the incarnation. However, Jesus did teach His disciples that an unending mark of true Christian ministry would be matching the preaching of the gospel with simultaneous ministry to the poor. In His description of the judgment on the sheep and goats, He says that the mark of true faith would be the care for the sick, the blind, the prisoner, or the hungry (Matt. 25:32–40). Actually, as Jesus' description of judgment continues, the very refusal to care for the poor is the only reason Jesus gives for banishing some into everlasting punishment (Matt. 25:41–46). It is evident from Jesus' life and ministry that caring for the poor was not tangential to His message, but rather was a necessary and essential verification of the truth of the freedom He proclaimed.

The Blessings of Poverty

The epistle of James provides what is perhaps the New Testament's most extensive rebuke of those who neglect the poor. Interestingly, James addresses poverty by first explaining the blessings of it.

To begin with, James explains that God has chosen to set His electing love largely on the poorest of the poor. James asks, "Has God not chosen the poor?" (James 2:5). James, of course, does not suggest that all the poor will be saved. But poverty does not place a person at a spiritual disadvantage in comparison to the rich. It is also true that God's choice does not imply any inherent merit in poverty. In fact, when a person is in poverty, his hopelessness cannot be masked. While the rich have the means by which they can temporarily mask the pain of living in a fallen world, the poor have no such refuge.

The fact that the poor have no recourse in this world (apart from God) provides a picture of the truth of Ephesians 2:8–9. There, Paul explains that people have no capacity to do anything that will merit God's grace. Every person is spiritually bankrupt and needy. When Paul says in Romans 5:8 that "while we were still sinners, Christ died for us," the implication is that our best efforts are filthy rags and are unable to help us attain God's mercy. This corresponds to the truth that outside of Christ, every man is a truly poor individual who can do nothing to assist himself, and is dependent upon the grace of God for life-sustaining aid. This is why poverty provides such an apt picture of the grace of God in salvation.

Another blessing of poverty is seen in the poor's reliance on God for daily sustenance; the poorer the person is, the greater faith he must possess in order to rely on God's provision for his physical needs. This demonstrates the countercultural view of God's kingdom: while the world seeks wealth and prosperity, in its quest it rejects the greatest treasure that can be found. By trusting in riches, the world rejects the only means of having a relationship with God. Those who have great personal wealth can live without the experience of intimately knowing a God who cares for His children. They do not have to pray for their daily bread, and they are content with what the world offers.

In poverty, Christians have found not only wealth through faith but they also have become "heirs of the kingdom" (James 2:5). This promise puts the focus not on temporal blessings, but on the future eschatological life. This is what Paul means when he writes that the sufferings of this present life are not worth comparing to the glory that is in the future (Rom. 8:18). This, Paul and James both say, is the foundation of hope for the believer in poverty (Rom. 8:24–25). When a Christian is living in poverty, he has an increased hope on the future kingdom of God.

To summarize, poverty can be a blessing because God has chosen the poor for salvation, because the poor believers can express a deeper faith in God for daily provision, and because they have a more sincere hope set on the future life.

FUNCTIONAL ATHEISM

Understanding the blessing of poverty is necessary to realize the force of what James writes next: "But you have dishonored the poor man" (James 2:6). The church's treatment of the poor was very different from that of God's. They had closed their hearts to the needs of their brothers and sisters in Christ, and in so doing had dishonored the very people that God had sought to honor through salvation. Their actions betrayed their pride and failure to remember the reality of their own spiritual poverty. By neglecting the poor they were failing the gospel requirement to recognize their own spiritual poverty.

When a Christian ceases to show compassion to the poor, not only has he left Jesus' model of ministry, but he is also demonstrating "functional atheism." The functional atheist professes to follow Christ, yet his lifestyle contradicts the example of Christ.

It is ironic when a "Christian" with wealth sees his brother in need, and closes his heart to him. When a Christian clings to his material wealth, he is rejecting the very tenants of his own salvation, and he is refusing to rely on God for his own provision. By closing his heart to the poor, he is actually closing his heart to God, and he is acting as if he alone is sufficient to meet his own needs. This is functional atheism, and it is the antithesis of gospel living.

James highlights this disparity by giving a stunning image of poverty inside of the church. He describes a brother and a sister who are poor (James 2:15–16). By using the Greek word adelphoi (ἀδελφοί, brothers), James is showing that these people are part of the Christian family. In addition to being Christians, they are so poorly clothed that James describes them as "naked." They are so hungry that they are described as "destitute of daily food." And while they are sitting there, outside the entrance to the church, believers pass by them and tell them to "depart in peace, be warmed and filled." It is difficult to imagine a more coldhearted response to a fellow believer in need.

This shocking scene is used by James to challenge believers to either care for the poor, or to recognize the worthlessness of their own faith. In so doing, James describes ministry to the poor as a hallmark of authentic faith. He rebukes Christians who would pass by, telling them that their faith is "dead" (James 2:17). For the Christian, there can be no more terrifying verdict. James essentially says that a person can call himself a Christian all he wants, but if his heart is closed to a brother in need, then his faith is dead. That person is not a real Christian, but a functional atheist.

The Severity of Neglect

Why does James make caring for the poor into such a watershed issue? Because it is in ministering to the poor that faith in a believer's life is most transparently represented. Only one who has abandoned his own self-serving and proud posture before God can understand true mercy. In extending mercy, even in an earthly and physical context, a person showcases his own transformation. In mercy, self-love has been replaced with love for others, and demonstrates recognition that God's love for the sinner is undeserved, and yet exists anyway.

Earlier in his letter, James had written: "Pure and undefiled religion before God and the Father is this: to visit orphans and widows in their trouble, and to keep oneself unspotted from the world" (James 1:27). This is James's way of telling his readers to be holy, as God is holy (see 1 Peter 1:15). It is a challenge to set aside the values of the world and live according to the values of the kingdom.

As children are to reflect the character of their father, so the children of God are to reflect the character of God, and God cares for the poor. If a Christian is to be an imitator of God then he must be a minister to the poor.

Underneath a person's—or a church's—refusal to minister to the poor is a refusal to imitate God in this area. God's compassion for the poor is one of His communicable attributes, which (like goodness, love, mercy, peace, righteousness, justice, truthfulness, patience, and forgiveness) Christians have the ability to reflect. All of God's communicable attributes can be modeled by believers, and they are all most clearly displayed within the context of human relationships. As believers love others, they are imitating their Father while simultaneously pointing the world to the love of God as displayed in the gospel.

This is significant, because it is in the gospel where the nature of God is made most clear. The gospel is the active illustration of God's self-revelation of His image, proclaimed in His Word and modeled by His Son. God loves believers who in turn love one another, and this love is most clearly demonstrated in the sacrifice of Jesus on the cross. God shows mercy to believers, and believers, in turn, are to show mercy to one another, and God's mercy is most clearly seen in the Cross. How incongruous it is when the very recipients of God's compassion, grace, and mercy refuse to illustrate the compassion, grace, and mercy of God to those in the world who need it. The age-old accusation of hypocrisy, well known to anyone who has attempted to regularly share the gospel, finds its validity in the unwillingness or disinterest of the church in caring for her members who are physically impoverished.

This is why Jesus distinguishes between the sheep and the goats based on care for the poor, and this is why James writes that a so-called Christian who passes a brother in need has a faith that is dead. This is a gospel issue; a person who is saved will want to proclaim the gospel to the world, and a person who refuses to show mercy to the poor is refusing to do just that.

A refusal to minister to the poor is a tacit admission that a person cares more about his own material wealth than about reflecting the attributes of God. When a person passes by other Christians in need, he is testifying that he does not follow the footsteps of Jesus, does not share God's heart for the defenseless, and that his faith is actually dead.

PRACTICAL APPLICATIONS

In some extreme forms of Hinduism, people refuse to help the poor. Some Hindus believe that the poor are poor because they made bad decisions in previous lives, and they need to suffer to purge themselves from the consequences of those previous lives. By that logic, helping the poor is actually counterproductive, because it will only mean that they will have to suffer again in the next life.

Sadly, this attitude is all too often shared by Christians. Consider these common responses to poverty: "Those people are experiencing the consequences of their sin," "They deserve what they're getting," or "If they really wanted to change their lives they could." These attitudes are closer to Hinduism than to Christianity. These excuses are a convenient way of missing this fact: the actual circumstances surrounding poverty are generally irrelevant to how believers are supposed to respond.

Christians are to recognize that we are all undeserving of God's help, yet God saved us. Without Christ, we were lost, hungry, culpable, and destitute. Spiritually, we were orphans, fatherless, and runaways. God held us responsible for our sins, and still we experienced His loving work of redemption. When Christians refuse to help the brother or sister in need, an inconsistent principle is being applied. The gospel is predicated on the underserved mercy of God demonstrated toward sinners, and those who have been saved by it are to demonstrate mercy to others.

This is not a call for cultural transformation; that will not happen until Christ returns. The mandate for ministry is not a charge for political activism; that type of action is ineffective and reveals misplaced priorities. The demand to care for the poor does not imply that the church should seek to eradicate poverty; the poor we will always have with us (Mark 14:7).

Moreover, this is not a call for indiscriminate giving to anyone who asks. Enabling a person to avoid working is not only poor stewardship, but sinful. The Scriptures command, "If anyone will not work, neither shall he eat" (2 Thess. 3:10). The Bible calls Christians to be discerning, not stingy. If Christians close their hearts to the poor, they are sinning (1 John 3:17). How tragic it would be if they closed their hearts based off of wrong assumptions about another's need.

Finally, there is an order to meeting the needs of the world. Christians are called to care first for their families (1 Tim. 5:8), then for other believers (Gal. 6:10). If a person passes by his brother or sister in need, he is hypocritical and devoid of the compassion of God (James 2:15–17; 1 John 3:17). The early church did not feed every widow, but only older widows, who where church members and had a reputation for good deeds (1 Tim. 5:9–16). The Jerusalem church did not share their needs with everyone on the street, but with one another (Acts 2:45). Lastly, after having provided for the needs of family and Christians, believers are stewards of what they have as they show love and compassion to the world around them.

The bottom line is that Christ extended the kingdom to Gentiles, prostitutes, thieves, and adulterers. Even today, some of the richest evangelism is seen with the poorest people. It is often the poor sinner who is quickest to embrace salvation, because he has no earthly hope. The believer should be most present in the places where the poor are found. This is the opposite of the contemporary church growth strategy. The poor are nobody's target audience.

The commands to exercise mercy and evangelize are not competing or mutually exclusive propositions. For the gospel to be maximally effective, one must exercise consistency between his life and the message. The complement of compassion and commission is critical because the mandate for mercy is the same as the mandate for missions. Without the preaching of the gospel, men and women, rich and poor, will never be afforded the chance to experience the greater riches of the mercy and grace of God. Feeding the hungry, ministering to the sick, and serving the poor are not ends unto themselves, but rather a means through which Christians encounter individuals who need the transforming work of God. Mercy is not a means to bring about the kingdom. Mercy is the means to bring about the glory of the gospel through seeing people come to Christ.

International Missions: The Selection, Sending, and Shepherding of Missionaries

Kevin Edwards

There is a biblical model for missions. It involves carefully selecting, training, sending, and supporting missionaries. The entire process—when done correctly—is a close partnership between the missionary and the sending church. This partnership is the backbone of missions, and can be an immeasurable source of encouragement for both the missionaries and the churches. This partnership will give a church's missions effort more focus, and will make it more effective in the cause of evangelism.

In the late 1800s an unparalleled missions movement began. Never before nor since has a generation of students exhibited such evangelistic zeal for the lost around the world. More than twenty thousand men and women set sail all over the world as a part of the Student Volunteer Movement, while more than eighty thousand supporters cheered them on and backed them financially. These students formed nearly half of the Protestant missionary force in the early 1900s, many of them serving in well-developed societies, and a high concentration of them in China and India. These student volunteers "were driven by an intensity of purpose that has rarely been equaled, and they were committed to evangelizing the world by whatever means was necessary."[1]

The Student Volunteer Movement that started in 1886 peaked in 1920, and then suddenly began to decline. The story of the decline of such intense missionary zeal serves as a vivid example of what can happen when a missionary endeavor is undertaken without following the process for missions that God has laid out in Scripture.

LESSONS TAKEN FROM HISTORY

While many factors could be considered, there are three principle causes for the decline of the Student Volunteer Movement. First, despite the evangelistic zeal of the students who went out as missionaries, many of them had a faulty theological foundation. Their theology differed from that of their missionary predecessors in that it was not born out of an education that had been centered on the Bible.[2] Heavily influenced by Protestant liberalism and an interest in world religions, the students' theological drift resulted in a compromising ecumenism. "The movement had a fruitful genesis but ended in a theological vacuum, because the original leaders had a pragmatic based philosophy coupled with poor theological training."[3]

Second, the local church was not the source of students being sent to the mission field. The shaky theological foundation of the Student Volunteer Movement included not only a faulty ecclesiology but also a lack of understanding of what role the local church should play in missions. This led to missionaries being sent out without the affirmation of, or partnership with, any local church. "Many books have been written on the history of the SVM, and very few of them even hint of a concern on the part of the SVM leaders to encourage volunteers to return to their local churches to be first accredited and then sent to the mission field by them."[4]

Third, the movement lost sight of the mission of the church. Due to a lack of theological foresight and discernment, the Social Gospel took over the Student Volunteer Movement. At its peak in 1920, the Student Volunteer Movement held a convention where even the salvation of the students participating was questioned. "There was more interest in race relations, economic improvements, and international peace than in sharing the gospel."[5] The history of the

Student Volunteer Movement is a story of how social ministry replaced the call to proclaim the powerful gospel of salvation in Christ.

These three lessons from the history of the Student Volunteer Movement demonstrate the pitfalls that churches commonly suffer when considering what types of mission movements to be involved with and what types of people to send to the field. When churches choose partners for their missions work, they need to carefully select missionary candidates from organizations that are theologically grounded, focused on building the local church, and centered upon fulfilling the Great Commission.

Sending missionaries is a part of what it means to be a church.[6] If a group of believers and their elders are seeking to grow in Christ and are striving to be faithful to the biblical plan for evangelism, they will be passionate about missions. Faithfulness to the Lord's command to make disciples of all nations will include a directed effort, regardless of the magnitude, at reaching the regions beyond any one church's immediate reach. The local church will have a missions program where it participates in selecting, sending, supporting, and interceding for special Christians who are sent out from it to reach the lost in other places.

The early church considered missions a matter of extreme importance (Acts 13:1–3; 14:27; 15:36–40). It was not a secondary or minor program. The apostles knew that they were involved with something global and monumental in God's redemptive program. The Great Commission was given to the apostles at least five times, if not more (Matt. 28:18–20; Mark 16:15; Luke 24:46–48; John 20:10; Acts 1:8). These men had left everything to follow Christ, and now they were to bring the message to the world. They then handed the baton to others, who have passed it down to us. For this reason, every church, whether large or small, should have its own involvement in the great missionary enterprise of the body of Christ.[7]

Today there is a variety of missionaries and ministries with which to partner. It seems like every week I get letters asking for support and partnership from sports ministries, social justice ministries, English language camps, youth outreaches, construction projects, leadership training, music outreaches, church planting, publishing, radio ministries, and the like. With this many requests, it is essential to have an understanding of what the church's priority should be in missions.

Selecting Missionaries

In selecting missionaries, Scripture lays out three principles to follow: prayerful selection, affirmation of the selection, and confirmation of the selection.

Prayerful Selection

First, the leadership must make a prayerful selection. Leaders need to seek the Lord for His direction. When the Antioch church considered its sending efforts, its leaders were found fasting and praying (Acts 13:2–3). The reason this principle must be followed is because missions is the outflow of the character and purposes of the Triune God. He must be sought because the spread of the gospel is the work of the sovereign Spirit as He gives increase to the Word of God around the world.

Affirmation of the Selection

Second, the church's leadership must affirm their selection. This means that they are choosing people who are qualified and gifted for gospel ministry.[8] The biblical qualifications for an elder in a local church, highlighted in Titus 1:5–9 and 1 Timothy 3:1–7, should apply to any missionary who is sent out.[9] If a missionary is sent out to proclaim the gospel and see new local churches established, then he should be particularly gifted to lead the task of planting and leading new churches. Missionaries who are involved with this kind of ministry should be held to the same standard as the elders of the local church, especially regarding his giftedness to teach the truth (1 Tim. 3:2; Titus 1:9). It does not make sense to send a person not qualified or gifted to pastor a church in his own country to plant a church in another.

Ephesians 4:11–13 makes it clear that the God who gave us the Great Commission also gives the church the means to carry out that task by gifting certain people in His church, such as evangelists, pastors, and teachers. When selecting missionaries, the leadership of the sending church must carefully evaluate the giftedness of the individual as evidenced in their local church. This includes evaluating the person's abilities, and assessing his call to ministry. In fact, when the Antioch church sent out Paul and Barnabas in Acts 13:1–3, these two men were apparently part of the teaching team of the Antioch church. They were not simply gifted men who were also qualified for ministry; they were also part of the team of leaders of the church in Antioch. The Antioch church sent its best men out to preach the gospel.

Taking the time to thoroughly examine potential missionaries, both for character and giftedness, will save heartache in the end and will help to ensure that a missionary is able to deal in a godly way with the challenges of ministering in a foreign culture. Missionaries who are sent out must be examples to the flock, particularly in the areas of holiness, humility, and prayer. Furthermore, men who are sent out need to be examples of courage, who are gifted in the ministry of the Word, and able to carry out their ministry in a context of many new challenges. Without this, their leadership will not be effective, and the mission will suffer.

If the local church decides to delegate authority for the missionary's ministry and partner with a mission agency, perhaps due to the agency's expertise in the field or the level of care that an agency can offer on a particular field, the church must not allow a sending agency to usurp the role of the local church in assessing giftedness and character. Many mission agencies have reduced this type of assessment and pre-field preparation to a battery of psychological tests and some rudimentary training. The only place to effectively prepare a missionary for service is in the context of a local church whose leadership is lovingly and intentionally preparing men for ministry.

Confirmation of the Selection

Third, the selection process culminates in the commissioning of the selection. This step, often known as ordination, acknowledges the work of God in preparing and evidencing the giftedness of the man to be sent out as a minister of the gospel. Typically the leadership of the church affirms their partnership with the one being sent out through the laying on of hands (Acts 13:3), where the church visually demonstrates its role as the mediating sending agency of God. Interestingly, there is a twofold sending in Acts 13:3–4. In verse 3 the Antioch church sends the missionaries, but in verse 4 we read that the Holy Spirit sends them. Through the laying on of hands, the church expresses its affirmation, support, and identification with this missionary as the Lord's representative. Peters writes:

By the laying on of hands, the church and the individual missionary become bound in a bond of common purpose and mutual responsibility. It is thus not only a privilege and service; it is also the exercise of an authority and the acceptance of a tremendous responsibility.[10]

PARTNERSHIP WITH MISSIONARIES

The relationship between the missionary and his sending church is best explained as a partnership. In sending out a missionary, the church is responsible to truly partner with the missionary in at least four ways. First, the sending church is obligated to train the missionary for his ministry. Regardless of the particular type of missions work the missionary will be involved in, most of his training should be in the ministry of the Word. Whether a missionary is involved in planting new churches or training national church leaders, the missionary often has a foundational role in the national church. As one to whom the national church will often look for answers, particularly in the training of national church leaders, the missionary must be able to explain the Bible when questions arise relating to the life of the church, biblical leadership, and theology. A poorly trained and inadequately prepared missionary will fail at this point, leading to potentially disastrous consequences.

As one can learn from the Student Volunteer Movement, an initial missionary zeal is not the only qualification for ministry. An insufficient or wrong theological foundation will result in leading people away from God's Word, often toward a pragmatic or Social Gospel. Regardless of the specific ministry to which a missionary is appointed, every missionary must be trained and equipped to handle the Scriptures accurately.

On a practical level, this means missionaries should have in-depth training in theology and in properly interpreting the Bible, ideally being able to study and explain the text of Scripture from the original Hebrew and Greek languages. While there are certainly other types of training that a missionary needs, failure to adequately train a missionary in this foundational aspect will prevent him from accomplishing his primary task. The sending church demonstrates its partnership with a missionary by providing, investing, and ensuring that missionary candidates are adequately trained to accurately handle the Scriptures (2 Tim. 2:15).

Second, the sending church must pray for the missionary. On a number of occasions the apostle Paul sought the partnership of churches through prayer. He asked the Ephesian church to pray that he would be bold (Eph. 6:18–19), the Colossian church to pray for an open door and for clarity of the message (Col. 4:2–4), the Roman church to pray for protection (Rom. 15:30–31), and the Thessalonian church to pray for the spread and glorification of the Word, as well as for protection from evil men (2 Thess. 3:1–2). Thus, a partnership in missions requires the senders to be prayer warriors who stay aware of the needs on the mission field and fervently pray for Almighty God to do what only He can do.

Third, a church must shepherd the missionary. A missionary's submission to the God-appointed leadership of his sending church does not end at his commissioning to the gospel ministry. Paul's return to the Antioch church following both his first and second missionary journeys (Acts 14:26–27; 18:22–23) illustrates his continued submission to his sending church. Because of the partnership of accountability that exists, missionaries need to keep their sending churches informed about what God is doing in their ministries, and they should invite counsel regarding future ministry plans.

Peters also adds that a missionary:

> recognizes the delegating authority of the church, identifies himself with the church, submit himself to the direction and discipline of the church, and commit himself to be a true and responsible representative of the church. He operates within the doctrinal framework and spirit of the church, conscious of the fact that he is a representative of his Lord as well as of his church, to whom he also acknowledges accountability.[11]

While some missionaries may start autonomous local churches, the missionary himself never becomes autonomous from his home church. Critical decisions regarding the ministry of the individual should be brought before the sending church for the input of the leaders.

The accountability relationship between the sending church and the missionary works both ways. The sending church must be actively involved in shepherding the missionary through the difficulties of ministry in a foreign country. It should provide encouragement and pastoral care. The apostle Paul faced great discouragements in ministry. In addition to opposition and physical persecution, he also carried a burden for the growth of the churches he had founded. At times he referred to himself as depressed (2 Cor. 7:6) and in need of spiritual refreshment (1 Cor. 16:18). If the great apostle Paul was susceptible to these needs and challenges, how much more susceptible are missionaries today? In the same way that Paul was often encouraged by a visit from another believer, so also today missionaries are encouraged by those who partner with them in the gospel.

Fourth, the church should partner with the missionary financially. The missionary needs to know that the church truly is with him in full partnership as he goes to serve. The apostle John said that missionaries should be sent in a way that is worthy of God (3 John 6). Thus, the glory of God is at stake in how we send our missionaries.

It is the biblical precedent and mandate that churches participate in the financial support of missionaries. John wrote to the early church that men who go out for the sake of the Name should not be expected to take money from those to whom they minister (3 John 7). Furthermore, the apostle Paul anticipated support from the church in Rome as he attempted to go to Spain with the gospel (Rom. 15:24). One of the primary ways that the Philippian church expressed its partnership in the gospel was through financially backing the apostle Paul (Phil. 4:15–16).

There are really only two possibilities when it comes to financially supporting missionaries. A church can either support many missionaries at small levels, or it can support very few missionaries at high levels. Certainly if the sending church is faithful in the first three elements of their partnership (training, prayer, and shepherding), there is a limit to how many missionaries it can faithfully assist financially. A church that has a missions committee of five people, but attempts to partner with twenty-five missionaries, is probably not partnering in a way that is fully involved.

In the same way, partnering with a missionary has to involve more than a token monthly offering. True missionary partnership involves caring for a missionary financially in a manner worthy of the Lord. Few churches can afford to cover the total cost of sending out a missionary. In fact, for many missionaries (depending on their field) their cost of support exceeds the pay of the church's senior pastor. But more sending churches can and should accept the financial accountability of covering much of the expense of supporting a missionary in the field.

Churches generally make a greater impact for the kingdom of God when they have a targeted and involved approach to a few missionaries, rather than a broad and general approach to many missionaries. A church that supports twenty missionaries at five percent of the missionaries' support level is not really shepherding any missionaries. It seems that churches have a bigger involvement in the great commission when they can fully involve themselves with one or two missionaries, rather than diluting their focus, money, and leadership over a large pool.

This looks the same in a small church as it does in a larger ministry. The elders should identify the right missionary, have him demonstrate his faithfulness and giftedness in the context of that local church, then commission him, send him out, and support/shepherd him through is ministry. This approach calls for a substantial investment of time and energy from the church.

The benefits of an ongoing investment in a missionary are great to both the church and to the missionary. The church provides encouragement at a deeper level, and allows for more intense accountability and shepherding between the church and missionary. This also allows missionaries who return to the sending church between terms or assignments to spend more time with the sending church, not having to crisscross the country briefly visiting a dizzying number of supporting churches.[12] In this way the body is best encouraged with detailed reports of how the Lord is using their missionary to make disciples of Christ, and the missionary is best equipped, encouraged, and refreshed for further effective service. Shallow partnerships miss out on this. Deeper partnerships between sending churches and their missionaries best honor the Lord.

THE GRACE COMMUNITY CHURCH EXAMPLE

I want to share with you how Grace Community Church handles our missions department. I do this not because it is the only way, or even necessarily the best way. I am sure there are other churches that do aspects of this better than we do. However, our church has sought to put into practice the biblical principles this chapter has explained. Furthermore, our church puts a significant amount of resources into missions, and also has a very large corps of missionaries. I hope that our example will be helpful to you as you think through how to approach missions in your own church.

We view the missions process as having two distinct parts: the selection of missionaries and the support of missionaries.

The church's sending process begins with the selection of missionaries. This process is not divorced from an individual's sense of calling by God to overseas missions, but this subjective calling is examined in light of how a candidate's spiritual giftedness is being demonstrated and developed in the church. Because the calling of God to missions is a call to the ministry of the Word, candidates are quickly eliminated if they are neither elder-qualified nor gifted, at least in an elementary sense, in teaching the Word. All ministry endeavors grow out of the context and life of the church. This allows for the Grace Community Church elders to be able to select people for missions whom God has clearly gifted as leaders to preach and teach the Word.

In our church these gifts are primarily evidenced in the context of our fellowship groups, or what some call Sunday school classes. These groups each have multiple home Bible studies that meet during the week, and it is in these small groups of fifteen to forty people that young men are able to practice and develop their giftedness in making disciples of Christ in the body. Through these groups these men are also able to lead others in taking the gospel to those in the greater Los Angeles area who do not yet know Christ. Ample opportunities for cross-cultural ministry exist in our church and our community, including many Bible studies and outreach groups for immigrants. Those men with evident giftedness in teaching and evangelism, coupled with a clear calling from God for exercising this giftedness in a cross-cultural setting, are those who become missionary candidates.

Closely tied to the evidence of spiritual giftedness in a missionary candidate is his growth in training in the Word. All missionary candidates undergo rigorous preparation in how to study and preach the Word, and the Grace Community Church elders must see them growing in their ability to teach the truth as they are trained to more accurately handle the Scriptures. This training occurs at The Master's Seminary, which is conveniently located on the campus of our church. Few churches have the privilege of such an arrangement, but this is essentially a mandatory step in our church's process of preparing missionaries for effective service. Therefore, initial evidence of giftedness is affirmed by a growing giftedness under intensive training in the Word.

Once a man's giftedness is clearly seen in our church, the elders begin to look for a mission field with opportunities that best fit his gifts. Some men are more gifted to be pastors, and others are more gifted to teach and train leaders. The reality is that any man in the ministry of the Word, regardless of the country in which he ministers, will find himself engaged in both of these aspects of ministry—the frontline ministry of church planting and shepherding, and the behind-the-scenes ministry of training up faithful men. So the elders attempt to place a missionary candidate on a missionary team where his particular giftedness will best complement the team's mission, whether that be evangelism, church planting, church strengthening, leadership development, or Bible translation.

The ability of a missionary candidate to work on a team is another important aspect of assessment and preparation for the field. Missionaries must be able to function on many levels within a team, including working under authority, working closely with teammates as peers, and leading in a team context. Once again, our church's Bible studies provide the perfect opportunity for the assessment and development of a candidate's ability to work on a ministry team as he ministers under the supervision of a fellowship group pastor, works alongside fellow teammates in the Bible study, and leads people in understanding and living out God's truth.

Deciding where to send a missionary involves several aspects. Choosing a field and choosing a mission agency are usually simultaneous decisions. At Grace, almost all of our missionaries go out under our church's sending arm/ agency, Grace Ministries International. The principal decision we face is where our missionaries should go. Some missionaries, especially those headed into a technical ministry like Bible translation, will go out under other mission agencies. These other agencies can provide training and support for specialized ministry to the missionary's target population. Often a missionary candidate, along with members of our church's outreach team, will take multiple preliminary trips before choosing a target nation. Ideally, a gifted leader even recruits others to go with him, as his passion infects other potential teammates with a desire to take the gospel to this nation. In this way the Lord raises up a missionary team from within the church, sometimes including other qualified men from partner churches.

As the Lord brings together a missionary team, the final step before being commissioned and sent out is to raise the necessary financial support. The whole support discovery process is an important part of missionary training. It is in this process that missionary candidates learn valuable lessons on how to patiently trust God while developing the communication skills necessary to convey their passion for their ministry. The new missionary raises support from individuals within our church, as well as pursuing other individuals and churches whom he knows. By the time he goes onto the field, the missionary will have developed a prayer and financial support team consisting of churches and individuals whom he has forged a relationship with. As the Lord brings his supporters together, the missionary candidate learns the importance of faithfully telling others about His vision through any means possible. While our church provides much of the financial support needed by our missionaries, we would not want to deprive either the missionary or the supporters the joy of participating in the Lord's provision for His work.

Grace Community Church partners with our missionaries financially in three ways. First, all of our missionaries are supported corporately through the regular donations from our members to the church.

Second, our missionaries are encouraged to seek the support of individuals in our church. This occurs primarily through the fellowship group and Bible study where a candidate ministers in our church, but also includes other ministries within the church that welcome the candidate to share about his upcoming ministry oversees. People in these groups get excited when they hear about the gospel ministry in a foreign land, and invariably they want to give and pray. This readiness is the result of their pastor's obvious devotion to preaching and excitement about missions.

Third, our church takes regular special offerings to fund the sending of missionaries to the field and to keep them there when they encounter financial setbacks. These three avenues of financial support do not supply one hundred percent of a missionary's necessary support, but together they do add up to most of his support. At our church we have never seen the Lord fail to provide the needed support for a missionary to get to the field. We praise the Lord for His continued provision for more than sixty missionaries on six continents.

Before a candidate and his family leave for the field, he receives specialized training in language acquisition. The missionary will also go through the process of ordination at our church.[13] The final step before departure is commissioning, which usually happens at the end of the worship service on the last Sunday before a missionary departs for the field. Missionary men are commissioned to the gospel ministry by the laying on of hands by the elders while the pastor prays for the missionary. After the commissioning, a reception is held to celebrate this momentous occasion and to give the church body one more chance to express their love to the missionary family as they head overseas.

After missionaries leave for the field, our church's support for them escalates to an even higher level. The whole process of preparing for the field has been bathed in prayer by our church, but once they leave, it is possible to pray for their on-field ministries, including their joys and challenges. Again led by the example of genuine concern and care for our missionaries by our pastor, our church body truly supports our missionaries in prayer. Every week our church bulletin highlights a different missionary team's current prayer needs. We often have special articles in the bulletin from missionaries or from short-term teams who have returned from serving alongside our missionaries. These articles highlight their ministries and encourage our church to pray for specific needs that will advance the gospel around the world. When our elders gather for prayer every Sunday morning, they are always alert to any special prayer needs that our missionaries have.

Two corporate meetings each month focus solely on hearing reports from our missionaries and praying at length for their specific needs. One evening a month, the church body comes together to spend time praying for the current needs of our missionaries, in addition to hearing encouraging reports of the Lord's work from both candidates and missionaries who are in town. The women in the church also meet weekly during the day for the same purpose, to pray and to hear missionary reports firsthand.

Our church hands out prayer cards, calendars with pictures of our missionaries, fliers highlighting their families and needs. We strive to find ways to remind the church to pray often for our missionaries. Our partnership also involves careful shepherding of the missionaries, a task overseen by church elders primarily responsible for the care of our missionaries. In addition to regular updates via e-mail and phone, our elders visit the missionaries as needed. These visits are simply to encourage and help the missionary family. Often these visits address an important upcoming ministry decision where the church leadership's counsel is needed. All of these factors amount to a missionary force that is visited often by our church leadership.

When missionaries return from the field to report, to rest, or to request counsel, the elders meet with them. Issues that frequently arise relate to personal and family life, key ministry decisions involving new directions in the ministry, and the pursuit of further education by the missionaries. Our missionaries appreciate and depend upon the active involvement of our church leadership in their lives and ministries.

All missionaries eventually return to their sending country for good. For some it is not really their home country anymore, and these people need shepherding and care as they look for the right ministry to settle into. A church that celebrates, welcomes, and shepherds the return of missionaries from the field will be a great help to a missionary family as they uproot and relocate to what often appears to them as a foreign country.

These practices are based on the biblical principles described in the first half of this chapter. They are not unique to larger churches, but with intentionality can be implemented in any church, regardless of size. When churches catch a vision for the shepherding and care of their missionaries, the church benefits hugely, the missionary is served and equipped, and the Lord receives maximum glory.

And of course the entire process has this scene as its goal:

A great multitude which no one could number, of all nations, tribes, peoples, and tongues, standing before the throne and before the Lamb, clothed with white robes, with palm branches in their hands, and crying out with a loud voice, saying, "Salvation belongs to our God who sits on the throne, and to the Lamb!"

All the angels stood around the throne and the elders and the four living creatures, and fell on their faces before the throne and worshiped God, saying:

"Amen! Blessing and glory and wisdom,
Thanksgiving and honor and power and might,
Be to our God forever and ever.
Amen." (Rev. 7:9–12)

21

Short-Term Missions: Supporting Those We Sent

Clint Archer

The new fad in church missions is to replace long-term missionaries with short-term missions (STM) teams. Many of these teams are unprepared, untrained, and ultimately unhelpful. This is a shame, because STM teams can be such a valuable part of a church's approach to missions. This chapter explains what role these trips should play in a church's attempt to fulfill the Great Commission.

As William Carey, widely regarded as the father of modern missions, volunteered for his pioneering mission to India, he often compared his departure to a dangerous climb into a very deep mine. "I will venture to go down," Carey said to his closest ministry partners as he bid them farewell, "but remember that you must hold the ropes."[1] They continued to hold those ropes for forty years, until Carey's death in India.

The echo of that challenge is still heard today. It is a call for churches to support those whom they send into the field. Carey was willing to leave his country, his family, and all that was familiar to him. What he asked in return is for the churches who sent him to support him. This call is what drives churches to continually explore more effective ways of encouraging and assisting their missionaries. Employing short-term missions is one significant way of tightening your church's grip on the ropes of support.

The very phrase "short-term" may conjure up images of ill-conceived ideas, shortsighted goals, and skin-deep impressions. Short-term missions, however, reflect God's eternal endeavor to extend His fame to all the people groups of the earth. The effect of a short burst of ministry can last for all eternity. The power of a bullet is not measured by the time spent in flight, but instead by the impact it made on the target; STMs prove that ministry effectiveness can never be measured by a stopwatch, but the effectiveness is seen in the encouragement of the long-term missionaries in the field.

Misconceptions of STMs

Perhaps nothing hinders effective STMs as much as wrong ideas about the purpose of one of these trips. Ideas of STM trips are as abundant as youth pastors who want a free ticket to an overseas adventure. But understanding what these trips are, and what they are not, can help shape an effective outreach strategy for your church and can make a short burst of energy resound with lasting results for God's kingdom.

First, STMs are not replacements for long-term missionaries. An annual two- to six-week visit abroad does not have the same effect a lifetime missionary does. The misconception that an STM trip is the same as supporting long-term missions leads to churches falsely thinking they are doing missions. As a pastor in Africa, I see no shortage of churches in the United States with zero full-time missionaries, yet they think they are active in missions work because they send a group of people overseas for a few weeks a year. I have even had a pastor tell me that his church sends out more missionaries than any other in his city because they send dozens of STM trips abroad. But these STM trips are not missions.

Missions occur when called, trained, and commissioned Christians and their families uproot from their homes to be transplanted on foreign soil. They sacrifice the comfort, familiarity, and safety of home for one purpose: to propel Christ's gospel enterprise to yet another corner of the globe. To call a three-week trip to dig a well in a village a "mission" is to undervalue the sacrifice of those who have "left houses or brothers or sisters or father or mother or wife or children or lands," for Jesus' sake (Matt. 19:29). This is not to say that STMs are unrelated to missions work. Though we are not living in Carey's "pit" with missionaries, we can hold the "ropes" of financial support, fervent prayer, and physical assistance.

Second, STMs are not a valid form of church planting. The STM endeavor can never be divorced from the local church. To separate the work of an STM team from a local church in the field can lead to false teachers and false converts scattered abroad potentially doing more harm than good. Without seasoned believers in the field helping the visitors, the potential for creating cultural misunderstandings, offending the few believers that may actually be there, and causing long-term damage to the gospel witness are real possibilities. Neither the sending agency nor the receiving group should be free from the careful oversight of an established local church.

"But," the objection goes, "what if there is no established church to which we can send a team?" After all, the desire of missions-minded believers, naturally, is to plant churches. But STM trips are not the right tool for this goal. Church planting is a ministry that takes training, long-term strategy, and enduring support. It requires cultural understanding, language acquisition, and the training up of local believers to be elders. It is not the place of the STM team to usurp this ministry, but to support it.

Unfortunately, some trips are less effective than they could be because teams are sent to an "unreached" region. There, the team preaches the gospel; souls are "saved," and then the team returns home abandoning fledgling believers to a new spiritual life with no church to incubate them. The team may even report with great excitement to their home church that they "planted a church" on their two-week excursion. But at best there is a loosely affiliated group of brand-new believers with no qualified leaders and no suitable pastor.

This is why STM evangelism is most effective in conjunction with an already established, native, local church devoted to the equipping and nurturing of the new converts. Short-term missions have an important role to play in church planting—they should focus on supporting and building up churches rather than starting them.

Third, an STM trip is not an opportunity for immature believers to gain maturity. Some churches treat STMs as a tool to help struggling believers, or those with stagnant spiritual lives, to have an experience that will boost their walk with the Lord. In these cases STMs are treated like a Christian day spa for spiritual invigoration, as if the solution for those who feel their walk with the Lord has reached a plateau is to give them a shot of spiritual adrenalin. But it is disastrous on many levels to think that STMs are the appropriate tool for revitalizing a person's waning passion for Christ.

A team populated primarily with immature believers is prone to problems. STM trips are often very difficult to cope with; they require great levels of patience, wisdom, humility, sacrifice, and even physical endurance. They may have the desired result that the members of the team learn and grow a lot, but this will happen at the expense of the effectiveness of the trip. The usefulness of the team depends largely on the spiritual maturity of its members. The trip is not a time to *become* spiritually mature, but to *be* spiritually mature. Make sure any STM team you build and send consists of strong, spiritually mature church members.

Finally, STM trips are not a poor use of funds if done correctly. Some churches refuse to participate in STMs because they think that STM trips are an inefficient use of money. This common objection stems from the misconception that if there was no STM trip in a given year, the money used on the trip would be allocated to some more worthy project. But STM funds are generally raised by the team members from family and friends, not just paid for by the church. The reality is that money is not being diverted from one project to another; it is being raised and designated for the STM.

Experience has proven that the money raised for STM trips is almost always given by those who have a personal connection to the travelers. The donors usually give to someone they know because of their relationship with that person. If that traveler was not going on an STM trip, it is not necessarily the case that a donor would increase his contribution to the church's building fund. Also, many donations for STM trips come from those outside the church. A church member would probably not ask coworkers or extended family to contribute to a building fund, but would ask for contributions to support personal travel abroad for missions.

Another reason people object to the cost involved is because it seems like a waste of money to do a project that locals could do more cheaply. The logic goes like this: a team of twenty people going from Colorado to Guatemala to dig a well has to raise around $30,000. But if they would just send that money to Guatemala, the well could be dug for less money by people who need the work more than Americans do. Frankly, some STM trips do waste money; they are essentially overpriced ways of accomplishing what a donor's check could allow local workers to do better.

The blame for this belongs to the sending church. When a missionary needs a roof repaired, he can either request the $2,000 it will cost him to buy the materials, and hire unemployed locals and skilled artisans, or he can ask his sending church to send ten unskilled teenagers at $2,000 per ticket to patch together a roof for him. Unfortunately, experience has shown that he is more likely to get his sending church excited about the inefficient, ineffective STM trip than he is to get an unglamorous check.

To be a good steward of their resources, the STM team needs to see their objectives as being more than overpriced manual labor. A carefully selected STM team can do what local artisans cannot do: minister to the missionary family, encourage the local believers, be an example of sacrifice and selfless service to young believers, and play other spiritually supportive roles. In a sense, the water tower they build is incidental to the relationships they forge, the lives they affect, and the spiritual encouragement they bring. You cannot put a price tag on that.

STMs in the Bible

Sending out short-term missions is not a novel idea. The concept was not hatched by a retired tour guide; in fact, the book of Acts models this concept. Although Scripture does not command STM trips, we certainly see the example of brief visits being employed in the initial spread of the gospel in Europe and Asia Minor. The apostle Paul was the archetypal STM leader in his day. Throughout Acts, we read of Paul spending three Sabbaths here, and three months there, visiting churches to strengthen their faith, to encourage them, and to see them face to face (Acts 17:2; 19:8). We see collections being taken up to help him on his journeys (Rom. 15:24; 1 Cor. 16:6; and 2 Cor. 1:16). Most of what we refer to as "Paul's missionary journeys" could be more accurately called "Paul's STM trips."

Some of Paul's journeys were neither church planting nor primarily evangelistic in nature. Instead he had a goal of encouraging those who were in the church plants. One example is found in Acts 15:36: "Then after some days Paul said to Barnabas, 'Let us now go back and visit our brethren in every city where we have preached the word of the Lord, and see how they are doing.'"

When Paul himself was detained for long periods, away from his home and in need of fellowship, we read of him requesting small bands of believers to join him for the purpose of bringing supplies and to minister to him. For example Paul asked for Mark to come to him with parchments and a cloak (2 Tim. 4:13). This is what STMs do best: encourage, minister, and bring resources to those who are laboring for the gospel away from home.

Though one must always be careful about drawing instruction from narrative, it is clear that the New Testament church considered STM trips to be worthwhile endeavors. When the churches sent out the right people for the right reasons, the churches supported them financially, even if their trip was to be a short-term one.

God's command to believers to spread the gospel to the ends of the earth is clear. Long-term relationships between churches, including visits from established churches to church plants, are an effective method of global partnership for the gospel. STM trips are one way to support and strengthen those relationships.

GOALS OF STMs

When done well, STMs are a valuable tool for international outreach. Rather than being a burden on the receiving church, STM trips can provide encouragement for the weary missionary couple, company for lonely missionary kids, examples of godliness for the community, and helpful assistance in building projects, vacation Bible schools, and community evangelism outreaches.

Short term mission trips export the soothing balm of fellowship and encouragement to the missionaries, and bring a slice of the missionaries' homeland to them. The role of STMs is to bolster the missionaries' capability for ministry and reinforce their frontline assault on the enemy's fortress. *Our* mission is to assist them in *their* mission.

Conversely, a poorly planned STM trip can place unnecessary burdens on missionaries. Imagine you had to host twelve rambunctious, immature teenagers who are constantly whining about the local food and demanding to be taken to the local tourist attractions. Those three weeks would not seem "short-term" to you.

There are choices that groups can make early in the process of planning an STM trip that can make all the difference in how effective the venture is. Careful planning and considerate decision making can go a long way to making the long journey worthwhile for everyone involved.

Select the Right Target

As with all of the Christian life, the ultimate goal of STMs is to further the gospel and increase glory given to God. In the field, STMs can have an impact on five basic groups. I have arranged these in a suggested order of importance: the missionary, the local believers, the sending church, the local unbelievers, and finally the STM traveler. It is possible and preferable for the trip to have an impact on all these targets. There is always overlap. But the primary target—the bull's-eye—needs to be the missionary. Focusing on the wrong target causes your trip to miss the mark of its optimum effectiveness for the kingdom, and it can leave donors, missionaries, and travelers disillusioned. We will examine this list in reverse order.

The STM Traveler. Perhaps you have seen advertisements for STM trips in church bulletins promising a life-changing experience as the primary draw for the trip. It reminds me of the cheerful U.S. Navy posters I used to see that invited potential recruits to "Join the Navy, See the World" as if the primary objective in having a navy was to provide sightseeing opportunities to bored young men. Unfortunately, this strategy of marketing a trip is missing the point of STMs. Yes, there will be personal benefit for the traveler (and obviously the whole trip is impossible without the team members), but if enriching the STM traveler is the goal, the trip will be organized around what is best for the team, rather than what brings the most benefit for the missionary and the field.

Unbelievers. Another target group that may receive benefit, but should not be the primary focus of the team's efforts, is the local unbelievers. Converting the lost so that they bring glory to God is the ultimate goal of missions, but it is not the primary focus of the STM team. Unbelievers are best reached by the long-term witness of a faithful missionary, not the blitz-evangelism of visiting travelers. When the STM leaders bear this in mind, they can plan a trip that will support the missionary's long-term strategy for that region.

If the goal is to evangelize unbelievers, a trip may be organized apart from any native local church. For example, a church might send ten travelers to a random "needy" area to preach the gospel with no knowledge of what local churches exist there. One of three possible scenarios will develop. First, the team is disappointed at the lack of converts, and the expense and effort feels like a waste. Second, eager for results, the team interprets the least sign of interest as a certain conversion story to report to their home church The group might declare confidently, "We had fifty converts!" because fifty people repeated the sinner's prayer after an open-air sermon. Third, many people are converted, but then are left as spiritual orphans with no local church leadership to guide them. Evangelism without a connection to a local church is extremely problematic. This is why STM trips actually strengthen their evangelism through working with a local church.

Sending church. The church that sends the STM team will undoubtedly receive blessings that accompany sacrificial giving. They will also gain an appreciation for global outreach, an enlarged sense of God's redemptive worldwide work, and a cadre of enthusiastic travelers who, on return, will inject zeal into the missions work of the church. But, like the above groups, the sending church should not be the primary target.

If the sending church is treated as the primary focus, the team can end up being a burden on the missionary. The church will send teams to more exotic locations or ministries where the fruit of ministry is more tangible. The sending church will get most excited when it receives reports of conversions, sees slides of very foreign-looking places and people, and hears that buildings were erected (however shoddily the work was done). But the ministry with the greatest need might be one without much glamour. The people might be the same color as those in the sending church. The fruit might be something as simple as encouraged missionaries and an increased witness in the community—not results that can easily be captured in a slide show. So these important opportunities in Europe can be obscured by the exotic dust of an exciting barn raising in Africa.

Local believers. Planners frequently do not see native believers (e.g., converts who were saved under the missionary's ministry) as a viable target group for STM trips. Yet this is one of the more helpful activities a team can be involved in. Often these local believers are the minority who need exposure to other people who believe the same teachings they do. We cannot overestimate the value of a team of godly strangers who give up vacation time and money to spend time in fellowship and discipleship with these isolated saints. It is immensely encouraging to meet people who are like-minded, and to experience the instantaneous bond of love that Christians enjoy.

Relationships with foreign visitors forged in service and fellowship that begin on STM trips can last a lifetime, and can be a great source of encouragement. Also, the congregation can see that what they have been taught by the missionary is not as marginal as it seems in their country. By developing spiritual friendships with like-minded believers from around the globe, the transcendent truths of the gospel become emphasized in a person's life.

Missionary. So how is it that a short-term blitz mission can have a lasting impact that serves the kingdom of God? Perhaps the greatest answer lies with the in-field missionary. The missionary is the STM team's target. He is the one who has the training, experience, and cross-cultural expertise to plot a long-term strategy to reach the lost in his field. The policy of an effective STM program is simple: give the missionary what he needs. Your task is to support his task.

Start with the missionary's expressed needs and desires, not what you can offer. If the two do not match up, tell him you are unable to meet that particular need at this time. Do not be a desperate matchmaker for an unsuitable pair.

Here are some questions to ask your missionary to ensure your team meets a real need:

1. Do you want an STM team this year? Do not skip this question. Many churches assume that their team is God's gift to the missionary. Many missionaries, however, think of the teams as a test of their sanctification. Remember your missionary is the one who knows his field best. Some situations are volatile and require sensitivity to the culture for which an STM team may not be well suited.

2. What time of the year would the team be most effective? Often a missionary has a long-term strategy that requires a team at a particular time of the year suitable to his country's school calendar. Your Christmas break might not best suit a Muslim calendar, and your vacation period might coincide with a formidable Russian winter (quite an obstacle to outdoor street evangelism in my experience).

3. How many STM members do you want? If you open up your trip to everyone who has a passport, your missionary may have to commandeer a school bus to get you home from the airport. Think of how many people he can physically drive around. Will he have to find another driver? Rent a van? Where will everyone stay? Is it safe or legal to have a group stay in the church? These numbers will differ drastically from field to field, so consult your missionary before you tell applicants they are accepted.

4. What are your goals, and whom do you need to help you accomplish those goals? A missionary to Ireland might not jump at your suggested group of elderly ladies qualified to teach English as a second language. He may want to run a sports outreach that year, and was hoping for your energetic youth group. But a team of older ESL teachers might be a huge blessing if your church has a missionary who wants to do an English camp in Croatia, for example. Figuring out what exactly the missionary needs, and when he needs it, is foundational to developing a successful trip.

5. How much do you think the trip will cost the missionary? After gaining as much information as you can, make sure you talk about the finances. Many missionaries will not volunteer the fact that the teams cost them money, unless they are pressed to do so. Some find it unspiritual—until they have to feed an army of hungry teens. Getting an accurate estimate of what the trip will cost, taking into consideration the economic climate of the country the missionary will be traveling to, will help you build it into the price of the trip, and will help ensure that the STM team blesses the missionary, rather than costs him.

Once the STM team is in the field, do all that you can so that the STM trip will not cost the missionary a single peso, quetzal, or rupee. Horde every receipt for every tank of gas he pays for, and hijack every restaurant bill before it gets to him. Come with lavish gifts for his family, and get ideas of what they need, including books, baking ingredients, local magazines, and football jerseys for the kids. Strive to make the experience not only spiritually profitable, but materially a blessing as well.

Select the Right Task

An effective team will have realistic expectations and organized goals. Your team cannot do everything. So decide what you can do, and strive to do that with excellence. Some examples of types of tasks usually done by STM teams include evangelizing, supplying manual labor, running camps, and providing specialized ministry services.

Evangelism. Trips that focus on evangelism are most useful in a local church context. Take the missionary's lead on when, where, and how to approach people with the gospel. In some countries, having foreigners witnessing is novel, and can be quite effective. In other countries, it could pose a burden for the missionary and the local church.

Labor. Building projects can be done only if the team has skilled workers on it. These trips can be useful if building projects are part of the missionary's strategy to witness to the community, as well as to provide skills that may not be available locally. If the team's labor could be provided instead by local workers for less money, the STM trip may be missing the point of its ministry. Sometimes providing labor is only the backdrop for the real ministry the missionary has in mind for the team. Make sure the team is prepared to do the other tasks the missionary has in mind while wielding a hammer, such as sharing testimonies, engaging unbelievers in conversation on the building site, and discipling local believers in host homes.

Camps. Sometimes the presence of foreigners attracts people and lends excitement and even credibility to a project the local church has in mind. For example, when Americans run a vacation Bible school in Japan, more parents in the community are likely to send their children, in the hopes that they can practice their English. Sending Americans to do a soccer clinic in France as an outreach may be met with skepticism, but having them do a basketball camp might be widely popular. The missionary in the field is the best person to determine what ministry would be most effective.

Specialized Ministry. The local missionary may need the resources of specialized skills to accomplish a task. Examples of these trips include those providing medical needs, teaching in seminaries, conducting music outreaches, and teaching English classes using trained ESL teachers.

Select the Right Team

Tour organizers accept any travelers willing to pay for the trip, but the selection of STM teams needs to be done with more discrimination if they are to succeed.

Spiritual qualifications. If you select a team full of immature Christians, be aware that the leader will need to provide extensive oversight on the STM trip. This is not to say that everyone on the trip must have a Bible degree or be elder qualified. STM trips can be a good stretching experience for a young believer, as long as the leader is aware of that need, and the trip can use young believers effectively. I have been on many trips where one ungodly person brings down the whole team because the leader was not able to keep that person's whining complaints at bay.

Skills. Make sure that the team has people with the skills needed to accomplish the desired tasks. If the water tower you build collapses, no one will remember the collective Bible knowledge of the team, just the cost of repairing shoddy work.

Travel experience. There should always be someone on the team who has had travel experience. A calming voice of experience can help when people get lost on the subway (and they will), lose their passports, or lose their patience. Someone who has haggled over a rickshaw fare in Kolkata is less likely to burst into tears when the team's taxi driver begins negotiations.

Once the right target, task, and team have been selected, arrange as many training sessions as is reasonable. These times should include prayerfully familiarizing the team with the missionary family, preparing for the tasks, and making bonding time for the team.

A Thoughtful Gift

Full-time missionaries have made tremendous sacrifices for the cause of the gospel. They have left their families, cultures, and the surroundings of home. They are serving in the pit, and they need support from those who sent them there.

Your STM teams can benefit your missionaries if careful thought and planning go into the endeavor. The team can make them feel loved, appreciated, missed, and supported. But when STM teams are sent without the correct strategy in place, money is wasted, efforts are frustrated, and the burden on missionaries is increased rather than alleviated. STM trips should be treated as valuable ways of prolonging and deepening the ministry of missionaries.

The tighter you hold the rope, the longer and deeper missionaries can bring God's light into the pit.

Notes

Chapter 1

1. For more on this, see John MacArthur, *Hard to Believe: The High Cost and Infinite Value of Following Jesus* (Nashville: Thomas Nelson, 2003), 19.
2. Ian Murray describes the error of hyper-Calvinism especially well, and focuses on how Charles Spurgeon responded to it in *Spurgeon v. Hyper-Calvinism: The Battle for Gospel Preaching* (Edinburgh: Banner of Truth, 1995).
3. Gail Hoffman, *The Land and People of Israel* (Philadelphia: Lippincott, 1963), 25.
4. Jonathan Edwards, *A Treatise Concerning Religious Affections* (Philadelphia: G. Goodman, 1821), 266.
5. Ibid., 293.
6. Ibid., 326–27.

Chapter 2

1. George Peters, *A Biblical Theology of Missions* (Chicago: Moody, 1984), 173.
2. For more on this promise as it relates to Jesus, see James Hamilton, "The Skull Crushing Seed of the Woman: The Inner-Biblical Interpretation of Genesis 3:15," *SBJT* 10, no. 2 (Summer 2006): 31.
3. For one example, see W. Bryant Hicks, "Old Testament Foundations for Missions," in *Missiology*, ed. John Mark Terry, Ebbie Smith, and Justice Anderson (Nashville: Broadman & Holman, 1998), 61.
4. Walter C. Kaiser Jr., *Mission in the Old Testament: Israel as a Light to the Nations* (Grand Rapids: Baker, 2004), 17. Kaiser calls the Flood and the separation at Babel two "great crises in the promise-plan of God" (16).
5. Scott A. Moreau, Gary R. Corwin, and Gary B. McGee, *Introducing World Missions* (Grand Rapids: Baker, 2004), 30.
6. Walter C. Kaiser Jr. explains this promise's impact on missions. See Kaiser, "Israel's Missionary Call," in *Perspectives*, 4th ed., ed. Ralph D. Winter and Steven C. Hawthorne (Pasadena: William Carey Library, 2009), 12.
7. In this way, the Abrahamic covenant has both universal and exclusive implications. It is exclusive in that only Abraham's God can restore peace between God and man. It is universal because he will be a blessing to the "nations." Nobody can be saved apart from Abraham's God, and nobody is outside of that exclusivity.
8. For more on this plan, see Gailyn Van Rheenen, *Missions* (Grand Rapids: Zondervan, 1996), 29.
9. Justice Anderson observes that the phrase "light of the world" has ethical implications, and implies that it is good deeds, specifically deeds of compassion,

that are the light (Justice Anderson, "An Overview of Missiology," in *Missiology*, 21–22).

10. Christopher J. H. Wright, *The Mission of God* (Downers Grove, IL: InterVarsity, 2006), 368–69.

11. Gustav Stählin writes that the goal of their obedience in general, and their kindness to strangers and aliens in particular, was "to bring aliens into the people of God" (Gustav Stählin, "ξένος," *TDNT* 5:11).

12. Kaiser, *Mission in the Old Testament*, 22.

13. Wright, *The Mission of God*, 371.

14. Richard D. Patterson, "The Widow, Orphan, and the Poor in the Old Testament and Extra Biblical Literature," *BSac* 130, no. 519 (July–September 1973): 224.

15. Wright, *The Mission of God*, 377.

16. Some may argue that Jonah was an exception to this rule. David J. Bosch explains why this is not the case: "Jonah has nothing to do with mission in the normal sense of the word. The prophet is sent to Nineveh not to proclaim salvation to non-believers, but to announce doom." He adds, "Neither is he himself interested in mission; he is only interested in destruction" (see Bosch, *Transforming Mission: Paradigm Shifts in Theology of Mission* [Maryknoll, NY: Orbis, 1996], 17).

17. Kaiser argues otherwise in *Mission in the Old Testament*, but is ultimately unconvincing because the passages he cites as having the imperative of going to the world are not only limited to Isaiah, but they are also all Messianic, and thus future.

18. Michael Grisanti has a careful explanation of this term. See Michael A. Grisanti, "Israel's Mission to the Nations in Isaiah 40–55: An Update," *MSJ* 9, no. 1 (Spring 1998): 39–61.

19. Peters, *A Biblical Theology of Missions*, 21.

20. Wright, *The Mission of God*, 378–79.

21. I am grateful to John MacArthur for pointing out this example, and for noting the absurdity (and impossibility) of Jesus' request for the family to keep silent about the resurrection.

22. Clearly, there are textual issues with the Markan passage. However, even if the passage itself is not canonical, it still stands that the addition of the Great Commission there is evidence of its importance to the early church.

23. Anderson, "Missiology," 22.

24. Peters calls this "a turnabout in methodology but not in principle and purpose" (Peters, *A Biblical Theology of Missions*, 21).

Chapter 3

1. James Hastings, John Alexander Selbie, and John Chisholm Lamb, eds., *Dictionary of the Apostolic Church* (New York: Charles Scribner's Sons, 1918), 2:665.

2. Sun Tzu, *The Art of War*, trans. Lionel Giles (Charleston, SC: Forgotten Books, 2007), 3.
3. William Hogeland, *The Whiskey Rebellion: George Washington, Alexander Hamilton, and the Frontier Rebels Who Challenged America's Newfound Sovereignty* (New York: Simon & Schuster, 2006), 238.

CHAPTER 4

1. Robert L. Reymond, *Faith's Reasons for Believing* (Ross-shire, Scotland: Mentor, 2008), 18.
2. William Lane Craig, "Faith, Reason, and the Necessity of Apologetics," in *To Everyone an Answer*, ed. Francis Beckwith, William Lane Craig, and J. P. Moreland (Downers Grove, IL: InterVarsity, 2004), 19.
3. Cornelius Van Til, *Christian Apologetics* (Phillipsburg, NJ: P&R, 2003), 17.
4. R. C. Sproul, John Gerstner, and Arthur Lindsley, *Classical Apologetics* (Grand Rapids: Academie, 1984), 13.
5. W. Edgar, "Christian Apologetics for a New Century," in *New Dictionary of Christian Apologetics*, ed. W. C. Campbell-Jack and Gavin J. McGrath (Downers Grove, IL: InterVarsity, 2006), 3.
6. Ronald B. Mayers, *Both/And: A Balanced Apologetic* (Chicago: Moody, 1984), 8–9.
7. Sean McDowell, *Apologetics for a New Generation* (Eugene, OR.: Harvest House, 2009), 17.
8. For more on these different approaches, see *Five Views on Apologetics*, ed. Steve B. Cowan (Grand Rapids: Zondervan, 2000).
9. The claim is made more than 2,000 times in the Old Testament alone that God has spoken that which is found in Scripture (Exod. 24:4; Deut. 4:2; 2 Sam. 23:2; Ps. 119:89; Jer. 26:2). This theme carries into the New Testament, where the phrase "word of God" is found more than 40 times (e.g., Luke 11:28; Heb. 4:12; see also 2 Tim. 3:16–17). Repeatedly throughout its pages, the Bible claims to be the very Word of God—inspired by His Spirit (1 Pet. 1:21) and sufficient for every spiritual need (2 Tim. 3:16–17; 1 Pet. 1:3).
10. K. Scott Oliphint, *The Battle Belongs to the Lord* (Phillipsburg, NJ: P&R, 2003), 13.
11. K. Scott Oliphint and Lane G. Tipton, *Revelation and Reason* (Philippsburg, NJ: P&R, 2007), 1.
12. Voddie Baucham Jr., "Truth and the Supremacy of Christ in a Postmodern World," in *The Supremacy of Christ in a Postmodern World*, ed. John Piper and Justin Taylor (Wheaton, IL: Crossway, 2007), 68.
13. See Stanley J. Grenz, *A Primer on Postmodernism* (Grand Rapids: Eerdmans, 1996). Grenz notes that postmodernism is characterized by "the abandonment

of the belief in universal truth" (163) and "the loss of any final criterion by which to evaluate the various interpretations of reality that compete in the contemporary intellectual field" (163). It further questions the "assumption that knowledge is certain" (165). By contrast, Christians claim that God and His Word is the final criterion of absolute truth.

14. David F. Wells, "Culture and Truth," in *The Supremacy of Christ in a Postmodern World*, ed. John Piper and Justin Taylor (Wheaton, IL: Crossway, 2007), 38.
15. Reymond, *Faith's Reasons for Believing*, 18.
16. Craig, "Faith, Reason, and the Necessity of Apologetics," 19.
17. Francis Schaeffer, *The God Who Is There* (Chicago: InterVarsity, 1968), 140.
18. John Frame, *Apologetics to the Glory of God* (Phillipsburg, NJ: P&R, 1994), 54.
19. John Piper, *Let the Nations Be Glad* (Grand Rapids: Baker, 1993), 14.
20. Ibid.
21. Antony Flew, *There Is a God* (New York: HarperCollins, 2007), 158.
22. Antony Flew and Gary R. Habermas, "My Pilgrimage from Atheism to Theism: An Exclusive Interview with Former British Atheist Professor Antony Flew," *Philosophia Christi* 6, no. 2 (Winter 2004). Online at http://www.biola.edu/antonyflew/flew-interview.pdf.
23. If we forget the Christ-centered message of the gospel we run the danger of teaming up with other theists, including non-evangelical Christians, in an effort to convince nontheists to become theists.
24. John Frame, *Apologetics to the Glory of God* (Phillipsburg, NJ: P&R, 1994), 6–7.
25. John Frame, "Presuppositional Apologetics," in *Five Views of Apologetics*, ed. Steven B. Cowan (Grand Rapids: Zondervan, 2000), 209.
26. For an explanation of how a presuppositional commitment to biblical authority can work together with a secondary appeal to extrabiblical evidences, see Nathan Busenitz, *Reasons We Believe* (Wheaton, IL: Crossway, 2008).
27. Along these lines, R. C. Sproul, John Gerstner, and Arthur Lindsley observe, "The most frequent objection to apologetics is that it is an exercise in futility, given the fact that no one is ever argued into the kingdom of God. The work of regeneration is the work of the Holy Spirit and cannot be achieved by apologetics, no matter how cogent" (*Classical Apologetics* [Grand Rapids: Academie, 1984], 21).
28. Schaeffer, *The God Who Is There*, 140–41.
29. Humility does not mean a lack of confidence. We would strongly disagree with those who equate humility with a lack of certainty about the gospel. Here is one example of an approach to which we would object: "We Christians do believe that God has given us the privilege of hearing and embracing the good news, of receiving adoption into his family, and of joining the Church.... Above all, we believe that we have met Jesus Christ.... [Yet,] for all we know, we might be wrong about any or all of this. And we will honestly own up to that possibility.

Thus whatever we do or say, we must do it humbly" (John G. Stackhouse, *Humble Apologetics* [New York: Oxford University Press, 2002], 232).

30. James E. Taylor, *Introducing Apologetics* (Grand Rapids: Baker Academic, 2006), 25.

31. H. Wayne House notes the effects of depravity in apologetics with these words: "All evangelical apologetics agree that human depravity is total and that sin has permeated the entirety of each human. This separates men and women from the necessary association with God required for eternal life, and it also causes people to reason wrongly. [But] is it to be acknowledged that the unregenerate cannot do anything on the human plain? Surely not!" (see House, "A Biblical Argument for Balanced Apologetics: How the Apostle Paul Practiced Apologetics in the Acts," in *Reasons for Faith*, ed. Norman Geisler and Chad V. Meister [Wheaton, IL: Crossway, 2007], 60).

32. This is not to say that apologetic efforts to show the reasonableness of believing in God are wasted efforts. On the contrary, they can be very helpful and affirming to the faith of believers. However, based on these biblical assumptions, it is not necessary to have detailed philosophical discussions about God's existence in order to be a faithful evangelist.

CHAPTER 5

1. Bill Bright, "The Four Spiritual Laws" (Orlando, FL: Campus Crusade for Christ, 2009). D. James Kennedy, *Evangelism Explosion*, 4th ed. (Carol Stream, IL: Tyndale House, 1996).

2. This drama is recorded by the Roman historian Tacitus in Annals. See also Victor Dury, *History of Rome and the Roman People*, vol. 5, ed. J. P. Mahaffy (Boston: C. F. Jewett, 1883).

3. Note the perfect tense in the Greek of 1 Peter 2:4 expressing past action with ongoing results. See Karen H. Jobes, *1 Peter*, BEC (Grand Rapids: Baker Academic, 2005), 152–57.

4. Leonhard Goppelt, *A Commentary on 1 Peter*, ed. Ferdinand Bahn, trans. John E. Aslup (Grand Rapids: Eerdmans, 1993), 144, 146.

5. Peter uses the strongest negative particle in the Greek to affirm this promise, "οὐ μὴ" (ou mē).

6. Jim Elliot's journal, entry from October 28, 1949. See Elisabeth Elliot, ed. *The Journals of Jim Elliot* (Old Tappan, NJ.: Fleming H. Revell Company, 1978), 174.

7. *De captivitate Babylonica ecclesiae praeludium* [Prelude Concerning the Babylonian Captivity of the Church], Weimar Ausgabe 6, 564.6. For more on Luther's understanding of this concept, see Norman Nagel, "Luther and the Priesthood of All Believers," *Concordia Theological Quarterly* 61 (October 1997).

8. Everett Ferguson, *Backgrounds of Early Christianity*, 3rd ed. (Grand Rapids: Eerdmans, 2003), 80.

Chapter 6

1. Richard L. Pratt Jr., *1 and 2 Corinthians*, Holman New Testament Commentary (Nashville: Broadman & Holman, 2000), 151.
2. Craig L. Blomberg, *1 Corinthians*, NIVAC (Grand Rapids: Zondervan, 1994), 184.
3. The NKJV translates v. 19 as "I have made myself a servant to all." But the HCSB is closer to the Greek here with "I have made myself a slave to all." The Greek word here literally means "to enslave" or to "bring under subjection," and is a much stronger word than "servant" implies.
4. Another subtle but important distinction: if a person thought that the dietary restrictions or Sabbath observance were still binding to Christians, Paul would have opposed him and denounced that teaching (cf. Col. 2:16–20). In Romans 15 (as well as Acts 15), the issue was not people who thought these laws were binding, but people who thought it wise to keep the laws in place.
5. It is both sad and noteworthy that the recent push toward a more worldly form of evangelism comes from people that generally otherwise hold to reformed soteriology. But the idea that in order to win a person to the gospel you have to live like them is absolutely contrary to the reformed teaching that God is sovereign in salvation. If a person believes that God is the one who draws people to Himself, it simply does not make sense to also believe that an evangelist needs to live like the world or the gospel will not go forth.
6. Pausanias, *Description of Greece*, 5.24.
7. William L. Bevan, "Games," *Dictionary of the Bible* (ed. William Smith; New York: Hurd & Houghton, 1868), 1:864–866.

Chapter 7

1. Certainly God still answers prayers for healing today. The difference is that the events in Acts 5 confirmed the authority of Peter, while now when elders pray for healing, it is the Lord who heals based on prayer, not an apostle who heals based on a gift (James 5:14). For more on this distinction, as well as a fuller explanation of the cessation of the sign gifts, see John MacArthur, *1 Corinthians*, MNTC (Chicago: Moody, 1984), 358–62; and John MacArthur, *Hebrews*, MNTC (Chicago: Moody, 1983), 48–50. For an understanding of why these gifts were given to the apostles, see 2 Corinthians 12:12, and an in-depth explanation in John MacArthur, *2 Corinthians*, MNTC (Chicago: Moody, 2003), 414–16.

Chapter 8

1. Of the sixty-one occurrences of preach in the New Testament, all but nine directly refer to the proclamation of the gospel. Of the nine, three refer to John the

Baptist's preaching (Matt. 3:1; Mark 1:4, 7); three refer to personal testimonies by individuals who interacted with Jesus (Mark 5:20; 7:36; Luke 8:39); two refer to Paul's sarcastic comments regarding the false gospel (Rom. 2:21; Gal. 5:11); and one refers to the angelic proclamation of the Lamb opening the book with seven seals (Rev. 5:2). The two synonyms of kēryssō, κήρυγμα (kērygma, message) and κῆρυξ (kēryx, preacher) appear eight and three times in the New Testament, respectively. The noun kērygma always refers to the gospel message, except in Matthew 12:41 and Luke 11:32, where it refers to the preaching of Jonah. The noun kēryx twice refers to Paul as the preacher of the gospel and once to Noah as the preacher of righteousness. See John R. Kohlenberger III, Edward W. Goodrick, and James A. Swanson, *The Greek-English Concordance to the New Testament* (Grand Rapids: Zondervan, 1997), 427–28.

2. In Ephesians 4:11, Paul says that Jesus gave gifts to apostles, prophets, evangelists, pastors, and teachers. In the New Testament, Philip is the only individual who is called an "evangelist" (Acts 21:8); however, in Matthew 28:18–20 every believer is commanded to proclaim the gospel, and 2 Timothy 4:5 makes this command especially specific to pastors. The gift of evangelism manifests itself in numeric successes in evangelistic preaching whether private or public. Refer to Robert Thomas, *Understanding Spiritual Gifts* (Grand Rapids: Zondervan, 1999), 192–94; 206–7.

3. D. A. Carson, *The Cross and Christian Ministry: An Exposition of Passages from 1 Corinthians* (Grand Rapids: Baker, 1993), 38. He goes on to call Paul's preaching "gospel-centered" and Paul himself as "cross-centered."

4. J. C. Ryle, *Holiness* (Moscow, ID: Charles Nolan, 2002), 376.

5. John Jennings, "Of Preaching Christ," in *The Christian Pastor's Manual*, ed. and rev. by John Brown (n.p., 1826; repr., Ligonier, PA: Soli Deo Gloria, 1991), 34.

6. Origen was a proponent of the allegorical method and saw three senses in Scripture: literal (earthly meaning), moral (relates to religious life), and spiritual (relates to heavenly life) (*De Principiis* 4.2.49; 4.3.1); see also, Roy B. Zuck, *Basic Bible Interpretation* (Colorado Springs: Cook, 1991), 36.

7. Lewis Drummond, *Spurgeon: Prince of Preachers* (Grand Rapids, Kregel: 1992), 222–23. For more on Spurgeon's philosophy of preaching behind that line, see R. Albert Mohler Jr. "A Bee-Line to the Cross: The Preaching of Charles H. Spurgeon," *Preaching* 8, no. 3 (Nov/Dec 1992): 25–30.

8. Dale Ralph Davis provides one of the more helpful examples of connecting every passage to the gospel in a way that honors the author's original intent and avoids allegories or unnecessary symbolism and hidden meanings. See especially Davis, *1 Samuel* (Ross-Shire, England: Christian Focus, 2008), although he also has similar books on Joshua through 2 Kings.

9. Thomas Brooks, *The Works of Thomas Brooks*, 4 vols. (Carlisle, PA: Banner of Truth, 2001), 4:35.

10. A. E. Garvie, *The Christian Preacher* (Edinburgh: T & T Clark, 1920), 311.

11. See also Galatians 4:12. Heinrich Greeven, "δέομαι," *TDNT* 2:40–42.
12. Charles Spurgeon, "The Wailing of Risca: A Sermon Delivered on Sabbath Morning, December 9th 1860," in *The Metropolitan Tabernacle Pulpit* (Pasadena, TX: Pilgrim Publications, 1986), 7:11.
13. Clark Pinnock, "The Destruction of the Finally Impenitent," *CTR* 4, no. 2 (1990): 246-47.
14. William C. Nichols, introduction to *The Torments of Hell: Jonathan Edwards on Eternal Damnation*, ed. William C. Nichols (Ames, IA: International Outreach, 2006), ii, iv.
15. John Frame, *The Doctrine of God* (Phillipsburg, NJ: P&R, 2002), 122–23.
16. Horatius Bonar, *Words to Winners of Souls* (Boston: The American Tract Society, 1814), 33.

CHAPTER 9

1. John MacArthur, *Ephesians*, MNTC (Chicago: Moody, 1986), 143.
2. Homer Kent, Jr., *Ephesians: The Glory of the Church* (Chicago: Moody, 1971).
3. *b. B. Bat.* 8b. See also: *m. Pe'ah* 8:7; *b. B. Metz.* 38a.
4. It is noteworthy that the apostles elevated their own prayer and study of the Word above being personally involved in the mercy ministry of the church. These priorities go against much of the popular anti-preaching sentiment that is sweeping the modern evangelical world.

CHAPTER 10

1. http://www.jesus2020.com/.
2. http://www.creativebiblestudy.com/knowchrist.html.

CHAPTER 11

1. Elements of this chapter have been adapted from John F. MacArthur, *The Gospel According to the Apostles* (Nashville: Thomas Nelson, 2000), 193–212.
2. Billy Graham, *Six Steps to Peace with God* (Wheaton, IL: Crossway, 2008). Al Smith, *Five Things God Wants You to Know* (Voice of Faith, 1980).Bill Bright, *Have You Heard of the Four Spiritual Laws Pocket Pack* (Peachtree City, GA: New Life Publications, 1993). "Three Truths You Can't Live Without," http://3things.acts-29.net/. Matthias Media, "Two Ways to Live," http://www.matthiasmedia.com.au/2wtl/. GetYourFreeBible.com, "One Way to Heaven," http://www.getyourfreebible.com/onewayenglish.htm.

This is not a critique of these specific presentations, but is merely an observation that we seem eager to produce and use "plans of salvation" that enumerate and consolidate the gospel message.

3. One particularly helpful resource is Will Metzger, *Tell the Truth* (2nd ed.; Downers Grove, IL: InterVarsity, 1984). Along with very practical information, Metzger also decries the reductionist trend in evangelism I have described, and he includes a very insightful section contrasting God-centered evangelism with man-centered evangelism. Another helpful book is Mark Dever, *The Gospel and Personal Evangelism* (Wheaton, IL: Crossway, 2007). He gives a very practical approach to personal evangelism.

4. For an excellent book that traces how evangelistic conversations in the Bible are started, see Richard Owen Roberts, *Repentance: The First Word of the Gospel* (Wheaton: Crossway, 2002).

5. When I use the term law, I do not necessarily mean the Levitical Law or the Ten Commandments, but rather any biblical teaching that confronts sin. For more of an explanation on this, see John F. MacArthur, *Romans 1-9,* MNTC (Chicago: Moody, 1991), 107–10, 138–43.

6. The concept of a Christian as a slave only makes sense when Jesus is understood as Lord. See my book *Slave* (Nashville: Thomas Nelson, 2010), especially chapter 2, for more on the relationship between understanding Christians as slaves and Jesus as Lord.

7. A. W. Tozer, *The Root of the Righteous* (Harrisburg, PA: Christian Publications, 1955), 34. See also pp. 63–65.

8. If baptism were necessary for salvation, Paul certainly would not have written "I thank God that I baptized none of you except Crispus and Gaius ... for Christ did not send me to baptize, but to preach the gospel" (1 Cor. 1:14, 17).

9. Charles Haddon Spurgeon, *The Soul Winner* (repr., Grand Rapids: Eerdmans, 1963), 38.

10. T. Alan Chrisope, *Jesus Is Lord* (Hertfordshire: Evangelical, 1982), 57.

11. Ibid., 61.

12. Ibid., 63.

CHAPTER 12

1. David E. Garland, *2 Corinthians*, NAC (Nashville: Broadman & Holman, 2001), 295.

2. C. H. Spurgeon, "A Sermon and a Reminiscence," in *The Sword and the Trowel* (London: Passmore & Alabaster, March, 1863), 127.

3. C. H. Spurgeon, "One Antidote for Many Ills," (sermon #284, Nov. 9, 1859).

4. An excellent book on this topic is Randy Newman, *Questioning Evangelism* (Grand Rapids: Kregel, 2004). Newman has very helpful comments and advice on initiating and carrying out evangelistic conversations.

5. J. I. Packer, *Evangelism and the Sovereignty of God* (Downers Grove, IL: InterVarsity, 1961), 75.

CHAPTER 13

1. Al Mohler, "Sin by Survey? Americans Say What They Think," http://www .ellisonresearch.com/releases/20080311.htm.

2. Richard Owen Roberts, *Repentance: The First Word of the Gospel* (Wheaton, IL: Crossway, 2002), 23.

3. Walter J. Chantry, *Today's Gospel: Authentic or Synthetic?* (1970; repr., Carlisle, PA: Banner of Truth Trust, 2001), 52.

4. Stephen Charnock, *Discourse upon the Existence and Attributes of God* (London: Richard Clay, 1840), 49.

5. James Montgomery Boice, *The Gospel of John* (Grand Rapids: Baker, 2005), 4:1211.

6. J. Goetzmann, "Conversion," *NIDNTT* 1:358.

7. John MacArthur, "The Holy Spirit Convicts the World, Part 2," http://www .gty.org/Resources/Sermons/1559_The-Holy-Spirit-Convicts-the-World-Part-2 (sermon #1559); cf. John MacArthur, *John 12–21*, MNTC (Chicago: Moody, 2008), 197.

8. Martyn Lloyd-Jones, *Authentic Christianity* (Wheaton, IL: Crossway, 2000), 58.

9. R. L., Harris, *Theological Wordbook of the Old Testament*, ed. R. L. Harris, G. L Archer, and B. K. Waltke (Chicago: Moody, 1999), 571.

10. Ibid., 909.

11. George Abbott-Smith, *A Manual Greek Lexicon of the New Testament* (Edinburgh: T & T Clark, 1981), 287.

12. W. E. Vine, *Vine's Expository Dictionary of the Old and New Testament Words* (Nashville: Thomas Nelson, 2003), 525.

13. Johannes Behm, "μετανοέω, μετάνοια," *TDNT* 4:978.

14. J. Goetzmann, "Conversion," *NIDNTT* 1:358.

15. Thomas Watson, *The Doctrine of Repentance* (1668; repr., Carlisle, PA: Banner of Truth Trust, 2002), 23.

CHAPTER 14

1. J. C. Ryle, *The Duty of Parents* (1888; repr., Sand Springs, OK: Grace and Truth, 2002), 5.

2. Tedd Tripp, *Shepherding a Child's Heart* (Wapwallopen, PA: Shepherd, 1995), 99–114.

3. Ryle, *The Duty of Parents*, 4.

4. C. J. Mahaney, *Humility* (Sisters, OR: Multnomah, 2005).

5. Charles H. Spurgeon, *Come Ye Children: A Book for Parents and Teachers on the Christian Training of Children* (Charleston, SC: BiblioBazaar, 2008), 74.

6. John F. MacArthur, *The Gospel According to the Apostles* (Nashville: Thomas Nelson, 2000), 209.

7. Ibid., 210.
8. Dennis Gundersen, *Your Child's Profession of Faith* (Amityville, NY: Calvary Press, 2004), 31.
9. Ryle, *The Duty of Parents*, 8.

CHAPTER 15

1. At Grace Church, every volunteer in youth ministry is deacon-qualified and goes through written and personal interviews before joining our volunteer staff. Additionally, every staff member is currently involved in a mandatory accountability and discipleship relationship as an example to our students.

CHAPTER 16

1. Stephanie O. Hubach, *Same Lake Different Boat: Coming Alongside People Touched by Disability* (Phillipsburg, NJ: P&R, 2006), 25.
2. Joni Eareckson Tada and Steve Jensen, *Barrier Free Friendships* (Grand Rapids: Zondervan, 1997), 25.
3. Wolfgang Schrage, "τυφλός," *TDNT* 8:271–3.
4. Ralph Martin, *James*, WBC 48 (Nashville: Thomas Nelson, 1988), 52.
5. D. Edmond Hiebert, *James* (Winona Lake, IN: BMH, 1992), 126–27.
6. Joni Eareckson Tada, "Social Concern and Evangelism," in *Proclaim Christ Until He Comes*, ed. J. E. Douglas (Minneapolis: World Wide, 1990), 290.

CHAPTER 17

1. Edward T. Welch, *Addictions: A Banquet in the Grave: Finding Hope in the Power of the Gospel* (Phillipsburg, NJ: P&R, 2001), 35.

CHAPTER 18

1. This quote has been attributed to John Ryland (James Leo Garrett, *Baptist Theology: A Four Century Study* [Macon, GA: Mercer University Press, 2009], 169; Alfred Clair Underwood, *A History of the English Baptists* [London: Carey Kingsgate, 1947], 142). It is worth mentioning that after his father's death, Ryland's son insisted that his father was wrongly associated with the rebuke to Carey (Thomas McKibbens, *The Forgotten Heritage* [Macon, GA: Mercer University Press], 58). However, Thomas Wright, Ryland's own biographer, pegged Ryland with the quote. S. Pearce Carey, the foremost authority on William Carey, concludes with Wright that "the outburst [was] extremely likely from the gruff old hyper-Calvinist [Ryland]. Carey himself, at different

times told his nephew Eustace and Marshamn that he had received an abashing rebuke" (S. Pearce Carey, William Carey [London: The Wakeman Trust, 1993], 470). In fact, S. Carey describes the effect that receiving this rebuke had on forming William Carey's philosophy of missions (ibid.).

2. Other groups that were involved in missions such as the Moravians and Puritans had major funding support through either Parliament or prominent denominations. But the missions society that Carey proposed was founded and totally supported by churches of obscure little villages, going either totally unnoticed or openly criticized by the majority of British churches.

3. For more reading on William Carey's remarkable journey to the mission field, see S. Pearce Carey, *William Carey* (London: The Wakeman Trust, 2008); Timothy George, *Faithful Witness* (Birmingham, AL: New Hope, 1991); or Terry G. Carter, *The Journal and Selected Letters of William Carey* (Macon, GA: Smyth & Helwys, 2000).

4. This dynamic is not unique to the United States. Churches in urban centers across Africa, Europe, and Asia also find themselves surrounded by large populations of immigrants who are ethnically and linguistically distinct from the historical make up of the city.

5. Bryan M. Litfin, *Getting to Know the Church Fathers* (Grand Rapids: Brazos, 2007), 32–35.

6. F. F. Bruce, *The Epistle to the Galatians*, NIGTC (Grand Rapids: Eerdmans, 1982), 19.

7. Alex D. Montoya, *Hispanic Ministry in North America* (Grand Rapids: Zondervan, 1987), 68.

8. C. H. Spurgeon, *The Complete Gathered Gold*, ed. John Blanchard, 457 (Webster, NY: Evangelical, 2006).

9. At Grace Community Church, the only ethnic ministry that has its own Sunday morning worship service is the Spanish ministry. This has developed because of the mushrooming demographics of the Spanish-speaking population in our city.

10. For Grace Community Church's perspective on how to respond to illegal immigrants in the church, see John MacArthur, ed., *Right Thinking in a World Gone Wrong* (Eugene, OR: Harvest House, 2009), 169–75.

Chapter 19

1. Walter Rauschenbusch, *Christianity and the Social Crisis* (London: The MacMillan Company, 1907).

2. Gertrude Himmelfarb, *Poverty and Compassion* (New York: Vintage Books, 1991), 2–24. She writes that these social changes, combined with an opposition to the slavery and child labor, produced a "fierce compassion" in American Christians (p. 4).

3. See Micahel Horton, "Transforming Culture with a Messiah Complex," *9Marks* Nov/Dec, (2007), http://www.9marks.org/ejournal/transforming-culture -messiah-complex. Horton writes: "American Protestants did not want to define the church first and foremost as a community of forgiven sinners, recipients of grace, but as a triumphant army of moral activists."

4. John Stott's landmark book, *The Christian Mission in the Modern World*, acts as a foundation for many of the most egregious examples of this (John R. W. Stott, *The Christian Mission in the Modern World* [Downers Grove, IL: InterVarsity Press, 1975]). The idea that meeting "felt needs" in the area of social justice was a necessary component of evangelism was later furthered by Harvey Conn (Harvie M. Conn, Evangelism: Doing Justice and Preaching Grace [Phillipsburg, NJ: P&R Publishing, 1982], 41–56).

5. Tennent provides a brief summary of how this played out in the U. S. from 1960s forward. See Timothy C. Tennent, *Invitation to World Missions* (Grand Rapids: Kregel, 2010) 391.

6. John Fuder, *A Heart for the City: Effective Ministries to the Urban Community* (Chicago: Moody Publishers, 1999), 64.

7. Norris Magnuson traces some of the more well known results of this, such as the Salvation Army and the YMCA. Norris Magnuson, *Salvation in the Slums* (Grand Rapids: Baker Books, 1990). He focuses on a few of the deliberate attempts to attack the social order, rather than merely meet physical needs (165–78).

8. Incidentally, D. L. Moody stood out as an exception to this. He tried to live his life in such a way to demonstrate to more conservative Christians that one could be active in mercy ministry while still being concerned about the salvation of souls. See William R. Moody, *The Life of D. L. Moody by His Son* (New York: Fleming H. Revell, 1900), 85–90.

9. An often overlooked element to John Calvin's doctrine is his "theology of poverty." Calvin very much believed that one of the church's main functions was to care for the poor. He faced much opposition because of this, as people accused him of rewarding laziness. Calvin encouraged people to live essentially in poverty so that they could give away as much as possible, and he saw this as a basic element of Christian discipleship embodied by Jesus' decision to come to earth in poverty. A fascinating summary of this is: Bonnie Pattison, *Poverty in the Theology of John Calvin*, PTMS 69 (Eugene, OR: Pickwick Publications, 2006). Likewise, the Wesleyan side of Protestantism was equally concerned with mercy ministry. See Manfred Marquardt, *John Wesley's Social Ethics: Praxis and Principle*, trans. John E. Steely and W. Stephen Gunter (1981; reprint, Nashville: Abingdon, 1992), esp.123.

10. For descriptions of this effect, see William H. Smith, "Kyrie Eleison," MR 15, no. 6 (Nov/Dec 2006): 21, and Ian Bradley, *The Call to Seriousness* (Oxford: Lion Books, 2006), 30.

Chapter 20

1. Ruth A. Tucker, *From Jerusalem to Irian Jaya: A Biographical History of Christian Missions* (Grand Rapids: Zondervan, 1983), 262.
2. "Many had entered their work as laymen, quite unprepared for the type of ministry they had been sent to fulfill" (Ibid., 262).
3. Benjamin G. Eckman, "A Movement Torn Apart," in *For The Sake of His Name: Challenging a New Generation for World Missions*, ed. David M. Doran (Allen Park, MI: Student Global Impact, 2002), 40.
4. Ibid., 29.
5. Ibid., 26.
6. "Missions is not an optional enterprise; it is the life-flow of the church. The church exists by missions as fire exists by fuel. Missionary partnership must be built into the church from the very beginning, for without it no church will reach its full maturity" (George W. Peters, *A Biblical Theology of Missions* [Chicago: Moody, 1972], 238).
7. Alex D. Montoya, "Approaching Pastoral Ministry Scripturally," in *Pastoral Ministry: How to Shepherd Biblically,* ed. John MacArthur, (Nashville: Thomas Nelson, 2005), 62.
8. For an overview of biblical eldership, see the Grace Community Church's Distinctives on Biblical Eldership (http://www.gracechurch.org/distinctives /eldership/).
9. For an examination of the key biblical principles and a detailed explanation of the biblical qualifications for an elder, see John MacArthur, *The Master's Plan for the Church* (Chicago: Moody, 2008), 203–25, 243–64.
10. Peters, *A Biblical Theology of Missions,* 221.
11. Peters, 222.
12. I recently met a missionary in Italy who had more than forty supporting churches.
13. For details of the ordination process at Grace Community Church, see Richard Mayhue, "Ordination to Pastoral Ministry," in *Pastoral Ministry: How to Shepherd Biblically*, ed. John MacArthur (Nashville: Thomas Nelson, 2005), 107–17 .

Chapter 21

1. Basil Miller, *William Carey, Cobbler to Missionary* (Grand Rapids: Zondervan, 1952), 42.

Contributors

Clint Archer	Pastor of Hillcrest Baptist Church in Durban, South Africa; Former director of Short Term Missions at Grace Community Church
Brian Biedebach	Pastor of International Bible Fellowship Church in Lilongwe, Malawi; Professor at African Bible College, Lilongwe Campus
Nathan Busenitz	Professor of Theology at The Master's Seminary
Austin Duncan	High School Ministries Pastor at Grace Community Church
Kevin Edwards	International Outreach Pastor at Grace Community Church
Kurt Gebhards	Pastor of Harvest Bible Chapel in Hickory, North Carolina; Former Children's Pastor at Grace Community Church
Rick Holland	Executive Pastor at Grace Community Church; Director of the D.Min. Studies at The Master's Seminary
Jesse Johnson	Local Outreach Pastor at Grace Community Church; Professor of Evangelism at The Master's Seminary
John MacArthur	Pastor-Teacher at Grace Community Church; Chancellor of The Master's College and Seminary
Michael Mahoney	Spanish Ministries Pastor at Grace Community Church
Rick McLean	Special Needs Pastor at Grace Community Church

Tom Patton	Assimilation and Membership Pastor at Grace Community Church
Jonathan Rourke	Administrative Pastor at Grace Community Church; Director of the Resolved Conference and the Shepherd's Conference
Bill Shannon	Biblical Counseling Pastor at Grace Community Church; Professor of Biblical Counseling at The Master's College
Jim Stitzinger III	Pastor of Grace Bible Church, Naples, Florida; Former Local Outreach Pastor at Grace Community Church
Mark Tatlock	Provost of The Master's College

CPSIA information can be obtained
at www.ICGtesting.com
Printed in the USA
BVHW040436130222
628560BV00002B/6